STRATEGIC
PLANNING
AND
MANAGEMENT

STRATEGIC PLANNING AND MANAGEMENT

The Key to Corporate Success

DELMAR W. KARGER

Marcel Dekker, Inc.   New York · Basel · Hong Kong

Library of Congress Cataloging--in--Publication Data

Karger, Delmar W.
    Strategic planning and management: the key to corporate success/
Delmar W. Karger.
        p.   cm.
    Includes bibliographical references and index.
    ISBN 0-8247-8490-1
    1. Strategic planning.   I. Title
HD30.28.K355   1991
658.4'012-- --dc20   91--7511
                                                                        CIP

This book is printed on acid-free paper.

MARCEL DEKKER, INC.
270 Madison Avenue, New York, New York 10016

Current printing (last digit):
10 9 8 7 6 5 4 3 2 1

PRINTED IN THE UNITED STATES OF AMERICA

Preface

The primary market for *Strategic Planning and Management* is those people and organizations who need to know how to properly plan, those who have tried planning and failed to achieve outstandingly significant benefits, and those who have read reports that indicated both good and bad results and now want to know "the truth of the matter." This primary market also includes C.E.O.s, C.O.O.s, executives, and managers who see a need to improve the strategic planning and management of their organizations. The book will answer all of the above-mentioned questions in a straightforward and easily understood manner.

Naturally this text should be of equal importance to professors and students in schools of business and management, including those in programs aimed at managing engineering and research or managing technology. Moreover, most engineering professors at various times discuss the need for planning, but know almost nothing about the planning discussed in this text. Many of the factors discussed herein apply to these engineering courses. The planning process is often misunderstood by those in these market segments. This writer has worked in academia and has written a very significant number of books in these fields and in industrial engineering.

This text clearly explains why organizations that want to succeed, and *continue* to succeed, need to engage in the proper kind of planning. The author has researched in the field, has helped profit seeking and non-profit organizations to plan successfully, and keeps up to date in the field. This writing is not based upon speculations and unproven procedures and results. Moreover, he has written (with a coauthor) a two-edition planning manual.

With respect to the *academic market*, the book can be used as a supplemental text in courses on strategic management and policy courses. Moreover, it contains almost all of the material normally covered in such courses, only in this case information is also provided on how to use the material. All of the above make it a candidate as a text for such courses by combining its usage with case studies (applicable case studies can be obtained from the Harvard Case Clearing House), outside readings, and appropriate written student reports.

This text establishes beyond any reasonable doubt for rational-thinking, knowledgeable readers that success can only be achieved by utilizing strategic management concepts, which can only exist through proper strategic planning *and* operational/tactical planning.

Operational planning must be an extension of the strategic planning effort and it must have a long and a short term component. Finally, the strategic planning obviously must be long range, but the required near term actions also always involve short range plans. The same holds true for the operational planning, which must include *both* long (5 or more years ahead) and short range (usually 1 year) planning.

The need for operational/tactical long and short range planning is usually not perceived as necessary by most writers and executives. The apparent possible power of the strategic plan causes them to overlook the fact that some practical means of assuring its achievement must also be included in the approach. The only practical way to assure attainment is to include both long and short term operational planning and tie all of these plan objectives and milestones to a measurement and control system. This latter portion of the foregoing statement is the focus of Part III of this text.

The failure of U.S. corporations to achieve competitive success in today's business environment is largely due to their short range based actions—this fact is well documented. Few even plan for a mere 2 to 3 years ahead, for reasons later explained in this book.

There has been a major shift in the competitive position of nations, and the U.S. has lost the dominant position it occupied after World War II because of its short range outlook. Naturally, the recommended approach to regaining its winning ways includes long term thinking and actions.

This book consists of three major divisions or parts. Part I develops the necessity and rationale for developing or creating winning strategies and tactics through strategic (long range) planning. It also defines the required *scope* of strategic plans through examples and descriptive materials. In accomplishing this, the discussion also discloses the planning areas that need to be considered and generally defines their outer limits, both those external and those internal to the organization.

The first part of the text has four chapters dealing with these matters. The first two chapters concentrate almost entirely upon the external (to the organization) environments. Chapters 3 and 4 move the scene to the inside of the organization. However, Chapter 3 makes the move somewhat gradually since the first subjects considered (mergers, acquisitions, spin-offs, growth, and restructuring) involve both internal organization factors and external factors and forces.

A fifth chapter provides some important research results on planning, including the major positive quantitative effects upon corporate performance measures. It also provides a major overview of the planning process for the guidance of future strategic planners, and a small section discusses the importance of assuring implementation through the measurement of plan achievment. The effect of this action is greatly enhanced when combined with professional work standards.

The last portion of Chapter 5 briefly discusses the beneficial use of professional work standards associated with the use of a management by objectives (MBO) program and how MBO goals must evolve from the plans if they are to be successful. The further beneficial impact of financial incentives based upon progress against the MBO/plan work standards is also mentioned. All of the material mentioned in this paragraph is fully treated in Part III of this book.

Part II contains the procedures and instructions detailing how planners can successfully complete the required very complex planning process—even in a large firm. Few people have thought through this process, and still fewer have ever attempted to direct such planning. Also provided are sources of information necessary to help develop the plan and the steps involved in its development. This part, of necessity, is lengthy and consists of six chapters.

Reference is made throughout the text to numerous current business situations to illustrate the value of planning, to emphasize the hazards of not planning, and to help guide corporate planners in coping with identified situations.

Part III is vital to the success of Parts I and II since it assures *management according to the plan*. This is what strategic management is all about—managing so as to achieve plan objectives. At least an additional 10 percent in performance can be achieved if recommended financial incentives are tied to plan and MBO achievement. It describes how use can be made of the generally recognized and sometimes well thought of MBO activity.

However, MBO often has had a poor success record due to the fact that ordinary MBO objectives/goals (measurement standards) are built upon an incomplete knowledge base and they often are not based upon properly developed strategic and operational plans. Moreover, the MBO standards or goals used were not properly developed and/or stated.

Second, the usual failures are partially caused by the fact that the MBO standards were not used to bring about needed corrective actions when variances from them were detected. Using MBO in the manner recommended in this text will not only result in bringing about the necessary corrective action, but also provide a significant improvement in organizational performance.

Strategic Planning and Management is a very complete discussion of both strategic planning and operational planning. Both must be long range (5 or more years), but the operational planning must also include a short range component that includes objectives and milestones for the measurement of progress.

This text is a complete resource book on planning *and* it can be used as a planning manual which will guide an organization through the entire planning process. Moreover, the book has great value as a reference book and text on managerial knowledge and insights. It will guide an organization through the entire planning process. Finally, it was written to make one more attempt at producing a major correction in how U.S. corporations try to achieve success.

Each chapter is "laced" with management fundamentals and suggestions as to its proper applications and usage. This prompts one more comment: the text will be a good review for executives who may not possess a business or managerial education.

While the text focuses on business corporation success, because of the way it is written and through the use of a special appendix it is almost equally valuable to managers and planners in non-profit and governmental organizations. It even provides help for sub-unit planners when the units are seated in non-planning organizations.

A special acknowledgement is due Dr. Robert G. Murdick, who joined this author in writing and publishing *Long Range Planning and Corporate Strategy* (Karger & Murdick, Troy, N.Y., 1977, 1978). Many of the concepts and ideas used in this text evolved from *Long Range Planning and Corporate Strategy*. Both the first and second editions of the book were the forerunners of this text.

The author's daughter, Ms. Bonnie McCormack, deserves a special "thank you" for helping to proofread the book. Dr. George Yaworsky performed the final proofreading, in addition to contributing to superb Chapter 4, Manufacturing Considerations.

Finally, the author's wife Ruth not only has helped as a proofreader, but had to live through the author trying to write two books at the same time. The second book, with coauthor George Yaworsky, is the fourth edition of *Managing Engineering and Research*—also to be published by Marcel Dekker.

Delmar W. Karger

Contents

Preface   *iii*

**Part I   THE ENVIRONMENTS OF STRATEGIC PLANNING,
WHY ORGANIZATIONS MUST PLAN,
PLUS AN OVERVIEW OF PLANNING**   **1**

1   Competing Successfully—Globally, Nationally, and Locally   5

2   Competing Successfully—Political, Educational, and Social
     Factors   29

3   Internal Business Considerations, with Some External Factors   49

4   Manufacturing Considerations—Planning and Integration   65
     Dr. George M. Yaworsky

5   Research on Planning Benefits, an Overview of the Planning
     Process, and the Implementation Procedure to Assure Plan
     Attainment, plus an Introduction to Measuring Professional
     Work   85

ix

**Part II   THE STRATEGIC AND TACTICAL PLANNING
           PROCESSES, INCLUDING DISCUSSIONS OF
           ALL MAJOR AND RELATED ASPECTS   113**

 6   How to Introduce an Organization to Planning   115

 7   Establishing Corporate Values and Image   129

 8   External Environmental Analysis   145

 9   Internal Evaluations   161

10   How to Develop a Strategy   185

**Part III   MANAGING PER PLAN, MBO, AND PROFESSIONAL
            WORK STANDARDS   223**

11   The Long Range and the Short Range Plans   225

12   Achieving Plan Objectives and Attainment of Milestones
     (Specified Progress Points) through Performance
     Measurement Systems   241

Appendix   Planning Guidance for Sub-Unit Department or
           Division Planners in a Non-Long Term Planning
           Organization and Non-Business Type Organizational
           Planners   261

Index   *273*

STRATEGIC PLANNING AND MANAGEMENT

1

THE ENVIRONMENTS OF STRATEGIC PLANNING, WHY ORGANIZATIONS MUST PLAN, PLUS AN OVERVIEW OF PLANNING

This portion of the text will describe the general outer parameters of strategic and operational planning by discussing major factors determining competitive success in terms of today's world conditions and their trends. These are often minimally treated in management and policy texts and often are not perceived to be as important as the "processes of management." Further, this is evidenced by the fact that most U.S. businessmen do not perceive that these factors will cause failure or poor performance in their organizations unless they adapt to the changed conditions.

It is a fallacy of many planners and writers of strategic planning books that the big questions involved in establishing a corporate strategy are such items as (1) should the firm expand its geographic reach (territorial limits), (2) should it diversify, (3) should the firm centralize or decentralize, (4) should it grow and (by what means), and other such matters, without making any reference to environmental factors. Often, it seems to many that such decisions can be considered without paying much attention to what is happening outside of the company. The reader will soon see that these outside factors are often a life and death matter to the firm.

This is a serious attempt to make all readers substantially aware of many of the forces and issues that can affect management success. Many of these are equally important to the proper management of non-competitive and governmental organizations. Finally, it is a disclosure of what a firm needs to consider and do if it is to successfully compete in the

U.S. and international markets (for all practical purposes the U.S. *is* an international market; more on this later). All this should be at the root of corporate strategy.

The above would be useless without a practical prescription as to how management is to make strategic and tactical/operational (these are inextricably linked together in planning) planning decisions, define them and implement them. All this will be discussed in detail in Part II.

Without strategic planning, strategic management is an impossibility since its strategic actions must result from strategic planning. Therefore, plain ordinary successful management and/or strategic management is impossible in today's world without strategic planning as well as operational planning.

Strategic planning and the associated strategic management have become so important because there has been an enormous increase in business complexity and uncertainty. In the past, the C.E.O. and his/her managers could often guess about future plans since things did not change rapidly and the degree of complexity was relatively low. Today one can't risk such simple-minded actions since there are too many pitfalls and too many aggressive and savvy competitors. The best competitors are already using strategic planning!

A further complication is that strategic planning (long range planning) must include or be associated with related and unrelated operational planning. The operational/tactical planning (both terms are often applied since both are involved) concerns both the long and the short term (usually 1 year) planning. Planning, strategy, and tactics are so intermixed that it is difficult for most writers and teachers to discuss them without creating some confusion in the minds of readers or listeners. This aspect of the problem will be treated in Part II.

Having brought up the relationship between strategic planning and strategic management, a bit more needs to be said about the matter. No dictionary, not even *Management* by Peter Drucker (Harper & Row, 1974), defines "strategic management." All discussions or definitions of strategic management associate it with strategic planning and strategy. Strategic management is management that implements and attains the objectives set in strategic planning—that is about as close as one can get to a definition of strategic management. Planning is the only logical route to follow in order to develop the strategies to be implemented by management; if a management does this it deserves to be called strategic management.

Chapter 1 attempts to identify major global, national, and regional/local factors currently having the greatest impacts on the direction and thrust of strategic management decision making.

Chapter 2 delineates important political, educational, and social factors affecting the successful efforts of management. In a sense, these first two chapters concern matters external to the organization — but which have a major impact on an organization's competitive ability.

Chapters 3 and 4 move the scene to the inside of the organization. However, Chapter 3 makes the move somewhat gradually since the first subjects are mergers, acquisitions, spin-offs, growth, and restructuring. All of these involve internal and external factors and forces. While these subjects are an integral part of management, especially of strategic management of commercial enterprises, they are often not well enough understood by many of the "players" (planners). Hence, such members of management are somewhat of a handicap since they can not make a proper contribution to the planning without this knowledge. Therefore this author provides some additional descriptive and definitive material on these subjects aimed directly at the somewhat uninformed on these subjects. Those already fully informed and knowledgeable can skip over the descriptive material.

After the above material, Chapter 3 moves inside the enterprise and addresses a specific and costly problem found within the design engineering function. It adversely affects product quality, product features, the time required to design and debug a new product, and especially does it adversely affect manufacturing costs and the time required for the overall marketing effort — measuring time from the beginning of the conception of the product. The design function and particularly its design team composition, organization, and perception of responsibilities in most U.S. manufacturing firms is a major handicap to achieving competitive success.

An expert (working, teaching, and consulting in this area, located at the University of Michigan) estimates the number of firms having the views expressed in the last sub-section of Chapter 3 and which are reinforced in Chapter 4 and who have implemented these ideas as being 25–50. Even if it were a 100 firms, it should be a frightening fact for most industrial firms. Some management and engineering specialists realized most of these deficiencies in the late 1950s. They tried to convince audiences that such changes made sense, but they had little effect. In fact, The Strategic Planning Institute, which is supported by industry, speculated that the suggested cooperation made sense and should be tried. What is all this about? The reader will discover the answers in Chapters 3 and 4.

Chapter 4 examines management and its engineering and manufacturing organizational elements in terms of the use of modern manufacturing methods and equipment. It too will discuss the design team composition mentioned in Chapter 3 as to its composition and organization so as to act as an integrated unit. This matter plays a key role in correcting many U.S. firm deficiencies.

Currently most organizations earn an "F" grade in their efforts to correctly solve the problems involved — even the once great General Motors has almost completely failed in this area.

Having covered the areas deemed essential to the development of strategic plans in the first four chapters, a summary of the complete planning *process* is presented in Chapter 5. It will also briefly mention using plan objectives (strategic and operational) as part of the establishment of professional work standards which are based upon the basic Management by Objectives (MBO) concepts.

This latter material involves the implementation required by strategic change and development. Since steps/stages of progress are mentioned in the planning, it is logical to use these in an MBO program to assure that proper progress is being made. The MBO, in this case, is associated with a reward system to augment salary by bonus awards for above average performance. This is a much used concept for rewarding managers, except in this case the achievement required can be and is properly defined.

One final comment about strategic planning and strategic goals: Whatever is done *must* be done in such a manner that the decisions reached *make sense* to all of the planners. These people, in turn, have a responsibility of selling the strategic decisions to any other professionals who become involved in implementation. If essentially everyone, especially those in top management, does not agree, the effort will largely be a failure.

1

Competing Successfully — Globally, Nationally, and Locally

I. INTRODUCTION

The primary thrust of the first four chapters of this text will indicate why it is necessary for U.S. firms to stop emphasizing the short range view and to adopt the long term view—with emphasis on required strategic actions. The outer parameters of strategic planning will be approximately defined by the examples cited in this chapter. The fifth chapter contains research data on planning benefits as well as the previously mentioned overview of the planning process. Some of the benefits from research will not be completely described, but the sources of the data will be indicated so the reader can explore further.

As to planning benefits, the reader will conclude that after learning the facts as outlined in the first four chapters planning should make it possible for the firm to not only survive, but also excel and succeed. In fact, it will become increasingly clear that planning is the only way to overcome business competition.

The long term view can only be created and followed through proper long term planning—5 to 10 or more years into the future. Ideally, the plan should cover a time span equal to the length of the life cycle of the product having the longest perceived life. How to do all this will be explained in later chapters.

Under each topic discussed in the first four chapters the author will identify the current most important factors that must be considered in the planning. However, we live in a rapidly changing world, so it is always necessary to keep sampling new data to enhance and update the material in the text with new data.

Creating and establishing strategies through planning is a *very* complex process because of the tremendous amount of data required and the insights that must be gained from reading the data. However, the benefits are very substantial.

Unfortunately, there is no way to "short cut" the process of planning. If you are tempted to try to do so, you will not achieve the benefits later described. Keep in mind that these benefits continue to grow each year if the process is correctly accomplished.

The author supposes that some readers can not help but be convinced that some C.E.O.s and their staffs have succeeded without strategic planning. Of course that is true. However, keep in mind that in earlier times thing did not change as fast and neither was the world as complicated.

You will find in Chapters 1 through 4 that much of American industry is failing to achieve success because corporations are not taking note of developments about them. They are not acting or performing in a manner designed to beat their competition (often the Japanese) by making use of long term thinking through strategic planning and its implementation. Strategic planning and its intelligent use by management is about the only reasonably sure way of discovering what competitive actions are needed.

II. COMPETING IN A GLOBAL MARKET

American industry, just inside of the country's borders, is competing in a global market, and it is even affecting local retail establishments. This statement also holds true for firms located in most fully developed nations. Substantially over 50 percent of American firms have already experienced international competition (directly or indirectly) and the remainder will not have long to wait. It has even affected retail establishments and firms that thought they were in command of a niche market. The status and health of a company can change very quickly.

Foreign competition is coming from the developed nations that are as adept as the U.S. at designing, building, and selling products — high tech or low tech — at either high production rates or at very low production rates. Many of the competitors seem to be more versatile than many to most of the U.S. firms. Some can beat U.S. firms by a substantial margin.

Additionally, the U.S. is being impacted almost as much by competition from "less developed countries" (LDCs), virtually across the board. Examples are Taiwan, Singapore, Korea, Brazil, Hong Kong, and India.

The U.S. used to be able to feel comfortable with competition from foreigners because it was believed that they did not know as much as we did, or that they had a less educated populace, or that they did not have an equivalent financial muscle. This was largely true in the 1940s and 1950s. Today, the reverse is usually the case, especially as to education and knowledge, financial muscle, and the sophistication of their management and engineering.

Not too many years ago Americans felt they "had a lock" on high tech; today there are four less developed countries (LDCs) who are reputed to have atomic bombs — Pakistan, Israel, South Africa, and India. More countries are developing this capability. Others, like Libya, are developing equally horrible chemical weapons, since this is less expensive but probably as effective in influencing nations.

Still another problem, but not insurmountable, is that many LDCs act unfairly regarding patent protection on foreign products. Companies in Brazil for example, are producing sophisticated modern pharmaceuticals by copying U.S. products that have patent protection here and abroad and are selling them virtually everywhere else in the world but in the U.S. and possibly a few developed countries. In 1989 the U.S. government started to "make noises" at Brazil, but at this writing has not levied a punitive tariff on Brazilian products coming into this country in order to force them to compete fairly.

We must keep open markets, but there is no need to let Brazil's or any country's firms "walk over the dead bodies" of our industrial firms. U.S. firms are losing hundreds of million dollars every year from such actions by Brazil and other nations. The U.S. government does not back up our organizations in a prompt manner — perhaps because the involved countries owe our banking institutions very large sums of money.

However, our government is also often merely careless or ill informed, as is evidenced by the fact that it was not until 1989 that it signed the patent convention long ago embraced by most of the developed nations of the world. It is also possible that some industries did not want it signed because they were cheating. It is often difficult to sort out "the truth" when nations are involved.

The everyday presence of international competition must be taken into account in all planning since it affects virtually every major business factor. It is essentially as true for the non-exporting firm as for those firms that do export — moreover, a majority of U.S. manufacturing firms should endeavor to sell their goods into the international markets.

One trouble with this last recommendation is that our products often require some redesign in order to match the desires of different groups of foreign buyers. The U.S. firms often try to rationalize their action of not paying attention to the desires of foreign customers by saying (to themselves) "it is good enough for the U.S. so let 'em buy what we make." The trouble is they have a choice and they choose to not "Buy American." A lesson that should emerge from these paragraphs is that selling abroad likely requires the development of still another set of strategies and tactics, often for each targeted country.

Planning requires the identification of not only the planning organization's strengths and weaknesses, but also those of competitive organizations — regardless of whether the competitors are local, national, or foreign organizations. Without this knowledge it is impossible to develop a logical and rational set of strategies and tactics to overcome competitors. Strategies must be based upon taking advantage of an organization's strengths and minimizing the negative effects of its weaknesses. Further, strategy must also take into account the *significant* strengths and weaknesses of competitors. Finally, the firm's final strategic objectives and goals must also consider the probable future status of the strengths and weaknesses in the involved organizations.

The general discussion under the previously indicated subtitle is "Competing in a Global Market." Some entirely new considerations will likely appear to be affecting business activities during the next decade — and maybe for many more decades. Some examples follow.

Peter Drucker, the grand old guru of corporate economics, has just produced some interesting thoughts about the future in an issue of *The Economist*.[1] He says the course of the direction of international business in the future is already largely visible. Drucker believes that international politics and policies will dominate the 1990s.

It is recommended that the reader secure a copy of the article, even though some of the main elements of the discussion will be mentioned. This author believes *The Economist* (not just this discussion) is almost must reading if the reader is interested in international business.

Drucker says that the world will move toward subdividing itself into large trading blocks, and *reciprocity* between businesses in one block and another will tend to govern commerce more and more — on the basis of reciprocity. The bad thing about this, as pointed out by Drucker, is that this could degenerate into protectionism of the worst sort. However, he also says it can be fashioned into a powerful tool to expand trade and investment — and apparently he thinks this will be its role.

Drucker says that the trend toward reciprocity as a central principle of economic integration has become almost irreversible — like it or not. Reciprocity between organizations has long been one means of repaying favors. Trade matters will become more complicated with reciprocity as the guiding principle between trading blocks (mentioned above) and the companies in each.

A second prediction is that businesses will integrate themselves into the world economy through alliances. Examples are minority participations, joint ventures, research and marketing consortia, partnerships in subsidiaries or in special projects, cross-licensing, etc. Even non-businesses may become partners.

This kind of activity will make it more and more urgent for many middle sized and small firms to become active in the world economy. This does not spell the demise of small business, but it does indicate a new kind of possible vulnerability in attempting to achieve success.

A third prediction is that businesses will undergo more and more restructuring. However, it is not the newspaper kind of restructuring that we have seen in the press which generally merely emphasizes downsizing (letting people out of the organization) or spinning off (usually selling off) one or more business units.

Since modern firms are becoming information based firms, they, according to Drucker, will tend to follow two new rules. One is to move the work to the people (the opposite of what occurred in the past) and the second is to "farm out" work that does not offer opportunities for advancement into fairly senior management and professional positions (such as clerical, back office, drafting, etc.).

The first trend may confuse the reader, since what it means is not just finding a bunch of people, but finding or establishing a firm in a location where a needed service can be provided. For example, one insurance company ships some paperwork to Ireland because Ireland has people who can read and write in the English language — the insurance company's office is in Newark and the number of available literate people is small.

Drucker calls this the unbundling of the corporation. Think for a moment as to what this might do to a typical large city and its businesses. Even Japan has started this action.

Drucker's fourth point is that the governance of companies is in question. No longer do private investors largely control the board of a company: the big voting blocks are now the pension funds, which are interested in "the quick buck." The above is changing concepts regarding such aspects of business as "self perpetuating professional management," management accountability, management legitimacy, etc.

Raiders have been "pushing" the idea that it is acceptable to make the quick buck. All this activity is affecting how our government looks at such things, and new laws are just starting to be discussed. The governance of business will soon become an issue in most all fully developed nations.

All this will cause more and more firms to try to go private with a few large holders of the company's stock.

In closing, Drucker describes his predictions as the identification of trends, not forecasts. He classifies his comments as conclusions. Planners, take note! This is exactly what planning is all about—developing insights that will be of use to management trying to discern how to increase or maintain an adequate return on investment or capital or net worth.

Drucker, as usual, poses a VERY BIG QUESTION for all readers and this author to think about. It is, what do these predictions/trends mean for my work and for my organization? This is what planning is supposed to help management do, yet in the final analysis the ultimate results are what the planners eventually decide regarding the meaning of the data collected and how it is to be used.

There are no simple answers to the above big question. However, it is prudent and necessary to try to understand just how and why Drucker's "trading blocks" will emerge or be created. National politics as well as economic and trade considerations are involved. The normal supposition would be that these would usually be regional blocks, but this is not a sure result.

Some of the problems involved in forming or creating such alliances are:[2]

1. Such "trading blocks" or alliances must benefit all their members.
2. The business activities involved will tend to include trade, capital, technology, and tourism.
3. Their needs to be a willing leader that has sufficient "influence." Examples might be Japan for the Pacific Rim nations, and the U.S. for Canada, U.S., Mexico, and others. Will a reunited Germany become the leader for Europe? It has many political handicaps and this result is very doubtful.
4. The others must be willing to be led—the big handicap regarding Germany in point 3.

III. GLOBAL COMPETITION IN THE TWENTY-FIRST CENTURY?

Dr. Lester Thurow, Dean of MIT's School of Management, appeared on the Public Broadcasting Service (PBS) TV show The Nightly Business Report on Thursday, January 11, 1990, to present his thoughts regarding a significant possibility for a drastic change in global competition during the twenty-first century. He made no reference to Drucker's position, which was made before the vast changes occurring in Eastern Europe began to happen — the falling apart of the Russian monolith. Thurow's idea could replace Drucker's concept or merely alter the composition of some blocks.

The referenced event sets the scene for Thurow's views. His views also involve alliances, but the views and perceptions are focused a bit differently. It is still too early to be sure whether Drucker's or Thurow's views or both of their views will become reality — this author believes one or a combination of them will become a reality.

Thurow began his discussion by speculating that the 12 European Community (EC) nations could now become 25 nations (including those of Eastern Europe) with a population of 850 million people, instead of the 350 million now represented by the EC. Putting this combination together will be neither easy nor quick, but even if it is accomplished over a period of one or two decades it would be an event that all major firms must take into consideration. For the past century, the U.S. was the world's greatest market!

He first mentioned that there are no really poor people in the group of 25 nations. For example, when considering the Soviet Union and/or East Germany, residents have a per capita income which is two to three times greater than that of either Korea or Taiwan.

Next examined was education at the high school level. To begin with, our average high school student ranks substantially lower than those of most of these nations when a random sample of students worldwide are tested (more will be said on education in Chapter 2). Nations in the EC have the best educated high school students in the world. Moreover, at the top end, Hungary ranks the best in mathematics and the Soviets in physics.

Additionally, Germany is at the leading edge in process technology. So is Japan. Russia ranks at the top regarding research, just as does the U.S.

Relative to anything we could put together, the 25 nation combination would have the most people (850 million), the best educated high school students, and contain nations at the leading edge in basic research and in process technology. Our natural partners would be the Latin American countries, but they are not advanced and many seem to be declining from their already low level. Japan's natural partner would be China, which is now again retreating from "the world" and whose population is largely illiterate. Even if we could line up with Japan (a huge distance from the U.S.), we still would represent a relatively small market and fewer resources than an expanded European block of nations.

IV. COMPETITIVE WAGE RATES

Virtually all LDCs have far lower average wage rates than the U.S. However if proper long term strategies and tactics are pursued, it is possible to cope and to successfully compete with them.

First, it is necessary to start the planning of defensive and offensive processes before the firm is in serious difficulty—start early to fight the competitive battle. Lead time is extremely important because countering actions require time to identify what must be done, time to mount the attack and execute the actions, and still more time will pass before the benefits can be reaped. There is NO QUICK FIX!

Coping with competitors having low wage rates requires superior design for product features, for its visual appeal, for ease of producibility (which equates to being able to produce the product at a low overall cost), and for high inherent quality in the product. This requires that the design team include team *members* (not just observers capable of making suggestions) from industrial engineering, quality control, and marketing.

Using automation wisely and effectively can only be accomplished by the above design team composition. Marketing is certainly important since it knows (or should know) the customer's needs and their limits as to price vs features. The mention of price (meaning cost or dollars) brings to mind that the Japanese also include someone from finance/accounting on the design team.

No firm will win the competitive battle just because it invented the process. U.S. firms largely invented the radio, television, magnetic recording, solid state electronics, micro electronics, VCRs, recording techniques, etc. Yet competitors from abroad have essentially taken these markets away from them.

The U.S. can't claim to have invented the automobile (the French and Germans did), but our automotive firms thought they had a "lock" on the U.S. automobile market because they dominated it. Foreigners now own over 30 percent of the U.S. market. In each case American firms thought they were so superior that no competitor could beat them. Then, when they did, U.S. firms asked for government intervention instead of improving their products and management practices. If they had done the latter at the proper time, the foreigners would only have 10–20 percent of our market and the U.S. firms could have captured some of their market (Ford was the big winner in such an action in Europe).

The sad fact is that the Japanese took our knowledge and did a better job of using it. They beat the U.S. in product design, product quality, manufacturing, and especially in their management excellence. During all this the U.S. thought it was "the world's wonder" when it came to excellence in management.

Much of the above resulted because Japan took the LONG TERM VIEW AND PLANNED TO WIN IN THE LONG TERM — and so they did! They beat the U.S. on cost/price, product features, product quality, management practices, and marketing strategy and tactics — and virtually all of their knowledge in these areas came from the U.S!

As to the Japanese who mainly "did it" to the U.S., listen to some of the facts as related by Akio Morita, Chairman of Sony Corporation. This material was mostly taken from a column authored by Charley Rease which appeared in the *Pensacola News Journal* and other Gannett newspapers late in 1988. Incidently, Morita in the following did a little "picking and choosing," but essentially what he says is correct.

Forty percent of Japan's total imports come from the U.S. This includes 6 billion of agricultural products. The U.S. sells more to Japan than it does to France, West Germany, and Italy combined. Some 420,000 Americans now work for Japanese companies in the U.S. The U.S. buys one third of all Japanese exports, but a large part of these is bought by American industry from American subsidiaries.

Morita's main point is that American industry is not competitive: not because of what the Japanese do, but because of what the American industries do — really do not do.

The Japanese produce in the U.S. and still beat the U.S. industries as to price, quality, and product characteristics. What more needs be said to prove that it can be done in the U.S. as well as in Japan (or any other country)? America merely needs to pursue the correct strategies and tactics. These require the proper utilization of engineering and other such specialties. This is basically stating that the U.S. must do a better job of management!

Morita, per Columnist Rease, indicated that the U.S. needs to do the following to become competitive:

1. Use a well-educated workforce, provide the proper designs, tools, etc., and challenge the workforce with the proper goals. (The U.S. lower level education is rapidly failing and U.S. firms now need to spend more and more resources educating their workers.[3,4])
2. Demonstrate that workers and management are not "on opposite sides" — they must work together if they are to improve their respective lives. Actually the desires and aspirations of management and of the workers are very much alike. (In the last week of July 1989 the United Automobile Workers lost a $1\frac{1}{2}$ year effort to organize Nissan in Tennessee by losing an election effort.: 1622 workers said "no union" and only 711 voted in favor.[5,6])
3. Management should not be distracted by mergers. This activity often

is a snare and an illusion since it magnifies the desire for quick profits in the so-called money game (see Chapter 3).

4. Invest available resources to achieve LONG RANGE GOALS (author's caps, to emphasize a key ingredient), to develop new technology, and to redefine production productivity (the theme of this text).

Morita did not say much beyond what already is known, except that he told the U.S. that it is not doing the very things that it gives "lip service" to doing.

This portion of the chapter concerns low wage rates and how to compete (the Japanese originally had low wage rates), in part, with low wage rate firms in developing countries. Automation and organization integration are the keys to leveling this "playing field," but not as currently practiced in most U.S. firms. They should be used to aid labor (aid their efforts) and to add value to the product—not just to eliminate labor. This is part of the problem and it will be discussed in Chapter 4.

The other action required is to redesign the product so as to better optimize the number and quality of parts (components), and THEN use the automation to manufacture the product. This latter action implies increased use of flexible automated manufacturing techniques, which in turn permit product variety by means of quick changeover from one product design to another (also discussed in Chapter 4).

What has been essentially proven beyond any reasonable doubt is that "we goofed." We made some big mistakes, and we can not excuse the mess some of our industries and organizations are in because our competition is unfair. In some cases it is, but that does not mean we should give up. In fact, it was also essentially proven that "right thinking" and "right decisions and actions" can make firms in the U.S. very tough competitors.

V. THE LONG RANGE VIEW

Morita's last point emphasizes the long range view. The Japanese, who really have been trouncing us in the competitive game, virtually ALWAYS take the long range view. In contrast, almost no one will argue that U.S. organizations mainly operate on a short term basis. U.S. industry is largely short term oriented. It does not engage in long term (long range) planning. Why? Because industry executives are paid in a manner that makes it relatively easy to achieve maximum remuneration if top management maximizes short term results. The second reason is that once a long range plan is produced and published internally, the executives, officers, and directors know that their performance will be measured against measurable goals. They are scared about failure if they are measured, yet they want other workers to be measured against goals and standards.

Specific details will be presented in Chapter 5 about the effect of proper long range planning upon corporate results; but here we will only state that the difference between the planners and non-planners in corporate results is approximately 50 to 1000 percent per year. Yes, the advantage of the long range planners is that great.

The short range view has caused management to skimp on quality, and in some cases thereby increase profit for the short term. This action, however, always has a long term negative effect. The poor quality of American automobiles caused U.S. firms, at least to a large degree, to lose over 30 percent of the U.S. market. In fact, American automakers still have a quality image problem because most of them have not been willing to make the necessary changes.

Moreover, building products of low quality adds 10–20 percent minimum to costs over the long term. Why? Defective products need to be repaired in the factory and quite often after they have been sold. This not only generates rework/repair labor; it also requires replacement material (replacement parts). Probably of equal or greater importance is that there also is a steady market erosion for firms peddling shoddy products.

Then why do it? Simply because up to 50 percent of top management compensation is in the form of a bonus determined upon the current (short term, i.e., last year's profits) earnings trend and amount. The author once tried mightily to convince a major firm (New York Stock Exchange listed) to plan long term and include achievement of long term objectives into the bonus system. The C.E.O. and some of the C.E.O.s who were directors viewed this as "dangerous to their financial health" — but never really expressed this thought. However, their actions indicated that this was the reason for rejecting the concept.

The threat of corporate raiders has (probably inadvertently) pushed the short term view since keeping the stock price up by emphasizing the short run may fend off these people for a short time. However ultimately such firms will be gobbled up when they begin to stumble in performance — and this is a sure ultimate result of pursuing the short term view.

Proper planning counters the raider since it can ensure the most effective use of the firm's assets, which is exactly what the raider does to pay for the acquisition. Raiders sell off poorly performing assets (assuming there is no quick way to improve the assets performance) or they kill such assets that can not be sold. Good performing assets are expanded. This raises the stock's profit to earnings (P/E) ratio above the industry trends and the raider has won again.

Leveraged buyouts (LBOs) do the same things, plus they finance much of the takeover with considerable debt, sometimes using "junk bonds" and/or a lot of ordinary debt. If things go just a little bit wrong, the firm is driven into bankruptcy.

Shareholders (the owners of the corporations) have proven time and again that they will tolerate the effects of the long term view — the sometimes slower growth in sales and earnings because of investments in plant, new products, research and development (R & D), excellent engineering, etc. All of the above does not mean that a firm can only be in high growth and high profit businesses or that the firm can not start a project with a lengthy period of development during which there may be losses.

Rubbermaid and Emerson Electric, especially Emerson, usually have not had high growth (much above 10 percent). However, such firms can command a premium P/E because they are perceived as being very well run firms, which not only produce high quality products but also are generally consistent in their performance parameters.

Gannett started *USA Today* and lost big money on the project for years. It will probably break even or make a little money in 1990, and should soon be a financially successful publication. Now Gannett has launched a USA Today TV Show. It has not done too well in its initial exposure. However, the price of Gannett stock has consistently risen, albeit not at a breakneck pace. In the past 5 years it has risen 100 percent and in the past 10 years 200 percent! This author investor considers Gannett's performance as excellent.

Not taking the long term view through proper *long* and short range planning leads to losing large segments of good business. Look at the businesses U.S. firms have lost in the last decade simply because they let someone else win while they were playing a short term game and the competitors were pursuing the long term view.

The Japanese who took over many of our high technology businesses pursued the long term view by acquiring market share with good products and low prices — thereby acquiring market share. Often our firms simply capitulated. Once the major share of the market was acquired, the the Japanese were making good money at the low prices. The world has seen the effect of short term strategies, and if the U.S. keeps playing that game it will become a second rate power and much more of its industrial wealth will become the property of firms headquartered in other countries.

VI. THE DESIGN PROCESS

It takes years to correct many of the problems found in a large portion of American companies, often one of the requirements in designing and manufacturing better products. On the other hand, the Japanese require far less time to design a new product, place it into production, and get it on the market than do most U.S. firms. Moreover, they know how to design quality into the product. This makes the task of playing "catch up" all the more difficult.

The fact that the Japanese do an excellent job in design, production, and marketing and require less time to do it than similar U.S. firms means that they are more efficient and economical in the described processes — their use of management techniques is superior!

U.S. firms put greater emphasis on marketing start-up than any other step. Further, U.S. firms put much less emphasis on tooling, production processes, and manufacturing facilities than the Japanese — the Japanese excel in these areas. This usually puts U.S. firms at a competitive disadvantage because of quality problems, less sophisticated use of technology, and higher costs. Moreover, the Japanese applied R & D focuses more on production processes than the U.S. — which also provides them a handsome financial return.[5]

Furthermore, the Japanese integrate industrial/production engineering, quality engineering, marketing, and finance into the design team. A very few U.S. firms do this, but very, very few of them — much less than 5 percent. Peter Drucker is another advocate of the formula prescribed by this author and guest author Yaworsky. The Japanese indicate that their successful innovations are being turned out with people from marketing, manufacturing, and finance participating. Drucker additionally says that the best R & D is business driven.[6]

U.S. firms need to continue their productive R & D leading to new innovations, but they also need to copy the Japanese with regard to their execution of the processes leading to the marketplace. Not only must the mentioned functions be integrated into the design team, but the team must be given technologically oriented support so as to make the whole process more efficient.[7,8]

Simon Ramo in his book *The Business of Science; Winning and Losing in the High-Tech Age* offers a substantial number of insights and suggestions about R & D and the U.S. educational system.[9] He says that the U.S. does not spend enough on R & D and he is probably correct. However, there is knowledge about what percent of revenue a company should spend for varying strategies — without taking into account special factors pertaining to the firm doing the planning. These data are based upon extensive research on the financial and business performance of U.S. industry.[10]

One comment on education is that the U.S. must do something *now*, quickly, to improve the product turned out by our primary and secondary schools. More will be said on this subject in the next chapter. Our public schools are not adequately funded, and Ramo says that they must not be considered very important based on the inadequate spending and upon the fact that the Reagan administration wanted to abolish the entire U.S. Department of Education.

Dr. Yaworsky, when he read this manuscript, commented that our schools were very much better before the Department of Education with its group of pseudo-educators appeared—and that only real educational issues were funded at that time, not just the things that were "good politics." This author has to agree with that assessment. One must therefore wonder if Reagan was smarter than some people thought.

Ramo claims our companies have the size and money to carry out adequate R & D. However, foreign firms are likewise endowed and their governments help them, while our government only occasionally helps U.S. firms. Sometimes it even hinders such efforts.

Most failures are caused by poor decisions regarding the management of the firm's physical, financial, and human resources. Any failure is very seldom primarily caused by one shortcoming. These are very important insights that everyone reading this material should always keep in mind— if the reader does not make a conscious effort to do this, he/she is sure to fail many times.

Lester Thurow, Dean of the School of Management at the Massachusetts Institute of Technology, said "Wisdom starts with recognizing that there is no 'silver bullet'. . . . No ONE (emphasis added) ACTION—no matter how major—is going to cure the problem."[11] This applies to both small and large problems. It certainly applies to almost all of the problems enunciated in this book. This statement also includes the folly of "throwing money at a problem"—the favorite ploy of congressmen and senators and and other bureaucrats.

VII. THE IMPORTANCE OF QUALITY TO PRODUCT, SERVICE, AND/OR MARKETING ORGANIZATIONS

That the Japanese have severely beaten us in product quality is not new to many readers. However, their first efforts to export to the U.S. failed because of poor quality. Remember that after World War II we had the world's most envied industrial base and it produced the quality goods that defeated our enemies.

The Japanese determined why they initially failed and then set out to learn how to make products of even higher quality than those of the U.S.—and, of course, they also learned how to market the goods. From whom did they learn, especially about quality? U.S. experts! At that time very few in the U.S. would listen to the likes of W. Edwards Deming (who first lectured to the Japanese in 1950) and his colleagues.

Most U.S. firms believe high quality costs money, more than low quality. You can find "bushels" of quotes to that effect. They are about 100 percent incorrect.

Deming became one of the most popular men in Japan. He went around preaching the virtues of producing high quality products. The Deming Prize is Japan's most prestigious industrial prize. His message is that producing quality products saves the company money. For one thing, it eliminates the 5–20 percent of labor spent on reworking rejects, and it also eliminates the use of the many duplicate parts needed to make the repair (called rework and repair in the factory) — another source of losses that is also very high. Further, a failure to produce quality products often loses the firm's market for the product. Look at what happened to our auto industry. Today, the Japanese, and others, have well over 30 percent of the U.S. market for new automobiles. Yes, price was involved, but a VERY major factor was the high quality of competing products. Today their products are not cheaper, just better.

If the reader does not believe the above, pick up the April 1988 issue of *Consumer Reports* in your public library and look at the repair records of 252 models. Merely "eyeballing" the displayed data should convince the reader that few U.S. automobiles measure up to the Japanese. There are other publications with such comparisons to support these data.

It is not just product quality that has become poor, but most of our service providers such as garage repairmen, painters, carpenters, plumbers, air conditioning repairmen, hi-tech laborers, etc. now almost always provide poor service. The February 2, 1987, issue of *Time* magazine ran a major story about the poor service offered customers by various U.S. institutions. The lead title was was "Why Is Service So Bad?"[12]

It documented that good personal service has become a rare commodity because of a shortage of laborers as well as untrained, uncaring, underpaid, and unmotivated workers. Some blame this on economic upheaval. Yes, the U.S. did experience substantial inflation in the 1970s and early 1980s. Prices had to be reduced as industry saw the problems of marketing, otherwise profit margins would have evaporated. Good workers became scarce because of labor shortages. Service workers were often overworked because companies perceived that this kind of labor was expensive.

The reader can easily deduce how poor customer service of all kinds developed and what should be done about it. We in the U.S. almost invented the concept of good service on a mass market scale, yet our firms have done virtually nothing about the now identified and described failure.

The *Time* article concludes by describing firms that have succeeded in todays markets by providing excellent service (quality service)—and this is not just in one market or industry.

Nordstrom is a Seattle based department-store chain that has turned excellent customer service into a billion dollar business. The chain is expanding rapidly and now has over 45 stores in California, Washington, Oregon, Alaska, Montana, and Utah—and now it has opened stores in the eastern states. A friend of the author's asked several Nordstrom personnel how the company maintained such good service. The answer was always the same, "If an employee does not measure up, he's fired."

Byerly's is a supermarket chain emphasizing quality service. They even have rugs on the floor and a home economist available to help customers. Their prices, they claim, are competitive—and THEY NEVER ADVERTISE. They let the good service do the advertising.

Another such "quality service" mentioned is Mini Maid Services (started in 1973; 1989 revenues were about 10,000,000 dollars), started by a mother of three children. Finally, L.L. Bean of Freeport, Maine, attracts each year to their remote store about 2.5 million American customers who like their sensible, frugal, and unpretentious products. Even more millions buy from the firm's catalog; sales in 1988 were $308 million. All products sold carry a complete guarantee—some for lifetime usage. No employee has any dealing with a customer without 40 hours of training. The customer truly is king.

Just a few more words regarding quality. Remember Thurow's statement, that no one thing will cure a problem. Nowhere is this more true than regarding the manufacture of high quality products. It is necessary to start the creation of quality in the design stage. Too often, it is believed that if the design uses quality materials and the product provides the proper functions, then quality will result *if* the factory exercises the quality *control* function—inspection.

Unfortunately, quality MUST start with the design. Why? If one analyzes a large group of product failures, one finds that about 40 percent of the failures were *seated in the engineering design*. It was discovered by John R. Dixon, professor at Amherst and program director for Design Theory and Methodology at the National Science Foundation and by R. Duffy, a research engineer at the University of Massachussets, that 40 percent of a large group of products exhibiting quality problems had the poor quality designed into product. However, it was also true that poor quality could and did result from actions in purchasing and manufacturing. Quality must be considered in every step of the process of creating a design and producing it. The same holds true for providing quality service or quality banking or quality anything.

VIII.   THE FALSE IDEA THAT BIG LEADS TO SUCCESS

Previously several small firms were mentioned that succeeded in spite of being small, especially at the start — i.e., Nordstrom, Byerly's, Mini Maid Services, L. L. Bean, etc. Moreover, look at some of our former champion BIG firms. First, look at the *old* big steel firms: many are out of, or virtually out of, the steel business. Yet new small firms like Nucor and Florida Steel are howling successes, and beating the Japanese at their game. General Motors, the largest of our automobile manufacturers is now in a worse position than Ford or even Chrysler — or so it seems from the difficulties they have encountered in their efforts to swallow electronic data systems, designing and building competitive and quality automobiles, automating their production facilities, etc.

That big is not better or that it does not automatically lead to success is one of the key ideas expressed in Tom Peter's "Facing Up to the Need for a Management Revolution" in *The California Management Review* and IEEE's *Engineering Management Review*.[13,14] Others have expressed the same idea, but not as forcefully.

This "big" mentality was emphasized by our manufacturing facilities at the time of World War II when GM, Ford, Chrysler, and others built untold quantities of a variety of products with acceptable quality considering conditions and needs. Today, much of this concept still exists. Big is good and will produce suitable products. However, many of these big firms have faltered and failed to deliver the promised better corporate results.

The world today wants both variety and quality. It can be had, but it requires new thinking in engineering, marketing, and manufacturing, as will be described later in this portion of the text. Variety is a "natural" for the Japanese and European nations, neither has been captured by the "big is better" idea.[13,14]

IX.   INTELLIGENCE GATHERING — COMMONLY CALLED SPYING!

Yes, it is true that today more and more firms have turned to intelligence gathering, since such information often produces major financial benefits. If you do not know what your competitors are doing, how can you protect yourself from their competitive assaults or, just as importantly, how can you develop strategies and tactics to overcome their main attractions to customers?

Most readers will say this sounds reasonable. It is, because it is about the only way for a person to ferret out the information in time for the firm to protect itself. Beware, it is very important to not do ILLEGAL intelligence gathering. It is not necessary and, if one does, it will likely be very, very costly—in many ways.

Planning, in a like manner and for very similar reasons, must also start with an intelligence gathering effort by the whole organization. This probe must be directed inwardly, as well as the outward probe described above, since one must know the organization's real strengths and weaknesses. This is needed in order to take advantage of strengths and gradually eliminate weaknesses—the latter takes considerable time. Most organizations think they know their strengths and weaknesses, but planning experience discloses that this is not correct. This information is needed in order to evaluate the the "outside" probe material regarding competitors.

There is still another reason, beyond those mentioned above, why strengths and weaknesses must be determined. Management must primarily take advantage of the organization's strengths since correcting defects takes a lot of time—often years. Yes, correct the defects, but be absolutely sure to take complete advantage of the organization's strengths.

All U.S. TV manufacturing firms, when they still existed in the U.S., routinely engaged in "benchmark spying" or intelligence gathering. They tested and tore down competitive products in order to develop their own more competitive models. The author knows that this did occur since he participated in such actions, both in the TV and the truck manufacturing industries. Benchmark spying or testing is not an illegal act, but neither is it inexpensive or as easy as it sounds. In a sense, benchmark spying is an art as well as a science and engineering matter.

Benchmark spying is not merely having the product design engineering department examine a competitor's product, test it, and discuss it with marketing. The team performing the work should integrate the efforts of members from design engineering, marketing, industrial engineering, quality assurance, and purchasing. If only the product design engineers do the job, the result will fail to disclose most of the more important aspects. This is similar to the earlier remarks regarding the composition of product design teams.

The unsophisticated usually seat the project in design engineering and never add the above members to the team. If the design/product engineers merely brief the other required members, the engineers will almost totally fail to provide needed information to the above suggested departments. There is a simple reason for this: the design engineers do not know what else is needed, neither do they know how to recognize it.

Brian Dumaine wrote an intriguing article in *Fortune* about such activities.[15] He mentions that one of the most successful hotel/motel chains,

Marriott, has played this game very successfully and intelligently. They used the information gathered to become a "powerhouse" in their industry area. Is it illegal? It certainly is not! For example, they spent 6 months sending "spy" teams around the country checking out the competition (by sleeping overnight, making tests, observing, and eating at competitors' motels and restaurants) before starting to spend a budgeted $500,000,000 dollars to create a new hotel chain (Fairfield Inns), which would beat the competition in their selected "price bracket" in every respect. Some might term this effort "market research," but it really is not similar to ordinary market research projects.

The Japanese have long known the value of competitive research; in fact, they train managers to make competitive intelligence everyone's business. At Mitsui, a trading company, they have a motto, "Information is the lifeblood of the company," and the executives exchange a total of about 80,000 messages each day, many via satellite communications. Another example is McDonnell Douglas, who used intelligence gathering to get the jump on Boeing with its new prop-fan airliner.

It is not always a big item that is a "tip off" of a new thrust by a competitor. Xerox has trained, for example, 200 line managers to look for changes in pricing, new technologies, and even new competitors. Much of what is individually gathered and passed along is insignificant, but only by analyzing the bits and pieces together can the big picture be determined. This is one of the main thrusts of the message on *competitive strategy* in a significant article appearing in *The Economist*.[16]

If the reader has been convinced that intelligence gathering regarding competitors is necessary for business success, at least part of the author's objective has been attained. However, more importantly, it is hoped that the connection has been made that it is important to engage in internal and external intelligence gathering as part of any planning effort. This is the only way to capture the total business picture in a given market sector, or in a given organizational unit. The internal intelligence gathering effort consists mainly of having and using open communication channels.

X. MARKETING AND PRODUCT DEVELOPMENT STRATEGY

The competitor that has often upset U.S. industrial managers is Japan, and it did this with a marketing strategy that was "go" oriented. Go is an oriental game played in Japan (and China) in which each "piece" is equally valued and one wins by surrounding the opponent's pieces—thereby eliminating them. This is very close to what Japan has done in many of our markets.

Chess on the other hand, generally represents the U.S. approach. Here the important pieces have different values and one wins by launching a targeted attack on the opponent's position to win by checkmating the king. The U.S. is profit oriented, not market oriented (surrounding the enemy product). In a sense, the values of the pieces are a proxy for profitability.

Why does this strategy not work? With the "go" strategy, Japan killed the market by way underpricing the U.S. products, which meant that our products could no longer be sold at a profit. This meant that the "surrounded" firm no longer had a viable market for its product and they then generally withdrew from that product line.

The U.S. firms lost completely because they did not fight early in the competition when they had a reasonable chance of winning; they were then in possession of "market share." They were so committed to their short term strategy of "making a quick profit" that they took no long term actions that would have given them a good chance of winning in the long term. Managers have to be knowledgeable and smart enough to know that the sale of the product must be maintained by better design, better product features, marketing, quality, etc.

Japan is now playing a somewhat different business game than "go," as exposed in "The Name of Japan's New Business Game" in *The Economist*, April 9, 1988.[16] The current Japanese approach is evolving into something in between the above two approaches. Just because the Japanese thoroughly beat the U.S. by playing a market share oriented game is no reason to believe that this will not change if they think they have found a better way to play the game, perhaps because of new developments that they have detected.

In order to properly plan for the next 5 or 10 years (remember that Japan and many other players are long term oriented), U.S. market planning must take into account all that has happened to their business enterprises in the past and all that will affect these business interests in the future. This means that U.S. firms must forecast future events, in part by analyzing trends and in part by discerning the future by analyzing the importance of current actions being taken by competitors.

Of course, these competitors will also likely be trying to read future events to discern what they should do to produce a winning strategy. Remember, if a competitor is winning by pursuing a given strategy, he will almost surely continue to emphasize it—so one will have to counter it in order to stay in business. The U.S. will fail if it only depends upon "trend analysis"—this applies to each and every business competing with knowledgeable and well managed firms.

For example, the Japanese have been agonizingly slow to make business decisions, but often very swift to execute a decision. Japan does what U.S. management experts recommend: studies our past actions, identifies where change is required, and makes the needed changes as quickly as possible. Japanese firms recognized their past slow pace in decision making and seem to be reshaping themselves in this area.

Nippon Steel, for example, cut the number of approvals needed from 30 to 5 for implementing decisions. Matsushita made all its divisions into virtually separate companies that pay dividends to headquarters. In the past few years, Ashi Glass established 20 start-up firms that were told to act independently.

By now U.S. firms should know from Japanese actions that the Japanese look upon business war a great deal like a real war—destroy the enemy! It now seems that their "go" oriented marketing game is being modified, not abandoned. They now appear to be additionally seeking to add value to the corporate efforts by introducing new products and doing it faster and more often than their competitors. This strategy seems to be specifically used when entering new markets and in trying to dominate them. It has made their "go" technique more effective.

The time it takes the Japanese to go from product conception to marketing is 50 percent less (on the average) than for U.S. firms. This means they are twice as fast.

An important part of this speed is that they put new products into production in far less time than we do. This is only possible if the "factory" is part of the design process—and that is exactly what is done in Japan. Second, some of the decrease in time is also due to a speeded-up marketing process.

It should not require blueprints to lead one to the understanding that manufacturing and marketing, as well as almost all business functions, require a great deal of attention in the planning process.

XI.   RESEARCH AND DEVELOPMENT

In 1968 1.5 percent of Japan's GNP went to R & D. Now it is at 2.8 percent of GNP. This beats the U.S. and most of Europe and represents a sum greater than capital spending in many firms.

In Japan over three-fourths of this cost is paid for by the companies doing the research, whereas in the U.S. the corporate share is only about 50 percent because of related government funded R & D. By these and other actions Japan signals that it intends to lead the world into the next stage of the industrial revolution of the future. More is said on this subject in a later chapter.

Moreover, Japan seems to be determined to continue to be a country that makes things, *not merely services them*. This is a very important concept that we need to learn, and learn quickly. *Once they acquire the "making businesses," they can then gobble up the "servicing businesses" at their leisure.*

A related thought — Japan has not led the world in creating new innovations (or winning Nobel Prizes), so they will likely decide that the rote drilling of "facts" in their school system will need some modification, but not by the extreme amount by which we changed our educational system. More will be said on this subject in the next chapter.

XII.   A NEED TO REVITALIZE OUR FIRMS AND GOVERNMENT WITH NEW THINKING

It is hoped that it is now clear that many internal changes are needed in the concepts and thinking that drive U.S. business and government organizations.

The year 1988 was a time of frantic leveraged buyouts (LBOs), leaving some ex-shareholders richer. However, the acquired firms usually were greatly weakened by the addition of a very large amount of debt — much of it with little security behind it (i.e., junk bonds). Therefore, if pressed by adverse business events such a firm may well go into bankruptcy — certainly it will be a candidate for Chapter 11 proceedings.

Another trend of the late 1980s is that many of our companies seem to want to manage money — thinking that is where the money is to be made. However, not everyone is "gulled" into this non-thinking state and takes actions to manage money, even if this is a popular business.

Look at Kinder-Care. They were highly successful with their day care business — and still are successful in this area. Then they decided to "go financial" and acquired a substantial number of financially oriented businesses, diverting day care profits and assets to these businesses instead of further hastening the expansion of the day care side of the business. Even though these *seem* to have done well, perhaps some of it is "created" performance and some may have come from the returns of the day-care business.

Regardless of what Kinder-Care management thought was desirable, the price of the stock fell well over 30 percent. They did not fool most of the investors, only themselves. Moreover, they have left themselves vulnerable to being acquired and the parts split off. Or, was it their idea to do this to provide a better base for a management LBO? The management by mid 1988 finally "saw the light" and is attempting to restructure, reduce debt, and set the child care activity free to rapidly expand. All this, however, has hurt many investors and it has greatly reduced confidence in Kinder-Care's management.

Corporate planning used to be oriented to considering a very limited geographic area that most concerned the company and a few area competitors. Today, the actions of competitors half way around the globe must be considered not only for overlapping markets, but also for economic and political climates (past, current, and future). The stakes are so high, both for the firms involved and for the nation, that one can not merely guess or use intuition in his decision making.

The sad fact is that there are so many things wrong with the typical larger industrial firm that all of them require a fairly large number of corrective actions if they expect to compete in the next decade and the next century. The best way to find out what is wrong and how to fix those things that are wrong is to engage in the kind of planning described in this text.

REFERENCES

1. Peter Drucker, "Peter Drucker's 1990s; The Futures That Have Already Happened," *The Economist*, October 21–27, 1989.
2. D. W. Karger, "The U.S. Educational System—It Is A Failed System," Speech before N.W. Florida Council of Engineering Societies (Pensacola, FL) and Kiwanis (DeFuniak Springs, FL), February/March, 1989.
3. Gary Putka, "Learning Curve; Lacking Good Results, Corporations Rethink Aid To Public Schools," *Wall Street Journal*, Vol. CCXIII, No. 124.
4. "Unions Need Not Apply," *Time*, August 7, 1989.
5. Edwin Mansfield, "Industrial Innovation in Japan and the United States," *Science*, Vol. 241, September 30, 1988.
6. Peter F. Drucker, "Best R & D is Business Driven," *The Wall Street Journal*, New York, February 10, 1988.
7. D. W. Karger, "Some Management Concerns for RPI's School of Management," Conference on Management of Technology for Competitiveness— Can Education Contribute, Rensselaer Polytechnic Institute, School of Management, Troy, NY, February 27, 1988.
8. D. W. Karger and G. M. Yaworsky, *Managing Engineering and Research*, Marcel Dekker, Inc., New York, NY 4th Ed., 1992.
9. Simon Ramo, "How to Revive U.S. High Tech" (a book review, 2nd part), *Fortune*, May 9, 1988.

10. D. W. Karger, "Non-Technical Considerations in Applied Research, Development, and Engineering Project Selection," paper No. 85-WA/Mgt-1, presented at Winter Annual Meeting, American Society of Mechanical Engineers, New York, November 1985.

11. Lester C. Thurow, quoted from an article in *Science* and the *Pensacola News Journal*, December 18, 1987.

12. "Why Is Service So Bad?," *Time*, February 2, 1987.

13. Tom Peters, "Facing Up to the Need for a Management Revolution," *California Management Review*, Winter 1988 or *IEEE Engineering Management Review*, June 1989 (Summer Issue).

14. Tom Peters, *Thriving On Chaos*, Excel, Distributed by Alfred A. Knopf, Inc., 1987.

15. Brian Dumaine, "Corporate Spies Snoop To Conquer," *Fortune*, November 7, 1988.

16. "The Name of Japan's New Business Game," *The Economist*, April 9, 1988.

2

Competing Successfully—Political, Educational, and Social Factors

I. INTRODUCTION

This chapter will concentrate on the political, social, and educational areas of concern that are believed to have potential for causing a significant adverse impact on competition in business and industry in the 1990s unless they are properly countered by the firm. As with Chapter 1, these discussions also indicate the necessity for firms to plan if they want to continue in business, so as to detect other such situations. Some of the projected or forecast problems and problem areas could cause the failure of virtually all firms not properly adjusting to coming changes. Proper planning is about the only mechanism that will help solve these kinds of problems.

The discussions are aimed at helping readers make connections between the current status and likely future events in such a manner as to facilitate the proper operation of businesses and other kinds of organizations. They emphasize improving results in business enterprises, but they also apply in a similar manner to most types of organizations, including non-profit, university, community, social, and governmental organizations.

The factors identified and described in Chapter 1 are similar in character and importance to those in Chapters 2, 3, and 4. None of these factors emerged in a short period of time (1–2 years); rather, they each required many years to become very visible. All this means that the strategic and operational planners must look not only for the more obvious major factors, but also for less visible factors.

Much of what is discussed in the referenced chapters has been known to the people taking advantage of the situation (some were in the U.S. as well as in other countries). Those knowledgeable people were "bending" their organizations either to take advantage of a factor or to neutralize handicaps presented by taking other strategic actions.

The lesson in the above paragraph is that if the firm does not want to substantially risk failure and wants to succeed, it needs to detect important factors early and begin at once to either take advantage of them or else counter the adverse factors. It takes a long time for an organization to change directions. Moreover, the reader should reflect upon the fact that the things exposed have pushed many U.S. firms into poor performance or into selling/merging the firm in order to rescue/retain what value was left in the corporation.

Planning is not an easy or a quickly accomplished process. Moreover, it cannot be relegated to an expert to produce a plan for the firm or organization. The planning effort MUST involve all major elements of an organization. This group, through united effort and under the leadership of a director and the C.E.O., must create a plan that is usable and capable of improving the organization's performance. Moreover, it must be *believable*, since the entire planning group must be convinced that it will work in order for it to execute the plan in a proper manner.

Sadly, many governmental organizations, and a few industrial organizations, have what they call plans, but they were only produced to show constituents (in case they are asked) that they did the right thing and planned for the future. The governmental plans usually are produced by a consultant and are only for "show." It is a rare instance where they are put to any practical use. Moreover, such plans are almost universally produced by an "expert" consultant without significant help by the concerned governmental organization head or other KEY management personnel.

In some industrial organization cases the "show" plans were produced by the C.E.O., with little or no help from anyone in the organization. In fact, most of the employees, at best, only know that a plan of some sort exists. There is an occasional dusting of the cover when they show it to some of the organization's constituents.

This author, as a corporate director, was exposed to such a plan by the C.E.O. when they were riding an airplane on a business trip. The C.E.O. had borrowed another firm's plan from its C.E.O. who was a friend. This borrowed plan was used by modifying "the numbers" to fit the second organization. To this C.E.O.'s credit, he and his organization did eventually produce a *proper* plan, which reversed the organization's flat sales and negative earnings to a strong upward trend in both. This author acted as their consultant planning director on the initial planning effort.

Our federal government heads indicate that proper planning is important to military organizations and to such branches of the government as NASA. But plans are not used in any other element of our government. Congress is especially adamant about its not formally planning for the future and the Executive Branch has never, to our knowledge, espoused formal plans for the economy or for society as a whole. This author believes some of the problem is partially due to the politicians thinking this is only done in communist countries. Further, they do not want to be held responsible for non-performance when measured against plan objectives. Finally, one must also consider that politicians (especially congressmen) spend a lot of time campaigning for a job that they may lose by each "election."

Government does not plan, short or long term: it only *reacts* to correct "happenings and fires" that obviously must be dealt with on some basis. However, U.S. business organizations are competing with firms located in *countries* that do have long range plans and objectives for key or important business segments and for the major business firms in these segments. This is especially true for Japan. The Japanese companies plan, as does their government. Moreover, these plans are followed and are updated on a regular schedule. Japanese firms have been successful, to a large degree, because of governmental *planned* support actions aimed at achieving *long term results* in their industrial community and because of industrial organization long term plans that are in accord with those of its government's agencies.

II. POLITICAL FACTORS

In Chapter 1, Japan and the actions of its companies were often described. The Japanese have overcome or achieved market domination over many U.S. companies in certain markets because of their below cost exporting— "dumping." This was accomplished with the help and blessings of the Japanese government. Essentially the government approved the dumping of products and financed it by low or non-existent interest rates. Japan wanted more exporting of Japanese products, so the nation helped its industrial firms win major market shares in product areas the government deemed desirable. They drove out all or much of their competition with artificially low prices.

Producing and selling these goods also helped their government (in effect) export some social (welfare) costs. If their plants had not been busy, the government would have incurred unemployment costs. This saving of unemployment expense approximately covered the loan costs and made it easy for Japanese firms to purchase market share. Have no doubts, the government knew exactly what it was doing.

The Japanese have two key arms of their government helping their industry increase export volume. The Ministry of Finance has the power to change depreciation rates and accounting rules and it "works in co-operation" with another agency, one that *Japan invented*. It is the Ministry of International Trade and Industry (MITI) that targets the industries that are to grow or that are to be allowed to wither, as well as the markets that are to be penetrated. Yes, they do have a plan and they execute their plan.

By working with the Ministry of Finance, MITI can help make the apparent cost of products lower and can help the companies finance losses incurred in buying market share through the extension of low cost loans to involved Japanese firms—sometimes at no cost. Be assured that whatever Japanese industry does, it is the intent of the Japanese government for them to act along these lines.

Since the Japanese government was so successful with its policies, what will prevent other nations such as Korea, Taiwan, Singapore, Hong Kong (if it survives the Chinese government), Brazil, and others from doing the same thing? The U.S. government is beginning to note the problem, but so far we are only engaging in "fire fighting" actions.

Another political action of general importance, but one which is even more important to U.S. businesses, is that Japan believes in economic planning. Our government only believes in military planning. The Japanese economic planning helped keep the value of our currency high with respect to theirs so as to give Japanese firms help in their pricing actions in the United States.

As to the U.S. military planning, it is so fragmented and divided between the services that defense plans are seriously flawed and often worthless. It is this lack of proper integrated planning that often causes our government to make rather irrational choices between various weapon systems in its effort to protect some of our beleaguered industries or those that are "pets" of the military.

One past example of this flawed action involves the U.S. steel industry, the world's largest steel industry in the 1950s. Our government and the steel companies frittered away the advantage—both were at fault. First, our government used the industry as a "whipping boy" with regard to pricing and wage rates. The industry destroyed its advantage by not modernizing and upgrading equipment in later years.

In the last few years many firms in the steel and the associated "rust belt" industries that modernized survived and are now making substantial profits. Could the firms have competed during all the years of their decline? Probably, even with the adverse government actions and Japan's then lower wage rates—remember, Japan had to import iron and steel. In fact we have several small mini mill steel companies that are SUCCESS-FULLY competing with the Japanese "head-on"—and are winning big. Nucor is one of these, and it even beat the pricing and delivery of imported bolts.[1] These were causing much of our equipment to fail—this even jeopardized our Space Shuttle.

Only NOW are the old steel companies going to continuous casting, which we invented, and to modern rolling techniques. Their profits have risen very substantially. Naturally, they did have overcapacity, and had to junk some of those outdated plants. It seems we are slow learners.

This saga of steel is not yet complete. Japan's smokestack steel industry began to lose business because world steel prices dropped and Japan's steel profit margins evaporated (just as those in the U.S. had dropped). The prices dropped because Nucor and other such U.S. steel companies in concert with others from South Korea and Britain priced the Japanese out of their export markets. Like the U.S. mills when they got into trouble, the Japanese mills then decided to diversify and went on a buying binge, acquiring and starting companies in businesses in which they had no experience and/or expertise.

The six largest Japanese steelmakers set up no fewer than 500 new ventures during 1986–1988. Their margins dropped, so the Japanese mills began closing plants and they also began selling off their new businesses, which they did not know how to run. This eliminated 19,000 jobs. It is predicted that the workforce will be trimmed another 13,000 jobs by 1991. Despite reduced sales, the 1989 profits of Nippon Steel (for example) will be greater than those of 1980 by ¥185 billion.[2] The reader will find another example of improper acquisitions, mergers, and new business ventures in Chapter 3, which discusses mergers and acquisitions.

There are some lessons here that should be perceived and clearly understood. First, never take an action that has not been thoroughly thought through, from beginning to end, using the planning process de-scribed in this text. Second, do not try to buy and/or operate a business in which the company has no expertise. For example, where in the experi-ence of a steel mill manager would he acquire experience in consumer products or hi-tech design and manufacturing?

III.   MONEY AS A POLITICAL WEAPON

When our currency is expensive relative to the currencies of the countries to whom we are selling, it becomes very difficult to compete in those markets and relatively easy for them to compete in our market. U.S. currency becomes relatively expensive when interest rates are raised upward by our government and/or when they are significantly above those of the foreign governments involved. However, remember that the currency actions of a government can shift these values as described earlier.

In 1987–1988, U.S. interest rates were reduced to a relatively low level as compared to Japan and some other industrialized countries. The result was that our currency began to fall in value relative to their currencies. Then our key interest rates were boosted to "curb inflation" and our currency began to recover some of its losses. However, the increase in relative value is still not enough to cause us problems.

One other ploy used by some governments to help their industries to export is to make it possible to offer buyers "cheap credit." For example, a government can provide money for such loans at a low interest rate. Some governments even provide money to make up operating losses and R & D expense—Air Industries created by the EEC countries is an example of this kind of action.

All this information should make it clear that governments can affect the ability of our firms to compete in world markets. Moreover, our U.S. market, as well as those of the world's developed nations, has for all practical purposes become one vast world marketplace. No longer are we protected by "distance."

A "cry" that one often hears from the uninformed populace, and many of our politicians, is to protect U.S. jobs by imposing tariff barriers. The fact is that the worst depression of this century was very greatly deepened when most of the developed nations began to impose trade barriers on everyone else. Why? "To protect our jobs." The truth is that "the jobs evaporated" in all the nations. There are NO jobs if business cannot successfully sell the products or services they provide.

We are coming VERY CLOSE to not having a tariff barrier between the U.S. and Canada; the enabling treaty has been signed but it will be a number of years before everything has been eliminated. The European Economic Community (EEC) hopes to have this condition among its members in 1992, but some of these nations are already "talking up" *EEC* trade barriers.

In the world's marketplaces "import rules" and "trade goods inspections" can be substituted for tariff barriers. Japan has erected all three of these barriers and they are only VERY slowly reducing them. Our government must take action to try and get them to tear down these barriers.

If one learns the rules and carefully works at overcoming them in the long term, many U.S. firms can successfully compete with Japanese firms in Japan. IBM is an excellent example of such a firm—it is successful in Japan. The message is that when things are tough, figure out a way around barriers. IBM managed to accomplish this task, but it is also true that Japan likely also wanted IBM in their country (maybe to acquire some of IBM's technology?).

From the material just presented, another message should be perceived. Use political pressure in the right places to get the government to do what you think is necessary—meaning that such issues and factors also need to be considered when engaging in planning.

IV. PROBLEMS OF TRADE AND BUDGET IMBALANCE

Japan sells us more than we sell them, so there is a trade imbalance; however, the figures generally cited do not take into account all of the items involved and therefore are not quite as large as the figures usually mentioned. Ideally, we should sell each other goods having approximately the same monetary value, but remember that this sum is distorted by relative currency values. In trying to achieve a balanced situation, the currencies of the two countries involved should have approximately the same relative value as measured by some common yardstick such as the cost of necessities like food and/or shelter.

The U.S. has similar imbalances with other nations, and this requires us to indirectly finance such imbalances, which adds to an already massive national budget debt. President Bush, like his predecessor, has promised to reduce expenses and thereby reduce the amount we have to borrow. The fact is that if we separate out military spending and social security type expenditures, we spend less per citizen on the federal government than virtually any other developed nation. It is therefore likely that this expense reduction *cannot* come close to solving our debt problem.

Some in government are suggesting that the U.S. reduce social security (S.S.) taxes because we are using the S.S. trust fund money indirectly to mask the large sums the government must borrow each year in order to "keep afloat." As to S.S. support, the U.S. already spends less than most developed nations on this category of expense; in fact, the poor are worse off than they were 2–3 years ago. That leaves the military cost as the remaining possibility of reducing the difference between inflow and out-flow of funds. They obviously have been getting more money than they can spend in a proper manner.

A new factor has entered the scene, the disintegration of communist control in eastern Europe and throughout the U.S.S.R. This should provide many opportunities to cut military expense, but will Congress use most of the resultant savings to reduce debt buildup?

The military organization of the U.S. needs to be rationally organized. The present division between services and commands is foolish and has caused great unnecessary expense. The nation needs a *unified* command, which should then do a superior job in weapon system selection and design. This would provide the nation a considerable reduction in the cost of our military needs and at the same time increase its fighting ability. *Integrated* planning would help bring about this change.

It also clearly illustrates that organization structure and related matters must be an integral part of long range planning. Improper organization not only costs identifiable dollars in almost any size organization, but it is at its peak influence in large organizations (like the military or a large industrial firm like General Motors). It can cost huge sums in even a relatively small organization because improper organization guarantees having a poorly functioning business/manufacturing operation. The fragmented military only plans for battle strategies (i.e., weapons systems) and what it wants to spend for acquiring these weapons systems and how much it needs to operate (this is done by each service for its own perceived needs); no other form of planning ever seems to occur. For example, the Pentagon budgeting group develops plans, but it does not sensibly relate to the above-mentioned planning. A correct and totally integrated planning activity would lead to desirable changes and results.

There is another military budget problem: the budget is burdened by the cost of protection for most EEC nations and Japan. It seems obvious that all that needs to be done is to make these nations assume their own defense burden. They certainly have the money. If this were done it would appear that the problems would be solved. WRONG!

The elimination of certain protective actions is not yet possible, but the United Nations and its constituent members are acting more responsible and rational—e.g., in the Kuwait "affair" (1990). Ultimately, with the advent of a secure democracy in the Soviet bloc nations, then the U.S. can reduce the numbers of men and weapons. However a huge new competitive problem may be an EEC expanded to include most of the new Eastern European democratic nations.

V.   EDUCATIONAL FACTORS[3-11]

In late 1988 there was apprehension on the part of investors that the low unemployment rate in the U.S. (just above 5 percent) would fuel inflation because business would need to bid up the going wage rate in order to obtain employees.

Many businesses can't get the employees they need simply because most of the unemployed have no marketable skills and many are functionally illiterate. Even a large portion of the officially unemployed (those who lost recognized jobs) are illiterate!

In some areas of the U.S., businesses are being forced to help their employees learn how to read and develop computational skills. Others have begun to export jobs because of this problem. As mentioned in Chapter 1, one major insurance company located in New Jersey could not find enough people who could read, write, and compute at the high school level, so they EXPORTED their jobs to Ireland where graduates can read, write, and compute. They fly the data to Ireland for processing and either fly back the results or return it via satellite. Exporting of jobs is already a common practice for a variety of reasons.

If an employee cannot read directions, warnings, specifications, or operating instructions, perform simple computations, and write simple reports, he/she is of little use in the modern factory or even as a clerk in a store. Pure labor type jobs, such as ditch digging, have almost disappeared from the work scene.[4] Further, many do not want to perform house/room/hotel cleaning work — they consider it degrading.

Depending upon the state, county, or city involved, usually 30–40 percent read at or below the eighth grade level. The school dropout rates through high school range between 25 and 40 percent in a majority of places. Up to 50 percent or more get social promotions up to and through high school, meaning that most of these are functionally illiterate. The total number in the U.S. is over 90,000,000. Think a minute about the problem: industry will *have* to help educate these illiterates, but government must also be part of the process.[5]

Many of the illiterates never were employed in a real job and are therefore not included in the unemployment statistics — meaning the U.S. has 1 or more percent additional unemployed that have not been counted. The U.S. does have workers, but very many of them are unqualified for most of today's jobs. It should be obvious that finding and training workers needs careful consideration in the development of long range plans.

Our chief competitor (or so it seems) is Japan. It has an illiteracy rate of about 1–2 percent. The author recently had a professional Japanese friend as a house guest and she could not conceive it as being above 1 percent. Most people there subscribe to or read two different newspapers.

The Hudson Institute, a well known think tank, provided some information to *Business Week*[6] which says that 40 percent of the jobs being created between now and and the year 2000 will require reading skills that are beyond 75 percent of the *new* workers coming on the scene. Only about 22 percent of the new workers will be able to read safety rules and equipment instructions and write simple reports—the skill level required for a store clerk. They went on to say that only 5 percent of the new employees will be at the next highest level, which means the ability to read journals and manuals and write business letters and read reports. About 6 percent will likely possess professional degrees.

We once were the envy of the world for literacy, the quality of education, and the number of professionally educated people. Today, we have fallen substantially from that position. Unless we solve the ills of our educational system, our standard of living will decrease and our nation will slide backward. Even a substantial number of colleges are largely gigantic babysitting institutions that turn out FEW high caliber professionals.

When considering this problem, remember that it was under the guidance of so-called professional educators that our schools have failed to keep educating our youth. As mentioned before, up to 50 percent are being pushed through without having acquired any significant academic skills.

The mess can be turned around. The July 30 issue of *The Economist*[7] described what South Carolina did to correct such a problem. It ranked 49th out of the 50 states in how much it spent on each pupil—one above the bottom rung. It had the highest dropout rate and its students ranked dismally low in reading, writing, and arithmetic. Naturally, they were at the bottom of the SAT score sweepstakes.

In 1984 Mr. Richard Riley led a North Carolina campaign to pass a huge Education Improvement Act, but it required a fight. Most of the state legislature opposed the act because it would raise the state sales tax to 5 percent to pay for it. Business men, the PTAs of the state, teachers, and public figures backed it and the legislature backed down and passed it.

The act raised salaries ($17,000 to $25,000 in 1988), established remedial classes, provided a year-round gifted children program, and provided management training to school heads. Lagging schools were declared impaired and the superintendents could be removed by the governor. To monitor the success of the law, a new division has been created that issues a yearly report. The best schools get bonus payments.

For the following 4 years, South Carolina schools reported the largest yearly percentage increase in SAT scores. Other test scores are up, truancy is down, and high school students are enrolling in advanced placement classes at twice the national average. Morale among teachers is the highest in the country. What this shows is that improvement is possible and it is not necessary to tolerate the continuing fall of the U.S. public school educational system. There are other success stories, but on a much smaller scale.

Citizens (all citizens) must hold the people managing our primary and secondary education responsible. When they fail to perform, they *must be* removed and replaced by better school superintendents.

Some suggest that the U.S. must go to a voucher system to clean up the mess, especially since the school system is essentially governed by the teachers' union which does not want to criticize itself. The recommendation would make it possible for the parents to take their children to the schools that *really* educate their students. The teachers and the administrators at the non-performing schools would be discharged—and there would be no jobs for them in the school system. This idea has been used in a number of places.[3,6]

Unless the U.S. improves its lower level educational system immediately, there will be no workers to hire to perform the necessary work. Business will have to set up special schools and the introduction of new products/processes will be delayed so long that it probably will jeopardize the viability of our businesses. More importantly to the nation, the standard of living for ALL workers will be lowered unless we correct the situation.

The securing of such national and state government action needs the muscle of industry's lobbying power as well as that of other concerned organizations and citizens. This is another problem to consider in planning—but few readers except those at the head of giant firms will have thought about it without the above discussion. Readers should also note that business and industrial firms are now forming partnerships with some school systems—although there are reports of some of these early efforts failing to cause any improvement. Logic says they will fail and continue to fail as long as the same failed teachers and methods are used—only more money will be spent.

The grade and high school systems are not the only educational problem. Less than half of our engineering school graduates are U.S. citizens. Yes, many of the foreign graduates from our schools stay on to work in the U.S. and acquire citizenship. However, we now find that the home countries are successfully persuading many of these people to return and help their native country succeed. The current country successfully pursuing this tactic is South Korea. Business and industry must also keep providing financial support to our colleges and universities.

Throwing money at the problem will do no good. The largest reason for the record increase in education costs is not the salaries paid to teachers, but the huge increase in support personnel. This is equally true of elementary, secondary, and college level schools.[8-11]

Charles Schultz, Director of Economic Studies for Brookings Institute, recently said in a television program (The Nightly Business Program of public TV) that the quality of U.S. high school graduates is well below those of other industrial nations. Moreover, when it concerns science and mathematics, the U.S. is at the bottom or near it when compared to other developed nations.

He believes a good part of our problem is that there are no discernible (to the students) economic incentives to work hard—there is no link-up to academic performance since poor students seem to do about as well as good students with regard to salaries (at least it appears so "on the surface"). One reason for this is that American industry can't get good or reliable data on a person's school performance. Often little can be secured, and what is available is not standardized and cannot be relied upon. Remember high schools have social promotions and many to most colleges have severe grade inflation—and our educators defend these as reasonable and rational actions.

Schultz said that the results of standardized tests are available to employers in other industrialized countries. His recommendation is that the Labor Department (U.S. industry can influence it) should help by developing standardized tests and make them available to the schools. The schools should make these performance records available to an employer that has been approached by the student for a job. They should be certified test results. Schultz thinks (and so does this author) that they should at least cover reading, writing, mathematics, science, typing ability, computer knowledge and language (reading, speaking, and writing).[8-11] However, intelligent people must write these tests if they are to measure anything. Maryland had an essay writing type test for high school seniors which was so bad that some college professors could not do well on it while some near illiterates did do well. Could this have been because some not too bright people made up the test and scored it?

VI.   COLLEGE AND UNIVERSITY EDUCATION

The costs associated with education were previously mentioned because they have risen so much that they are hindering not only primary and secondary education but also college and university education—for exactly the same primary reason, the increased number of non-teaching personnel.

Yes, the cost of college and university education has risen at a faster rate than that of inflation.

There is a decrease in high school students with the necessary qualifying grades and credits to gain entrance to college. This is further compounded by a decrease in school population, plus the apparent unnecessarily high cost of education. Because of all of the above factors it is highly likely that securing and holding professional manpower will be a problem for U.S. business and industry in the next one or two decades—and the effort to keep them should be accorded a high priority.

Our colleges are becoming populated with an escalating proportion of foreign born students—in some technical and scientific programs the portion of foreign national students is 20–40 percent. True, these can often be encouraged (some need no encouragement) to join a U.S. firm. However, they often come from greatly differing cultures and their English language ability is sometimes lacking. Moreover, the foreign national governments are learning how to convince the graduates to return to their home country.

For technically oriented firms, the described situation can be an increasingly large problem in the future. Dr. John A. Armstrong, Director of Research for IBM said in a published interview[12] that he did not think people have any idea how much we (in the U.S.) are living on borrowed time. If we are not careful, he says, there is a good chance that we will not be able to save ourselves since we have not solved the problem of educating enough of our youth in science and mathematics.

Dr. Armstrong believes that our citizens need to be galvanized into prompt action to solve the problem. Incidently, he also agrees that it is much harder to keep foreign scientists working in our country. Armstrong is convinced that we must "grow our own" scientists (which also includes engineers).

VII. SOCIAL FACTORS

An obviously important factor to consider is the matter of personal social security and the responsibility organizations have toward employee welfare needs. Many view this matter as being taken care of by federal and state governments when they established Social Security and pension plans for government workers and by unemployment benefit programs. However, as most managers and professionals know, general social security considerations must also include company pensions, health and life insurance, educational benefits, child day care, an environmentally and occupationally safe workplace, and others. All of these factors are a part of a package of benefits that relate to social welfare and social responsibility.

These factors must be considered in planning activities. Complicating such consideration is the fact that the cost of many of the elements in the "package" are escalating at varying rates. The planning therefore must also consider what the firm should do to publicize to employees not only the benefits but their costs to the firm.

Job security, or freedom from the fear of the loss of one's job, is a danger that is always present to some degree. In industry, usually the higher your position, the more danger there is of this possibility—at least this is the assessment of many observers, including that of this author. The way to develop true job security for most professionals is to have enough capital (knowledge, money, and/or money equivalents) or to have tenure in a school or university, or the right civil service position, or be a career military man, or some other such relatively "safe" type of job. Knowledge capital is the most important of the three mentioned kinds of capital in many respects. If a professional worker has enough knowledge and ability, he can virtually always secure an equal or better job.

If one is a craftsperson (millwright, electrician, pipefitter, etc.) and he is in a large and well run industrial firm, seniority begins to provide considerable protection after about 10 years of service. Here, as for the above professional workers, knowledge and *skill* provide the ultimate security. If these kinds of workers will change job locations (cities) it works almost as well as for engineers, accountants, etc. These people, however, do not move about easily and therefore they are about as concerned about job security as the untrained workers.

It used to be that untrained union workers without identifiable skills and knowledge had considerable job security protection with 10 years of seniority, but with quantum changes in the health of firms and in the products produced at a given point in time in a specific plant, this aspect of job security has significantly decreased. The employees know this and are therefore concerned. The unions either have not recognized this fact or refuse to acknowledge its effect on the kind of work rules and employee protection needed.

It is obvious that job security and other social factors play a substantial role in the enthusiasm a worker has for hard work and in helping the organization to succeed. In case a job is lost there normally is some state unemployment compensation, but the benefits tend to "run out" quickly in a severe recession or depression.

Moreover, workers used to assume that Social Security (S.S.) benefits would be untaxed and not decrease in times of financial difficulty. Further, the pensions provided by employers were considered secure. But in the past decade these benefits have become very suspect. The government "tinkers" with Social Security taxation and it is using the Social Security surplus to finance the yearly deficit by investing it in government bonds that will need to be redeemed by the government soon after the year 2000 so as to be able to pay the S.S. benefits. Sad, but it is unlikely that the government will have the money or the will to go further into debt so as to provide all the expected benefits. All this will have an adverse effect upon labor relations and rational government.

Many companies consider the pension system their property, and some have prevailed with this view in the courts. As a result, sometimes they just eliminate the pension system and take the money. Other firms when they run into financial difficulty close down the system and take the money. Others close down the system, remove the surplus and then restart the system—all within 24 hours.

In spite of the above dangers that the hiring organizations pose to the welfare of the employee, and any doubts "sowed" by the unions, there actually is a great deal of loyalty to the hiring organization. However, the less secure employees always have some degree of pressure tilting them to worrying about their job security and are the least loyal to the organization's views.

Having said this, and not too many will admit to the above, it should be obvious that social considerations will play a BIG role in the enthusiasm a worker has for cooperating and playing a large role in helping the company/organization to succeed.

The Japanese have elicited a greater loyalty from employees because the company managements seem to have a feeling of greater responsibility for their employees than the managements of the American firms. Not only do the Japanese espouse lifetime employment for a major segment of work force, but they also do other things to engender a "good feeling" toward the company. Japanese workers are, for example, given a major voice in deciding how they should work, how to improve quality, how to improve the product, how to improve production, and more. Much of this is done in formal discussion groups, but some is informal two-way discussion.

In the February 13, 1989, issue of *Fortune*, Brian Dumaine, describes what various firms have done to GREATLY improve performance by speeding up the process through change.[13] One of the areas that could usually be improved is that of the speed of decision making.

When General Electric completely reorganized their old circuit breaker division, they consolidated six plants into one, and redesigned the product for simplification and automation, computerized design, order handling, and scheduling. More importantly, they also got rid of all line supervisors and quality inspectors and thereby reduced the organizational layers between worker and plant manager from three to ONE. Everything the middle managers did, such as scheduling vacations, quality assurance/improvement, and establishing work rules, was left to the 129 workers on the floor. These workers were divided into teams of 15–20, and the more the responsibility GE gave the workers, the faster the job got done. The plant now almost runs itself, and they have even installed an electronic sign to help the workers better determine how to schedule themselves— no, it does NOT tell them what to do, it merely provides production data.

Most businesses want flexible work rules, but if the employees do not trust management they will not agree to much of anything that management wants. Most companies desire high morale, but this is a subject left to the personnel department in a typical organization, and management ignores the problem unless the workers become so unhappy that it affects their work. There are a host of such problems in most organizations that need to be thoroughly and completely thought through in the planning process.

Another problem needing a solution is that of the use of drugs by employees. Until a solution to the general drug problem (including alcohol) is found, most firms and organizations will need to consider the implementation of random screening tests. In fact this will likely be a part of any rational solution. Management can not tolerate employees who are addicted to drugs. The effects can cost large organizations millions of dollars in increased indirect and direct expenses. Drug addicted employees can even physically endanger their coworkers. The author and many experts believe such actions will be required, or else some other solution must be found.

The author dislikes mentioning a big problem without at least mentioning a different approach to solving it. It is contained in an article "It Doesn't Have To Be Like This" in *The Economist*.[14] The article has a very detailed three page discussion on how to solve the mind altering drug problem. It is a sort of replay on an old solution for a similar problem. Basically, do what was done with solving our liquor problem which crested during the U.S.'s period of legal "prohibition"—make it legal and tax the h——— out of it and use the money to pay for extra police to regulate it and to rehabilitate those unfortunate enough to become addicts. Make sure the tax pays everything and also puts some in the coffers. However, do not make it so expensive that it becomes worthwhile to become an illegal seller of drugs (like liquor from the prohibition days). They say legalizing the drugs trade would be risky, but prohibition is a PROVEN failure.

This author, as with many older people, saw the failure of prohibition with alcohol. The first inclination of many such people is to agree that we should do the same with mind altering drugs. However, the addictive potential of alcohol on our population is probably in the neighborhood of 20 percent of the population. Drugs have the power to cause all who try it to become addicted and are a whole different kind of problem. Rehabilitation of addicts is very difficult, if not impossible in many cases. This makes this solution very "suspect" of having fatal flaws.

Since Part I of this text is an endeavor to explicitly expose the great variety and importance of the kinds of problems and opportunities that must be considered in planning, one more problem can be mentioned. It, and many of the things discussed to this point, cannot be discerned by extrapolation, guesses, or depending upon personal knowledge. Here, in this last item, is clearly illustrated the importance of managers reading a large variety of publications, not just those about the industry, or one profession, or only national publications or any such narrow view.

The next general subject is "Backlash Against Business," which loosely fits into the social factors category. The source of the information to be disclosed is a British publication, *The Economist*, which published an article with the above-indicated title.[15] It deals with the changing moods of the citizens and politicians of various countries toward the desirability of fostering business versus putting restrictions on business.

The more general national mood changes toward business (for or against) are cyclical, but there is some uniformity between countries, especially in the developed nations. In the 1960s business in the U.S. was everybody's whipping boy. Next came the period where business seemed to have much support. Now, it seems that evidence is accumulating that indicates a reverse swing will occur and that by the end of the 1990s it will be rather clear to observers that a change in attitude has occurred. Similar indicators are found in other countries. For example, a distaste for all the "bad" business activities in the U.S. has already surfaced. Even if business "shapes up" it may be too late—the distaste may become much worse and result in negative legislation. This could affect many firms.

There seems to be no sure or easy way to prevent it by planning, but planners can take actions that will protect the firm from most of the possible harm that could come to it because of this change in perception and also bring about a change in attitude of the firm's employees about how management really treats their employees. If you want to increase the feelings of the employees for the firm, take action now. Do not wait until things really get bad.

The approach in this chapter has been to cite a problem and then try to suggest ways of coping or benefiting from the described situation or factor. Right thinking will often make possible the identification of an opportunity, rather than merely perceiving a factor or a problem.

For example, most professional employees and a large portion of all office employees spend two or more hours per day reading—reports, technical articles, instructions, procedures, methods, correspondence, memos, etc., at a speed of 300–400 words per minute. In most of these cases it is possible to reduce the reading time by 50 percent or more. How? By teaching such employees "speed reading" and improving their reading speed to 800 plus words per minute. Up to 1200–1500 words per minute is possible for some really accomplished speed readers. It is teachable, and speed readers understand and retain as much as slow readers. However, it will not work when reading highly technical and involved material, like a mathematics book or problem.

If the organization does the teaching internally, the ensuing cost will be almost negligible. Calculate how much that hour per day saved for each professional who finishes the course is worth to the firm over each future year that the employee is employed. This really has little to do with planning, other than to illustrate another kind of matter that can be considered when planning.

VIII.   CONCLUDING REMARKS

The factors discussed in these first two chapters have exposed some very major problems faced by the modern business firm. They will not vanish for either business firms or other organizations. It is therefore necessary to rationally plan to overcome such problems—or better yet, to take advantage of them.

The reader should also review the specific bibliographies at the rear of each of these first two chapters. Note that these important findings were located in general and business oriented publications.

The professional literature often is blind to these kinds of situations. This is because those associated with the specific professions involved in the subject do not like to talk about defects, simply because they would be talking about how to correct flaws that they themselves created.

As to forecasts of the future by governments or governmental bodies, be cautious. They tend to be "self-serving"—"bent" to shore up or "bear out" something they want to do or want to have happen because it will make voters happy.

One other low profile suggestion that the reader should note is that political actions can have a drastic effect (good or bad) upon the firm. Therefore, do take political action when it may help your organization.

One final observation—the author, who has over 80 man-years of corporate board experience, has never heard a political issue or the support of a candidate ever discussed in a board meeting. If the approach is clearly focused upon the welfare of the firm, such discussions can be beneficial.

Finally, be sure to be prepared to find still other problems and opportunities described in the next two chapters. However, the scene will mainly be internal to the organization.

REFERENCES

1. John Merwin, "People, Attitudes and Equipment," *Forbes*, February 8, 1988.
2. "Japan's Smokestack Fire Sale," *The Economist*, August 19, 1989.
3. Delmar Karger, "The U.S. Educational System—It Is A Failed System," A speech delivered before N.W. FL Engineer's Council (in Pensacola, FL) and a "working paper," DeFuniak Springs, FL, 1989.
4. John Fischer, *The Stupidity Problem and Other Harassments*, Harper & Row, New York, NY, 1948, 1964.
5. "No Child Should Attend A Second Rate School" (an interview of Lauro Cavozos), *USA Today*, May 30, 1989.
6. Bruce Nussbaum, "Needed: Human Capital," *Business Week*, September 19, 1988.
7. "A Penny for Your Schools," *The Economist*, July 30, 1988.
8. Gary Putka, "Tracking Tuition: Why College Fees are Rising So Sharply," *The Wall Street Journal*, December 11, 1986.
9. Peter Brimelow, "Are We Spending too Much on Education?" *Forbes*, December 29, 1986.
10. Peter Brimelow, "The Untouchables," *Forbes*, November 30, 1987.
11. Philip Smith, "It's Ruining Our Schools!—A 600 Percent Rise in Workers Who Don't Teach," *National Enquirer*, March/April 1988.
12. IBMs Top Scientist, *The New York Times*, Business Section, page 6, Sunday, July 9, 1989.
13. Brian Dumaine, "How Managers Can Succeed Through Speed," *Fortune*, February 13, 1989.
14. "DRUGS; It Doesn't Have To Be Like This," *The Economist*, September 2, 1989.
15. "Backlash Against Business," *The Economist*, April 15, 1989.

3

Internal Business Considerations, with Some External Factors

Mergers, acquisitions, spin-offs, selling business units, and restructuring are all factors that must be considered when developing a strategic management plan—really a strategic long range plan. These factors or actions must also often be considered in both long term and short term tactical planning.

This and the other material in this chapter mostly involve internal considerations. Yet some of the above mentioned items also involve external considerations. Be advised that internal considerations are as important as external considerations in a majority of cases. Further, as mentioned in the introduction to Part I, many planners are essentially not knowledgeable about the above mentioned actions. Unfortunately mergers et al. are an essential part of most strategic planning efforts of large and many smaller firms.

Since many planners need to become informed regarding the above activities, the discussion of them will include basic descriptive information as well as strategic considerations. There seemed to be no easier or better way of accomplishing both required tasks.

The factors mentioned above (Mergers et al.) must be considered in most efforts to develop a strategic long range plan since they relate to such actions as the following:

1. Growing the company.

2.   Trying to escape being acquired.
3.   Restructuring, involved in 1 and 2 as well as in trying to increase profitability.

The initial discussion will center upon mergers and acquisitions. Mergers almost always involve an acquisition, but a merger generally is a "somewhat" friendly action where two companies *agree* to merge, generally for perceived organizational benefits. However, one firm is usually in the lead position and wields a major influence upon what actually happens. In a few cases, a merger involves an attempt to mutually and equally share in the decision making that must follow the merger.

An acquisition is where one company attempts to buy another firm, usually by first acquiring a significant ownership position if its stock is publicly held and can be purchased on an active exchange. Such acquired ownership positions can range from about 5 to 20 percent. This may eventually result in a generally friendly acquisition (an ordinary merger) or it can involve a bitter struggle between the acquiring company and the company in danger of being acquired.

The three indicated actions will be addressed in the material which follows, as well as all of the components or factors mentioned in the chapter title. Moreover, the three actions (that often trigger the factors identified in the title) will be included in the discussion.

The process of "growing the company" naturally leads to considering mergers and acquisitions as a viable route to company growth. Moreover, management can grow the firm by internal actions such as expanding sales, increasing production capability, creating new products, acquiring new distribution channels, and a host of other such actions. Sometimes a firm which becomes a "target" for an expansionist company uses the same tactics (mergers and/or acquisitions) to grow itself out of the "range" or "reach" (becomes too costly a target) of the acquiring company.

Mergers are also sometimes used by a company trying to evade acquisition by seeking a merger with still another company that is perceived as being friendly—in essence, asking the so-called friendly company to acquire them via a merger. The friendly firm is referred to by the trade as a "white knight."

Such firms sometimes (but rarely) try to swallow a much larger firm and thereby make themselves too large to be acquired by a predator firm.

Since there are so many variables in the transactions, motives, and pressures driving the actions of the participants, the only way to sort out the facts is to consider the topics of the chapter heading individually and to cite which of the variables (reasons) are driving the action(s).

I. MERGERS

Most firms at one time or another must factor merger-relevant actions into their strategic planning. The effects caused by such actions are very important to the welfare of business and industrial firms.

First, mergers will be discussed as a part of the process of growing the company. Naturally, a company can be increased in size (sales and profits) by expanding the market area, advertising, introducing new products, revising or modifying its distribution system, reducing expenses/costs so as to increase profits, restructuring to make more efficient use of existing assets, and other such actions. However, one other route often taken is to use the merger route in combination with all or most of the above-mentioned internal actions. Acquisitions by purchase or unfriendly merger are also used to grow the company.

If the firm is operating in a fragmented market the usual action taken to grow the firm is to try to consummate one or more friendly mergers with selected target firms and gradually become the dominant firm. This may require many such transactions over a substantial period of years. Examples of the latter case are Service Corporation International and Gannett. This is just one of the many reasons why long term planning must precede short term planning.

In such transactions, the initial effort is to attempt to acquire the firm by an exchange of stock—this usually requires that the *acquiring* company's stock must be publicly traded. If the firms involved are relatively small, they are usually owned by one or just a few insiders. In this case, the merger is initiated by arranging to meet with the principal owner to begin the bargaining process. The "exchange" is often one involving cash.

There is no real reason to concentrate on unlisted firms, since listed firms eventually must also be approached—in most cases. In fact, if an individually owned firm is large enough, it might endeavor to acquire a publicly owned firm in order to secure a listing on a stock exchange.

The insiders who want to continue working in an acquired firm are usually "told" that they can continue in their previous positions—this is especially true if the acquiring organization does not have a depth of talent. In fact, where this is involved, it is usual to require the selling C.E.O. to continue serving for a specified period of years. If the firm is to be integrated into the acquiring company, it will be necessary to send at least one major executive to the acquired firm—often this person will have a financial background.

The above action becomes more complicated if the acquiring firm wants to grow, but is not focused on the same or related businesses.

An example now follows in order to illustrate what can and often does happen, even where people have broad experience and a lot of money.

If you are quite knowledgeable regarding these factors, you can skip over the details.

The example firm, in which the author was involved, wanted to grow from yearly $500,000 earnings and $1,000,000 sales to $100,000,000–$200,000,000 sales and secure a listing on a major stock exchange, not just NASDAQ. Without knowing the facts, the first part of the statement sounds silly, but the firm's product was hi-tech and made by an advantageous company confidential process—hence it *then* had a 50 percent profit margin.

The firm was able to beat the big users on price and product characteristics. However, these purchasers and potential purchasers were all vertically integrated and wanted to continue manufacturing their major raw product. They only bought from this specialty supplier when their customer needed a finished product that they could not manufacture with their own raw product.

The company involved was essentially owned by one very ambitious person with very deep pockets stuffed with big money. If it had not been for the last fact and that the C.E.O. was essentially of the genius type, the ultimate result would have been a major disaster. The driving motive was the availability of $500,000 each year from the parent firm (plus cash flow) and the very strong desire to own and manage a big industrial firm. Due to industry conditions, the existing business could not be expanded—other than by buying a finished goods manufacturer, which was not deemed advantageous or feasible. Ultimately, there also was a recognition that the technical advantage of the current product would be overcome with the passage of time since no strong patent protection was achievable—and this eventually did occur.

The aim was to achieve the expansion of sales and profits by purchasing firms. These firms had to be in unrelated businesses since there were no firms in the main business area that could be bought at an affordable cost except one, and this small firm was also purchased.

There was no long range plan specifying actions, industry and business areas, firm size, etc., because of known logical reasons. As opportunities arose, each possibility was examined, and the business evaluated on the basis of stated information and the financial statements, but not by people having experience in the business. Most of the deals involved an exchange of stock since the acquiring firm was a public corporation (price was listed in the "pink sheets"), although a majority of the stock was held by the owner. Some cash buyouts were also consummated. Most of the acquired firms were closely held, with some of the owners operating close to the borderline of legality.

Where is this discussion leading? Hopefully after reading this tale, the reader will never get involved in this kind of action without proper planning and business evaluations.

A small financial data service was acquired, which eventually was sold for about the purchase price to a much larger firm. Several printers, one in Richmond, Virginia, were purchased. They never made any consistent profits after acquisition. Lawsuits between the former owners and the acquiring firm also developed. Again, these were overcome. Two of the printing firms were sold back to the former owners. A large magazine and book distributor was acquired, but this too developed problems, including the leakage of profits and the discovery that the purchased inventory was not what was stated at the time of the purchase—the purchaser had no one in the firm who was qualified to do more than merely check titles and quantity.

It should be obvious that the big error in making these acquisitions was a lack of knowledge and experience in the businesses being acquired. Excellent legal advice, fairly competent accounting type financial advice, and the advice and consent of a board of directors containing some generally competent people will not substitute for this lack of essentially required experience and knowledge. The purchase actions were almost entirely based upon an analysis of financial statements, examining the operations, and looking at the physical assets.

An ordinary person would, early in the game, have had to give up on the effort and would have lost big money. Do not conclude that the acquired firms had shabby profit and loss (P & L) statements. They just did not continue to produce the indicated former returns—you can draw your own conclusions from this piece of intelligence.

The firm also acquired a rope manufacturing company and several spinning mills. It took years to introduce an excellent manager who could rationalize these remaining operations, properly integrate them, and learn how to manage them. However, this was accomplished, sales grew at a better than average rate to where they now are about $80,000,000–$90,000,000 annually, and it is an excellent and consistent profit producer. Another firm with a somewhat related product line has grown to about $25,000,000 annual sales.

How long did this take? About 25 years! Most of the junk was acquired and disposed of in the first 5–8 years. The rationalization consumed far too much time. Moreover, if the excess money had not been available and if the person had not been a highly intelligent person, the effort would have resulted in bankruptcy—he was a very quick learner.

Over the past 40 years there have been many attempts to grow by acquiring firms that were in businesses that were essentially in operational areas in which the acquirer had no expertise. In the vast majority of such cases the acquired firm eventually regretted such acquisitions.[1]

Most of the undesirable attempts to expand could have been eliminated through a proper long term focus through planning combined with industry and company growth studies, and securing outside expert advice — and listening to it if the needed expertise does not exist within the firm. The purchases would never have been made, especially if internal know-how (knowledge) or purchased consulting expert knowledge had been used by the C.E.O. Excellent legal and adequate financial knowledge was available and was used intelligently.

Excellent managers who can grow with the firm are invaluable and should be nurtured — meaning that there must be excellent personnel policies in existence. Some depth of talent in the acquiring company is an absolute requirement if the businesses are not to be combined into the headquarter location.

It would be improper not to suggest that the value of excellent legal counsel is worth every dime. The C.E.O. of the acquiring firm was never successfully legally overcome by disgruntled former owners or other participants in any of these activities — there were many attempts to do this legally. Neither was any trouble encountered with the Internal Revenue Service (IRS) or any governmental agency.

The most important lesson to be acquired from just this one example is that one should not acquire businesses in which the buyer has no real experience or expertise. First, it is advisable to acquire someone with expertise in the field one wants to enter (could be a consultant).

Keep in mind that the owner C.E.O. of a purchased firm often does not produce for the new owner. It takes several years for even a genius to acquire a meaningful experience in a new business. All kinds of businesses tend to be complex. A proper planning effort would have brought forth most of the above perceptions and prescriptions for success — and many other similar requirements.

There are many examples of successful growth via mergers and acquisitions. For example, Kinder-Care, before they decided to also become a financial services organization, steadily grew by opening new Kinder-Care locations. They also bought up smaller chains by merger or outright purchase.

Service Corporation International has grown almost entirely by well-planned buying and acquiring by merger existing funeral homes and funeral home chains. They they expanded into related fields such as cemeteries, flower shops, limo services, and a casket manufacturer — while all of the non-funeral home acquisitions relate to the central business, the company had no experience and knowledge in running such firms. Hence they are now divesting some of these. One of the latest acquisitions is an insurance company which is being used to supply guaranteed funerals.

Gannett is a very successful acquirer of newspapers and TV stations.

However, they also internally launched *U.S.A. Today*, a national weekly, in order to grow the company internally. Their plans are believed to have projected substantial losses for about 3–5 years; but it is taking a little longer to reach profitability in this venture because of adverse conditions in the newspaper and publishing sector of our economy. While they lost big money for several years, *U.S.A. Today* is now almost at the break-even point. They obviously are going to win big on this one since its circulation already exceeds that of *The Wall Street Journal* of Dow Jones. They also make money on TV stations which they own.

Their latest internal growth ploy was a joint effort to launch a "U.S.A. Today" national TV newscast, but results were so bad that this venture has been canceled. It had difficulty in finding a winning format for the program.

In spite of all the actions of Gannett, their earnings have grown at about 15 percent per year. In the past 5 years Gannett's stock price has increased about 200 percent. Dow Jones, mentioned above, also practices growth via mergers and acquisitions.

There is nothing wrong with the concept of growing a company, only do it in a logical and businesslike manner. Use every technique that will add to your advantage. The only firm in the above list that did not do this too well in the past several years is Kinder-Care which was mentioned in a previous chapter. Their failure to run a subsidiary geared to "managing money activities" caused a big drop in their stock price.

A bit more should be said at this point about "growing the company to become a larger firm." Some managements seem to attempt to grow the company because of a belief that big is better.

This concept was discussed in Chapter 1, but more needs to be said in this section on mergers and acquisitions (related activity). We gave one example of a firm that merely set out to get big by buying profitable companies. Most of these acquisitions cost the acquiring firms much money, money which could have been used to create increasing profits — usually because the purchased firms had no real relation to the existing business(es) and because the acquirer did not have the guidance of a long range plan where this kind of action would be considered in a rational and unemotional manner.

The somewhat incredible fact is that large so-called sophisticated firms frequently do as poorly as the firm mentioned in the example. Scientific evidence as shown by a hundred or more of studies indicates that big firms do not usually do well with acquired unrelated businesses.[2,3] In a 1956 study, Joe Bain examined the cost advantages of multi-plant firms versus single-plant firms and not one case was found that supported multi-plant operations.[2,3] Frederic Scherer studied the fate of 15 former subsidiaries of conglomerates which had been sold to their former managers. All but one showed improved performance.[2,3]

The above shows that we still have a lot to learn about managing "bigness." Further, if one has a number of different businesses, each in a separate plant or operation, then possibly a new concept of *complete* autonomy might be a helpful management structure.

Earlier, a number of examples of companies that grew large by acquisitions and mergers and which succeeded were presented. Yet one can cite many that failed to achieve benefits by such actions and which had to reorganize, downsize, or go into "Chapter 11"—i.e., Hospital Corporation of America, The Bank of America, Merrill Lynch, Campeau Stores, and others.[2,3]

One can also find many examples of firms that grow mostly through internal actions, including innovation leading to new products. An example to study, and many observers have done so, is 3M, Minnesota Mining & Manufacturing Co.

II.   ACQUISITIONS

Almost everything that was said about mergers also applies to acquisitions. Also, it can generally be stated that a friendly type acquisition usually results in a lower acquisition cost than an adverse approach. However, sometimes the friendly approach will not work and the extra cost cannot be avoided.

The author has some experience in this area and would cite one such attempt. The acquiring firm (NYSE listed) wanted to acquire another firm (also NYSE listed). The C.E.O. of the acquiring firm sat on the board of the other company. When he asked the author about submitting an offer for the firm he desired, he was told to go ahead. However he did not proceed in an open and straightforward manner. He did two things, acquired 5 percent of the stock and declared such ownership, raised the stake slightly, and then submitted an offer that was obviously much too low to be perceived as being fair. Do not ever do this because it merely gets the people at the firm receiving the offer angry. He was told by the board that the offer was entirely too low. Eventually, he acquired still more stock and submitted another offer. It too was turned down and he was then "talked" into signing a 5 year "stand-still agreement."

Every once in a while he tested "the waters," somewhat unofficially, and was always turned down for the same reason. The directors of the firm receiving these offers soon realized that they had better find a friendly (white knight type) buyer or this man would eventually get the company at too low a price after the stand-still agreement expired. Such a buyer was found and the buyer bid $55.00 per share. The first buyer initially offered about $33.00 per share and eventually raised it to slightly over $40 per share. Friendship will not count for much when such deals are evaluated, so it is prudent to make a fair offer. If the offer is far too low, the friendship advantage will be eliminated almost at once. Boards usually contain a substantial number of very knowledgeable people and they also secure outside advice as to the fairness of an offer from a major underwriting firm, as well as legal advice. Boards do not want to be sued for taking improper actions—it can be very costly to the company and/or the board members.

An unfriendly acquisition is always difficult, and it would be advisable to seek the very best advice available—both firms almost invariably engage the services of an investment broker in order to protect the board and thus end up at the best possible price. Consider all angles or possibilities and be sure you determine, before you start making offers, the maximum price you think the firm is worth *to your firm*. Keep emotion out of the affair as much as possible.

III.   SPIN-OFFS

The spin-off of a business unit occurs when a section of the business is perceived not to be of significant value to the main business of the firm. In some cases, it is "dragging down" the price of its stock because of variability in earnings; or its potential is not highly valued by most of the share holders and/or investors; or its profit margin is low; or its growth rate is low and likely will remain low; or it is viewed as a seasonal business (whereas the other businesses are steady); or some combination of these. In some cases it can be the opposite: the firm's value will increase if the spun-off unit is on the market as a separate company. Since the firm doing the "spinning off" retains some reasonable amount of equity in the new firm, any success it has also helps the firm spinning off the unit.

A strategically oriented management, which should also mean a management that engages in proper long and short range planning, should obviously study each business unit in their planning. If a business unit is believed to be undesirable for one or more reasons, then a decision must be made how to handle the situation with least damage to the firm. Sometimes it can be done in a manner that enhances the firm, i.e., makes a profit and enhances the shareholders perception of its value as mentioned earlier. A so-called raider always does this to help pay for an acquisition.

An example of a spin-off that did not harm the firm would be a spin-off by Adams-Russel Co., Inc. They spun off Adams-Russel Inc., (formerly Adams-Russel Electronics, Inc.), essentially the original company and therefore the *original* parent firm, in a share-for-share distribution to stockholders on July 14, 1986. Adams-Russel Co., Inc., was founded in 1958 (the parent firm identified above, they merely changed their name) as an electronics manufacturer. They eventually diversified into the cable television business in the mid 1960s. The cable TV business became the most important business.

Total earnings of the spun-off unit were in the range of $1.75 to $2.00 per share per year about 2 years before the spin-off. In 1987, right after the spin-off, the earnings of the spun off firm dropped from $1.06 per share to $0.20 per share. That probably was the motivation for the spin-off.

What then happened? The spun-off unit's stock sharply dropped, with little effect on the parent company's stock price. Yes, the spun-off firm did eventually correct its difficulties. It then became an acquisition target of M/A-COM, who offered $15.00 per share—and the offer was accepted. At this point, everyone was satisfied and happy. The reader might like to know who had shares besides the public. Directors owned 10 percent; an ESOP (employees stock ownership plan) 16 percent; TeleCable Corp., 14 percent; and Continental Cablevision, 9 percent.

The above complexity is about typical for spin-off. A sale of a business unit accomplishes some of the same objectives, but in a different manner and with different constraints.

IV. SELLING BUSINESS UNITS

Adams-Russel Co., Inc., probably could have sold the above described spun-off business, but they would not have received a very good price relative to the ultimate value of the asset because the business had just entered a down period. The expenses of the spun-off firm were too high, sales needed rejuvenating, and earnings had collapsed due to improperly bidding fixed price contracts, etc. Long term, with some fixing of problems, the firm again became a profit generator. M/A-COM saw the potential of Adams-Russel Electronics (really Adams-Russel, Inc.) and acquired it by recognizing its worth in the size of its offer. Sales at the time of the sale to M/A-COM were about $140,000,000.

Reasons for possibly selling business units include that (1) the unit is not growing, (2) it is not producing a good return in the way of earnings, (3) the unit is facing a decreasing market, and (4) the unit has increased its long term debt to the point where servicing it is subtracting from the company's value. There are other such reasons that only occur occasionally.

One consideration in strategic planning should be to sell such business units if at all possible for a reasonable value. If one sustains a loss in such a sale, it is usually still desirable to sell and to take a one-time loss on the disposal of the business unit.

In looking at a particular business unit, strategic planners should note that those that are weak performers and are not significantly improvable are a drag on the better performers. This is exactly what corporate raiders do, sell off the junk and poor performers and keep the good businesses that are capable of being grown and having their earnings performance improved.

Such actions are absolutely necessary to survival, especially if there is a great deal of long term debt. A great deal of debt is always present if the business was acquired by a leveraged buyout or if the purchase of subsidiary firms were purchased with junk bonds—an action which saddled the previously mentioned Kinder-Care with a lot of junk bond type debt.

With high debt, especially of the junk bond variety because of their high interest rates, it is vital to corporate survival to sell off the poorly performing units, especially those that do not seem to have a good future. This not only improves corporate performance (earnings), but it also usually brings in money to help reduce debt.

It is impossible to have an excellently performing company with many of the business units not making an adequate contribution to corporate performance. This is often what attracts corporate raiders, since they can sell off the junk and keep the desirable businesses.

In Part II all of the previously described planning considerations will be discussed from the "how to do it" view and it will be shown how one can create order out of the complex chaos exposed in Part I.

V.   PRODUCT DESIGN ENGINEERING

A.   Introduction

In Chapter 1 it was disclosed that Japanese firms bring new or significantly redesigned products to the market in about half the time required by most U.S. firms.

Mentioned was the matter of incorrect design team composition and the failure to properly share functional responsibilities in the efforts of U.S. firms in designing products. Because of mistakes involved in the design process, most U.S. businesses not only lengthen the process, but also significantly increase manufacturing costs and almost guarantee resultant low product quality relative to that achieved by the Japanese.

Some people say that we can ignore the Japanese. The facts show that we can't. Moreover, we must also consider the Germans, who also seem to do a pretty good job of competing. Additionally, there are the Taiwanese and the Koreans, and tomorrow there will be many other such savvy producers that can be added to the list.

What is so sad is that the Japanese and most other nations learned their management knowledge from the U.S. We really have no excuse for our poor performance. In many case we have simply allowed bureaucracy of large size to freeze into an action that does not work very well.

We in the U.S. know all the skills and "tricks" used by the Japanese and others; we just do a poor job of using our knowledge. We were and are delinquent in how we *manage* the processes involved. In fact, in the particular case of product design engineering, we have failed to innovate new organizational and responsibility-sharing concepts. Bureaucracy took hold and the people involved in product design refused to change organizational composition, structure, and the sharing of responsibility simply because they did not want to change. They were afraid because change sometimes is a wrenching process.

B.   The Product Design Team

There is an absolute requirement for engineering design, industrial/manufacturing engineering, quality engineering, and marketing to be full cooperating members of each product design team. Sometimes there may be some additional team members who should be logically added, but the above is an absolute minimum variety in team composition. All the indicated members from functions other than product engineering must be accorded equal stature and importance: they should be considered *as equal members of the team*. The Japanese often include a member from finance on the design team, probably an excellent part-time team member. This entire view is generally shared by Dr. Edwards Deming, who, as most readers know, is revered in Japan. Purchasing gets involved in securing quotations on purchased items going into the new product, so one might add such a member. However, this is not a necessity. However, these remarks will likely be viewed as heresy by most members of design engineering functions—this is based upon the fact that very few U.S. firms use this approach.

The author once tried to integrate industrial engineers into each design team at Magnavox in the mid 1950s, but the product engineering department would only accept one I.E., in each design engineering department (there was one at each major plant). This essentially neutralized this engineer since he could not be an active and effective participant on all the design teams found in each plant. In fact, they never agreed that he would ever become a genuine design team member. Moreover, they insisted that the industrial engineer's salary be on the design engineering budget.

Considerable additional information relating to the above concepts will be found in both the third and the fourth editions of *Managing Engineering and Research*.[4,5] This material was also discussed at Rensselaer Polytechnic Institute's celebration of its School of Management's 25th anniversary in "Some Management Concerns for RPI's School of Management" on February 28, 1988.[6]

Strategic considerations now indicate that the United States and other countries need to restructure the engineering design team in order to successfully engage in global competition. It was proven that the U.S. and most fully developed countries essentially already have a global market in their country for their major and many minor firms. This subject is discussed in detail in the fourth edition of *Managing Engineering and Research*,[5] which will be published in 1992. However, some of the highlights will be mentioned here in order to help planners reach a proper decision regarding the organization of the design effort.

This writer in his industrial jobs and in his consulting activities has seen at least $20–$40,000,000 wasted because of the way designs were accomplished and presented to the factory. The designs were deficient because of the lack of integration of the functions mentioned into the design team.

To the above excess costs one must add the other moneys wasted in the purchasing of repair parts needed to rework products that did not pass inspection and in the manufacturing process because the new or redesigned products were not designed for ease of productibility. The total money wasted by such poor design attributes probably exceeds $100,000,000 in just the plants where the author was involved. The total wasted funds in the U.S., when lost markets are included, will easily exceed one or more billion dollars in the course of just 1 or 2 years! This is an understatement if the "boners" made by the military and their contractors are included.

Many readers are personally acquainted with trying to find a part similar to something they know was previously designed and manufactured and which could be used in a new design if the drawings and specifications could be located. However, unless one has the catalog number of the part or the product model or part number, the search is equivalent to looking for the proverbial "needle in a haystack."

There is coding systems software that can communicate with a company's CAD/CAM system that solve this problem by using group technology techniques. These are described in W. Hyde's book *Improving Pro-*

ductivity by Classification, Coding, and Data Base Standardization,[7] and the software and related consulting service are available from a number of firms, among them the Brisch Birn Consulting firm in Ft. Lauderdale, Florida.

Product design engineers are supposed to design for low product cost, which includes ease of productibility, as well as for function. Yet they are not taught this in engineering schools and do not have the opportunity to acquire such information though experience working only in design engineering—neither do they have the educational background to work in industrial/manufacturing engineering, which is nominally located in the "factory."

Industrial/manufacturing engineers or people who know such techniques and are part of the manufacturing activity as well as an integral part of the design team are required to help accomplish the design function. They, in turn, need considerable computer software support, which is partially available[5,6,8] but is not being used in over 95 percent of the design engineering departments.

Similar software to aid the quality engineers on the product design team is needed, but this author knows of no available software of this type.

Marketing needs to be an integral part of the team so as to be able to promptly answer questions as to the desirability of product features, how quantity of product sold might vary with different product characteristics, etc.

These methods and approaches were presented since their recommendations are not "standard practice" in the U.S. even though the arguments for following these recommendations are overwhelming. Further, most firms do not even recognize that such a problem exists.

The reader should be aware that a whole new concept of engineering organization will likely be required, at least in some cases.[5] This concept would have the "factory" or "manufacturing oriented" engineers (with their chiefs) reporting to the company and/or engineering chief of the plant. This is one suggested way to organize. However, there is a second, less radical, alternative, which is also explored in the fourth edition of *Managing Engineering and Research.*[5]

REFERENCES

1. Robert B. Lamb, *Competitive Strategic Management; Corporate Planning* (introduction), Prentice Hall, Inc., Englewood Cliffs, NJ, 1984.
2. Tom Peters, "Facing Up to the Need for a Management Revolution," *Engin-*

eering Management Review, June 1989 (Summer Edition) and *California Management Review*, Winter, 1988.

3. Walter Adams and James Brock, *The Bigness Complex*: *Labor and Government in the American Economy*, Pantheon Books, New York 1986.

4. D. W. Karger and R. G. Murdick, *Managing Engineering and Research*, Industrial Press, Inc., New York, 1980.

5. D. W. Karger and G. M. Yaworsky, *Managing Engineering and Research*, Marcel Dekker, New York, 4th edition, 1992.

6. D. W. Karger, "Some Management Concerns for RPI's School of Management" (a speech at Rensselaer's School of Management 25th anniversary), Troy, NY.

7. W.F. Hyde, *Improving Productivity by Classification, Coding, and Data Base Standardization. The Key to Maximizing CAD/CAM and Group Technology*, Marcel Dekker, New York 1981.

8. D. W. Karger and F.H. Bayha, *Engineered Work Measurement*, Industrial Press, Inc., New York, 1987.

4

Manufacturing Considerations—Planning and Integration

Dr. George M. Yaworsky, Ph.D., M.B.A.

Technical and Management Consultant, Alexandria, Virginia

Historically in the U.S., top level long range planning for a business that manufactures a product has been largely a market planning effort. The marketing effort engenders feedback with the product designers to assure that the product includes features deemed desirable in the market analysis. Unfortunately, most organizational interaction diminishes significantly at this point. This leads to schedules which are then developed based on the market "window" identified in the market planning effort by the marketing department. Manufacturing, which traditionally is at the end of the cycle, is therefore scheduled to meet this marketing window, which usually makes developing a realistic manufacturing schedule impossible.

Most U.S. companies go about product development and decision making in a manner that excludes manufacturing from their strategic planning. Corporate strategic planning in the U.S. is primarily marketing and/or financially oriented.

Manufacturing is not given the opportunity to influence the design for ease of producibility, to develop processes, acquire the best equipment, or arrange the manufacturing flow to achieve improved, let alone optimum, efficiency. Even today, with much being written about treating a company as a system, product making companies often forget their basic reason for being in business—to manufacture and sell products!

Of course, 40 years ago, U.S. productivity led the way around the world. In the last 40 years, the total U.S. industrial production output has undergone rapid growth, while concurrently the number of workers on the production line has increased only slightly. This is attributable to improved manufacturing technology implemented on the shop floor. However, our *nonproduction* work force increased almost as much as the production output.[1]

All this implies that manufacturing technology has doubled the productivity of the production line worker on one hand while on the other hand it also implies that some of the functions normally performed by production line workers have been changed in content and are now being performed by nonproduction line workers. This increase in so-called indirect labor or overhead (and ensuing indirect costs) has had the net effect of actually decreasing the productivity growth rate.

This kind of productivity growth is actually a double-edged sword. Since the productivity of the production line worker is significantly improved, there is a reduction in production line workers and an ensuing reduction of the direct labor base over which to spread the overhead cost. The result is a doubly inflated overhead rate as shown below:

	Before	*After*
Direct Labor Base	$100	$ 50
Overhead Cost	100	140
Overhead Rate	100%	280%

Thus, the prime target for future planning of technology efforts is the indirect labor cost. Of course, more technology is only part of what must be done to address this issue. In fact, misplanned and misapplied technology can do more harm than good. The central issue in addressing this problem is managing to plan so as to synergistically integrate the complete set of objectives, resources, practices, and attitudes in an enterprise, such that ultimately the whole is greater than the sum of the stand-alone parts. This approach brings out value added in that it will significantly lower indirect costs—the main factor inhibiting productivity growth.

Studies have shown that the average part in a manufacturing enterprise spends as much as 95 percent of its time waiting and moving between machines. Furthermore, of the remaining 5 percent, less than 30 percent, or about 1.5 percent of the total time, is spent having useful work performed on it. Obviously then, machine automation alone is not the answer. What has to be done is to better deal with the complex real-time control, analyses, planning, and management necessary in an increasingly integrated enterprise.

How about the so-called service industries? It is true that there are no machine tools around, but such firms often deliver some kind of product. They do involve business functions, and always deal with analysis, storage, and flows of information. Thus a more integrated approach will be useful here also.

After all, what is manufacturing? Traditionally, it was said that manufacturing entails four processes: formation, reduction (includes machining), joining, and finishing. This view is still held to be true by many manufacturing professionals today.

However, in view of the increased power of the computer, this definition has been expanded. Today, manufacturing more and more simply means the conversion of raw materials into desired end products, be they television sets, hamburgers, books, or grand opera. One may then say— manufacturing is the "whole world." This is not quite true, but its newer methods, influence, and power are much more far reaching and relevant today than 40 years ago and are growing rapidly. In fact, the whole approach is called computer integrated manufacturing or CIM.

It is the aim of this chapter to address planning in an increasingly integrated CIM-like enterprise. In this context several ancillary practices such as design for manufacturability/quality control, just-in-time inventory systems, and flexible manufacturing systems will also be discussed. More detail and depth on all these topics (including CIM) can be found in the literature (references 2–10) and also will be addressed more thoroughly in the authors' forthcoming book.[11]

I.   THE INCREASINGLY INTEGRATED ENTERPRISE

In every enterprise there exist, to some degree, three primary areas that must interact. These are business management, design, and manufacturing functions. In addition there are various company-wide support functions such as networking, purchasing, and warehousing. Note that quality is increasingly being viewed less as a support function and more as an enterprise-wide planning and implementation necessity.

In the past 40 years much effort has been spent to modularly upgrade parts of these functions in a stand-alone manner. For example, a business function software module, prepared in the business environment setting, does not usually interface with any design or manufacturing modules. In fact, often various business function modules do not "talk" to each other.

However, all enterprise-wide functions have one common denominator—the specific product being produced. It is this common denominator that provides a specific point of interaction among the business, design, and manufacturing functions. Currently, each of these major functions recreates various elements of data concerning the product being produced. It is this redundancy and/or mismatch in the creation of data from the common denominator that is the primary source of errors and poor productivity. The present manual interactions between modules tend to increase indirect costs.

Computer integrated manufacturing is the total computer integration of all the functions in an enterprise. Every element of the organization would be working with and building on a common set of data. It is a total systems approach, which cuts through many traditional, management, technical, and economic disciplines. Currently, no one has achieved a total CIM factory. However, the implementation of progressively integrated enterprises is increasing worldwide. With good planning such systems have been shown to save money and increase productivity, especially in the longer term. Thus, an increasingly integrated enterprise is becoming not just a matter of money, but of survival in the international marketplace as well.

It is very important to note that strictly speaking, an integrated manufacturing approach is not new.[2] Until the late eighteenth century, manufacturing was a craft where craftsmen conceived, designed, tooled up, marketed, and repaired a product. Each such operation was complex, but it was completely integrated.

As the demand for finished products grew, the integration bonds began to break down very rapidly. Different people, aided by increased machine power, began to attend to specific individual component tasks. As product demand expanded further, more and more people performed not only fractionated craftsman type tasks, but also new jobs, which entailed enterprise-wide control of manufacture. This added newly required organizational layers and hierarchical echelons.

As the growth in productivity has diminished, this fractionalization resulted in the stage of diminishing returns. However, with man's increased ability to handle larger amounts of data more easily, an original data set describing the product to be produced will increasingly provide a mechanism by which the know-how of all the fractionated functions will be increasingly coordinated. Thus, mankind is in effect coming full circle—with increased computerization the enterprise is again becoming more and more integrated. The key to this integration is the concept of database management system.

Besides better data communication, integration involves compatibility, standardization, and greater flexibility in product design and quantity. In true craftsmanlike fashion, an integrated enterprise will be able to make more customized products with more flexibility in volume and general product mix. Computerization will thus also help ease the increasing skilled labor shortage. Manufacturing is not only becoming an increasingly important activity within an enterprise—it is also becoming *the* integrating function within an enterprise.

Besides the integration of software and hardware, it is important to consider various interfaces between people and organizations to achieve better teamwork. With increased integration the organizational structure and responsibility mix of many people will change markedly. Since various parts of an integrated enterprise compete less among themselves, any competition is increasingly relegated to the marketplace. Furthermore, integration results in a closer linkage between an enterprise, its suppliers, and its customers. This leads to a further restructuring of the organization.

The achievement of an integrated enterprise and the planning that goes with it must deal with many technical and management challenges and ramifications. These will be addressed at this point.

One of the great barriers to an integrated enterprise is the organizational structure of American companies. Most U.S. corporations not only have different organizations for design and manufacture, but these organizations have different drives and goals. Product design organizations are evaluated on the basis of product function and performance while manufacturing organizations are rated by such factors as production volume, inventory turns, and various costs. The design people often just don't address the manufacturability of a product in their design efforts. Any suggestions from manufacturing personnel for product improvement are often ignored while, on the other hand, any lack of understanding on their part is often not communicated to the design people. Frequently, a design is just "thrown over the wall" with no feedback of any kind. As a result, the whole enterprise suffers and much mutual blaming for any shortcomings results.

Furthermore, because of the management system of individual rewards, and the increased mobility of management, a manager often develops a sharklike attitude of seeking "to win over his peers"—rather than cooperating in setting up longer term corporate objectives. Because of his desire to be promoted quickly, a manager tends to emphasize short term goals. This is bad, not only because it neglects a longer term outlook per se, but because many of the newer techniques and practices in an integrated enterprise take more than a short time to fully implement. For example, the evolution of a flexible manufacturing system (more on this later) can take a few years, while a reasonably integrated CIM system can take even longer.

With this in mind, one must strive for increased initial cooperation, as well as continuing feedback mechanisms between design and manufacturing personnel. This means not just having senior industrial engineers taking an active part in the design team (along with people knowledgeable about product costs), but also increasing interaction between design engineers, industrial/manufacturing engineers, machinists, and other skilled workers on the shop floor. Quite often, an increased amount of knowledge about manufacturing processes will make for a better design engineer. Sometimes much can be learned from the skilled workers as well. A design can be such that the product works, but can be made much more easily and cheaply with increased manufacturing knowledge. Moreover, under such circumstances the product's quality is often substantially improved.

Traditionally, American corporations have emphasized a form of statistical quality control that supports the position that a product made according to specifications within permitted tolerances is of high quality. Such a "goalpost" philosophy (where if it's within the football uprights it's good) neglects continuous variation from target. Sure, in football, a ball kicked near a post scores the same as one going dead center. However, the analogy does not carry over into product performance. Moreover, a product made just within tolerance is not much better than one a little bit outside; yet in the goalpost philosophy one is within "spec" and the other is not. Consequently, some sort of continuous quality index, focusing on deviation from target, would be helpful.[6,7] Of course, this type of approach has been used by the Japanese for decades.

The "goalpost" philosophy also engenders undue emphasis on inspection since "everyone" knows that failures will be corrected by field service personnel if the customer complains. This, in turn, leads to unduly high levels of scrap, rework, inventory, and warranty expense, as well as the loss of customers—probably one of the most important losses.

In contrast, the Japanese and many European manufacturers have adopted the so-called "zero defects" approach. What this means is not that all defects vanish, but that a definite target, not just a "tolerance hole," is found to shoot at. This approach has reduced defects substantially.

Companies also discovered, often to their surprise, that the total manufacturing costs often declined as the number of defects decreased. What this means is that there was an optimal (usually small) defect percentage at which the cost was minimized. Moreover, it was less expensive to build a product in conformance with carefully thought out design parameters early, rather than use a procedure that required defective items to be detected, reworked, scrapped, and/or repaired—sometimes in the factory and often in the field. More details about such an improved quality approach can be found in the literature.[6,7,12]

Quality has to be improved significantly in every aspect of the organization, not just in products and services. Thus, much more attention and care will have to be paid to detail in the course of setting up the integration of various software and hardware systems to insure the proper flow of data between design and manufacture.

In this light, the question of various system standards must be thought out very carefully, especially in view of the fact that from a technical standpoint the current arsenal of standards is far from consistent, adequate, or comprehensive. One has to pass data freely and with integrity between different makes of computers, equipment, and machinery. Thus, various vendor and device independent specifications for physically connecting different hardware, transmitting information between different systems, as well as considerations related to systems configuration, operation, and support, have to be examined. Such support systems entail process models and systems to present information meaningful not only to different computers but also to a variety of functional organizations. One can't just mesh different existing systems together and hope to handle any problems later. The costs could and probably would be disastrous. Therefore, since more attention will have to be paid to detail, a deeper level of technical understanding will be required, right up through top management levels.[13]

Another facet of this problem is that performance of step-by-step integration without the guidance of overall strategic and operational plans invariably leads to serious problems. Consequently, when setting up any part of an integrated enterprise, one should try very hard to think ahead regarding further integration with possible future additions. This author has seen the relatively thoughtless acquisition of expensive equipment (often money saving in the short term) that later "boomeranged," since the equipment couldn't be integrated with any future additions without extreme expense. At best, such a practice results in piecemeal implementation, not integration.

Then there is the problem of training. In the U.S., most people who design the new equipment do not later operate it on the shop floor. Often, with the introduction of new hardware and software, the operators themselves are very poorly trained. This does not mean that they are not smart enough to learn. One cannot staff factories with just managers and engineers. A well designed system will allow for good training and retraining of a large part of the old workforces and creation of new jobs to boot.

Planning for increased inventory turns is another very important aspect in a modern enterprise. Traditionally U.S. companies have tried to optimize inventory via various kinds of so-called optimal inventory schemes. However, what happens if an enterprise eliminates a large part of its inventory? Could it be done?

The answer is yes. In the so-called just-in-time (JIT) philosophy, inventory is viewed as a waste to be minimized. JIT focuses attention on waste elimination by purchasing or manufacturing just enough of the right items, just in time, no sooner or no later. This implies that very carefully planned and executed schedules are an important part of JIT.

JIT attacks the idea that speed is tantamount to efficiency—faster is not always better. If drilling a hole takes 3 minutes and heat treating the part takes 60, why drill holes faster than the part can be heat treated? Such extra parts just add to inventory, *they are not adding value*.

It is very interesting to note that as inventory is reduced company wide, other problems that were masked by excess inventory begin to stand out. For example, if a company wants to protect itself against bad quality, either in what it makes or what it buys, it stocks up on inventory as a security blanket. Analogously, in a more everyday vein, how many people hoard various tidbits of information, that they never have any use for, to read more carefully at some later "proper" time? Most often such material eventually gets thrown away—unread.

Another motive for higher inventory is lack of supplier reliability. Still another source of high inventory is high setup times. If these problems were reduced, one could not only decrease the inventory, but have a better run company as well. Such synergistic effects have been instrumental in bringing about some very large productivity gains resulting from smaller inventories and subsequent lower inventory carrying costs.[14]

While computer integrated manufacturing (CIM) implies the total computer integration of all functions of a plant and is a *very* broad manufacturing function concept, a flexible manufacturing system (FMS) is product family oriented. Such systems have become increasingly useful and sophisticated in the U.S., Europe, and Japan, particularly during the later 1980s. Currently, an FMS often fills the niche between hard automation systems and stand-alone machine tools—thus paving the way to the integrated CIM enterprise.

While no two experts in the field will agree on precisely what constitutes an FMS, a general definition is "a controlled process which produces varieties of part types or products within its stated capability and predetermined schedule." Currently, an FMS is typically designed to run for extended periods of time with little operator attention and would likely include automatic inspection and cleaning equipment. It will include whatever processes are required to manufacture, or at least machine, a specific family of products. Such part families are coded and classified by attribute, process, or both and fall into the domain of group technology (also mentioned in the previous chapter). More material on this subject can be found in *Group Technology at Work*.[16]

Generally the "flexibility" of an FMS depends on careful *planning* and selection of the part family to which the system should be dedicated. For any part outside this selected family, the FMS will not necessarily be sufficiently "flexible." The FMS for the selected part family yields relatively short throughput times and low in-process inventories (synergy again). This is an important advantage and a limitation of an FMS.

Moreover, "flexibility" can exist in various forms, such as volume flexibility (economical production of variable numbers of parts), parts mix flexibility, routing flexibility (especially important during unexpected breakdowns), and design change flexibility (fast response to design changes). This all goes hand in hand with the need for an increasingly adaptable and flexible management. Management dealing with FMS and any other form of enterprise integration must be flexible also! Much effort, time, and money will have to be expended on management and implementation of change.

Often, integration efforts fail not because of inadequate thought but because of an insufficient length of allowed time. A longer term financial orientation than traditionally observed in the United States is a virtual prerequisite. It is plain foolish to just cry about lower wages overseas. The integration ideas and practices mentioned in this chapter (and the previous one) will far more than offset such a "handicap."

Furthermore, an integrated enterprise entails moving away from hierarchical organizations toward more flexible team-oriented management style. This further involves providing a more stable environment for all enterprise employees so that the people involved will not panic unduly in the course of any significant changes. If management is ready for a wider spectrum of eventualities and communicates its concerns, hopes, and aspirations throughout the enterprise, then even with a somewhat unclear future the workers will have a more positive attitude. This will not only enable them to handle changes better, but also enable them to contribute to solving problems as well. This will be helped by paying more attention to education programs, not only for workers, but for managers as well. Very often the managers are extremely threatened by interfunctional project oriented issues because of turf concerns or just plain lack of adequate knowledge. Under such conditions (and this author has seen this more than once), such "managers" may not only drag their feet, but may try to deliberately sabotage implementation of good positive planning.

II. PLANNING FOR AN INCREASINGLY INTEGRATED ENTERPRISE

So far, what has been discussed is the state of manufacturing (particularly in the U.S.), the increasingly integrated enterprise as a solution, and some of the concomitant practices and challenges that go with it. At this point, planning for such a case will be discussed from a more proactive "how to do it" standpoint. In this light, specific issues relevant to manufacturing and integration will be emphasized.

Although relatively sophisticated computer systems and associated technologies play an increasingly important role in an integrated enterprise, they are often not a necessity (at least not initially). Frequently, substantial progress toward integration can be made with a thorough understanding and application of standard and traditional equipment and techniques. This consideration is of utmost importance in any planning effort involving manufacturing, since there is usually no compelling reason to dash off and acquire expensive equipment in order to accomplish intended objectives.

A clear idea of objectives and goals (where one wants to go) has to be formulated and agreed upon. This has to be done from the highest management level downward. Overall business objectives need not be specified in great detail since their purpose is to serve as a guide and driving force for much more detailed strategies and eventualities further down the line. To accomplish this one must obtain TOP management involvement and commitment. This top management should include manufacturing-oriented personnel. Moreover, it is absolutely necessary to solicit participation of lower level operations management—not just the top management team.

Invariably, the pivotal figure in such efforts is the C.E.O. Since an integrated enterprise addresses all the factors needed to keep a competitive edge, and decisions can be very far-reaching, only the C.E.O. can properly lead and support the whole operation. In fact the C.E.O. should play the part of "chief integrator."[17]

In order to do this intelligently, the C.E.O. must have as thorough an understanding of what's going on as possible. The C.E.O. does not need detailed knowledge of every facet of an intended plan; however, he must have a good general grasp of the situation and be in agreement with its main specifications. Of course, more detailed knowledge should be readily available to any C.E.O. if he needs it.

If there is not sufficient capability to get started, one can hire competent consulting help. However, one should "grow one's own" planning team as fast as possible.[18] This does not mean hire and train a department of people—the main team should be the top management executives. Planning by planners who are not the officers and/or directors (and who therefore do not have a stake in the company) never works to a significant degree, at least not over any significant length of time.

Sometimes there may be enormous resistance to planning for a more integrated enterprise. This is particularly so if much of top management is relatively unfamiliar with the practices and ideas involved. In such cases, finding or hiring an internal champion who has a lot of relevant knowledge, experience, and credibility can be very instrumental in helping the C.E.O. lower resistance to integration. Such a champion can initially be a consultant; however, as mentioned previously, it is best if he or she eventually becomes a high level full-time company employee. Notice that the role of such a champion is not just that of providing information, but also one of lowering fear and spreading credible assurance as well.

Typical benefits of enterprise integration are[19]:

Reduction of overall lead time.
More inventory turnovers.
Increase in product quality.
Reduction of costs.
Increase of engineering analysis capability
Increase of production facility output.
Better customer interface and service.
Reduction of work-in-process (products in various stages of completion at any time prior to shipping).
Less waste.
More flexibility in design, volume, parts, or product mix.
Faster response to market demands.
Higher return on assets.

Such strategies should be constructed with extreme care to be both binding and yet robust enough to adapt to changed priorities or new technologies. All relevant enabling technologies should be considered carefully, as soon as possible after an initial statement of objectives. Throughout the whole planning process all possible constraints, be they cost, technology, people, equipment, time, or economic climate, should be considered. Furthermore, one should make every effort to anticipate such possibilities.

For example, a newly emergent technology can change matters significantly, which indicates that a provision should be made to have a technical staff that actually keeps up with new developments and has the intelligence, knowledge, and training to advise what should be done regarding it. On the other hand, the people more directly responsible for the planning should *understand* and carefully evaluate the given advice. In planning for integration, one must practice what one preaches.

What are the enabling technologies resident in a CIM enterprise? The following list is reasonably complete, although it may have to be amplified for more detail.

Computer modeling.
Simulation.
Computer scheduling and loading.
Numerical control equipment and any required programming.
Group technology (includes coding and classification).
Robotic technology.
Material handling and warehousing.
Network communications.
Computer aided process planning.
Database management systems.
Quality assurance planning.
Artificial intelligence.
Manufacturing resource planning (includes modules of various business
    related functions).
Computer aided testing.
Technology relevant to various standards and interface protocols.

For any strategic plan, particularly one involving a computer integrated
type setup, one should obtain the best people possible in various relevant
disciplines, who have a thorough knowledge of what's involved. There are
many so-called systems integrators who deservedly have low credibility. A
representative list of types of disciplines requiring experts that are necessary for integration is given below:

TOTAL SYSTEM INTEGRATION.
Computer integrated manufacturing.
Database management system.
Geometric modeling.
Communications/networking.
BUSINESS SYSTEMS.
Production control.
Financial services.
Manufacturing resource planning.
Business systems integration.
Office automation.
Procurement.
General management.
DESIGN SYSTEMS.
Design engineering (preferably including knowledge of experimental de-
    sign).
Design systems integration.
CAD systems (includes computer aided engineering, CAE).
Graphics.

MANUFACTURING SYSTEMS.
Manufacturing/industrial engineering.
Manufacturing system integration.
Production planning.
Computer aided process planning (CAPP).
SUPPORT ACTIVITIES.
Warehousing.
Material handling.
Plant/equipment maintenance.
Quality/experimental design (emphasis on plant-wide implementation).
Training.
Technology transfer.

Any strategic plan involves going from an initial to a final configuration. Therefore, it is essential to perform a self assessment of current conditions and capabilities (Chapters 8 and 9 of this text). To reach a goal, one has to know where one is starting from. It is still a source of amazement to the author that a significant number of strategic plans that he has seen are great at showing the promised land in the rosy future, but say nothing of the current desert and how to get from it to the promised land. Since the manufacturing function is a highly interdependent activity, one has to access as much of the enterprise as possible, not only the parts/factors that will be directly affected by the plan. Some of the aspects that should be considered are quality level, costs, schedules, suppliers, capacity, facilities, inventories, products, equipment (both software and hardware), processes, material flow, and needed skills.

The most important point here is objectivity. Thus, an outside consultant can be very helpful, not only because he has seen other companies, but also because he poses less of a potential threat to the egos involved in the status quo. Often the company is initially a lot further from the expressed goals than most insiders think, and the news may be far from pleasant. Furthermore, various internal groups and individuals frequently do not see eye to eye as to where the company stands. Therefore, an assessment of the current situation should not only accurately describe the status quo, but should help achieve consensus regarding it.

A study of the competition can be very important. How capably does a competitor perform his designs and produce his products? What do the firm's customers say about it? What do the firm's friends and enemies say about it? What price structures are used by competitors? Much information of this type is in the public domain and can be obtained and/or ferreted out in an entirely legal fashion through patient and resourceful research. For more detail see Chapter 8.

Often a system feasibility study approach can be of great value. Such a study should address not only how to obtain any particular system to perform a function, but also whether and how that system can be integrated into a company's present structure, in order to obtain a superior final product, price, and/or general configuration. Specific projects and targets for change should be identified. In doing this, one should not place undue credence on sales literature. The study should examine various factors necessary to assure success of a particular plan. A determination of the availability of a proposed system and any other necessary equipment (hardware and software) is also important.

Before specific projects that will engender the required changes are identified and targeted, one has to have a good knowledge of what is the state of the art. This not only sets a baseline for existing systems, but also helps put any newly created ones in better perspective. A basis for comparison between old and new approaches should be established. Thus, one would consider capability as well as feasibility in a given plan.

In the course of identifying specific project targets for the required changes, one has to decide what to make versus what to buy. Usually, it has been found that in making maximum use of company knowledge and facilities, an excess of either "make" (making everything) or "buy" (buying as much as possible) is worse than some middle path. As much support should be obtained from vendors as possible for items that the company cannot make advantageously. This has already been mentioned in the discussion of the just-in-time inventory philosophy.

If the proper enumerated tasks have been accomplished, one should now be able to chart, establish, and follow a logical sequence of steps necessary to achieve the plan. From a psychological point of view, often it is good to start with ideas one is most familiar with and/or those functions deemed most amenable to the new methods, procedures, and systems— even if the chosen systems are otherwise not of the highest priority. In other words, at least accomplish what can be done—then tackle a higher priority and/or a more difficult task.

A system of priorities of various plant functions which can depend on relative benefits, costs, time constraints, or other factors can be set up and followed. Any prioritization scheme is highly individual, depending on the requirements and constraints involved. The constraints can be external, such as technological or marketing factors, or internal, such as financial considerations, personnel (both quantity and quality), and general company culture. Also, as mentioned previously, training is extremely important.

The final steps involve monitoring and review of plans and results. One must realize, however, that planning is an ongoing iterative process which involves continuous feedback. Thus, one must always be prepared for change and expect the unexpected. However, if a project is well planned, most perturbations will not cause instabilities that warrant major changes. In fact, one can allow for crises and failure in the plan—and thus be able to deal with them when they occur.

Frequently, as a new system is introduced it is good not to immediately discard the old one. If possible, plan to run any old system parallel with the new one until things go smoothly. This is not just because the new system may have major faults, but also because a learning curve often exists—it takes time for people to adapt to change.

It is usually best for review persons or teams to be completely independent of the project team. Here senior staff and outside planning consultants can play a very important independent cross check role. Some issues relevant to such a review are:

1. The degree of plan success—are the various impacts and benefits more or less than planned? Why?
2. Unanticipated problems—How can they be solved?
3. Were various plan constraints such as money and time maintained? If not, why not? What are the possible resultant implications?
4. Are the benefits properly perceived throughout the company—especially by top management?
5. Would the project be tackled differently today? How?
6. What, if anything, is still needed to either make the system as successful as anticipated, or more so? Which ensuing steps should be done by the present project team, and if there are any changes in the team, what should they be?

III.   IDEF$_0$—A GOOD PLANNING TOOL

There are a number of tools that have been created to aid in strategic planning—particularly in an integrated enterprise setting. A particular methodology which this author has found quite useful is one of the U.S. Air Force's integrated computer aided manufacturing (ICAM) definition techniques called IDEF$_0$, or structured analysis. The subscript zero implies the possible existence of at least an IDEF$_1$. This is indeed so, as there are current IDEF$_0$, IDEF$_1$, and IDEF$_2$ modeling techniques. Only IDEF$_0$, the most widely used of these, will be discussed here. It has been tested in many different types of environments, particularly industrial, and has proven to be not only workable, but very successful. IDEF$_0$ is based on the Structural Analysis and Design Technique (SADT) developed by SofTech. In turn, SADT is based on cell modeling techniques

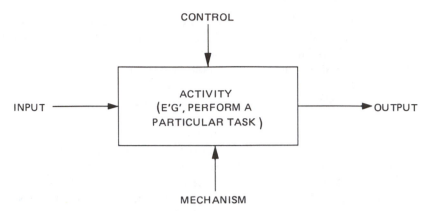

Figure 1   An IDEF$_0$ activity and its interfaces can be represented by a simple drawing. Obviously, each outgoing and incoming arrow can be connected to boxes representing other activities.

developed by Dr. Shizuo Hori during his work at the Illinois Institute of Technology Research Institute (IITRI).

Actually, all activities or functions, not necessarily those relevant to manufacturing planning, can be modeled using IDEF$_0$. An activity is represented by a box, and the interfaces between the functions are represented by arrows. Each activity may have an input, an output, a control, and a mechanism interface represented by arrows entering and leaving the box in question. This is illustrated by Figure 1.

Associated with this are a number of basic rules, which are:

1. Every process consists of a series of activities or functions which are represented by boxes. Activities are always named with an active phrase verb, not just a noun such as "planning," for instance.
2. Each activity often has an input (data, a design, etc.).
3. Each activity must, in some way, transform an input.
4. Each activity has various constraints or conditions imposed on it. These are called controls. Each activity box should have at least one control.
5. Each activity can have resources or mechanisms with which to work, e.g., computer, machine, planners, vendors, committee, etc.
6. Each activity must have an output, such as the completed function or some product, result, or report.

In some versions of IDEF$_0$, mechanisms can be combined under a more general control heading. They can also serve as inputs or be part of outputs. Input arrows show what will be used, while output arrows show the results of activities or the outcomes that are produced. Control arrows describe the circumstances under which the activity takes place, while mechanisms show how an activity is performed. The arrows indicate much more than a sequence of flows. They may not only branch and join, but also denote constraints, feedback, iteration, and overlap in time. A completed model shows a snapshot of all possible interactions between various activities in the course of a given process. This is very important in any planning endeavor.

If necessary, an activity can be decomposed in a top-down treelike hierarchical manner into more detailed component activities. In such a case the more general activity becomes the "parent" of all corresponding activities at the next lower level (the "children"). A particular child activity can in turn become a parent activity in a further decomposition scheme. This process is continued until the desired level of detail is reached. Various activities can be decomposed more than others, depending on the particular needs and constraints of the project.

Such a diagrammatic technique, along with supporting narrative, can bring matters into perspective quite rapidly. It focuses on the necessary activities and their interrelationships rather than on organizational hierarchies, as many modeling techniques do. $IDEF_0$ diagrams are not organizational charts, since a function can often be performed by any number of people not all reporting to the same supervisor. Likewise, one person may perform several functions, not necessarily situated adjacent to each other in a diagram. This technique is also a helpful aid in outlining and organizing written material. The result of such structuring is a more effective document that is logically and efficiently written.

$IDEF_0$ can be used not only to analyze a current as-is model, but also to set up a hypothetical improved TO BE model. This can be done either separately, or together in one diagram, as long as one can tell the two cases apart. In this way, one can compare various different configurations in any desired detail. This approach is very useful in modernization studies where one wishes to modernize a given production facility. It is much easier to set up an improved situation if the current one with all its facets and interactions is well documented and understood.

As mentioned previously, $IDEF_0$ can be applied to any endeavor, not just manufacturing. This is brought out in the simple example illustrated in Figure 2.

Note the inputs, outputs, mechanisms and controls. Often there are many adequate characterizations of an $IDEF_0$ model. Usually none is uniquely correct. The main consideration is that any model make "sense" and be consistent throughout. For example, one could well use both "ground" and "tender loving care" as controls, rather than as mechanisms

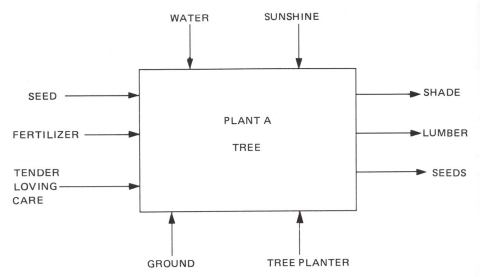

Figure 2   A very simple example of an $IDEF_0$ model—planting a tree.

and inputs, respectively. If the tree were a fruit tree, then fruit may be an output. Furthermore, one can get a little more fancy and add carbon dioxide as an input and oxygen as an output. It doesn't hurt to be as explicit as possible.

Of course, the example is quite elementary. More sophisticated and detailed cases can be found in listed references.[2,11,15] One can also obtain software to help format boxes and arrows. However, what to put in the boxes is obviously not given. The software is merely a formatting aide. It is called $AUTOIDEF_0$ and can be obtained for free from the ICAM Library, WRDC/MTI, Wright Patterson Air Force Base, Ohio 45433-6533. The software was designed to work with a Control Data Corporation Cyber 170 computer. For other computers, the program would need rewriting. However, these $IDEF_0$ displays could be generated on a PC type computer equipped with a proper graphics software package or likely with a CAD software package.

This modeling technique is very powerful, not only for planning, but also for diagnostic purposes in considering both the current state of affairs and possible improvements. It can also be used to identify those opportunities which would have the greatest beneficial impact over the entire process considered—not just a select portion of it. For example, one can assess the effect of introducing new technology on various parts of the whole enterprise, not just on a particular function. Too often, improvements are viewed only as they apply to a relatively specific problem, and a particular function may be improved at the expense of other upstream or downstream functions. Viewed from a limited "one function" perspective, the return on investment can easily be thought of as insufficient to justify the investment. However, when viewed from a total systems perspective, a new technology may provide benefits throughout the entire enterprise, thus providing a much more acceptable return on investment.

$IDEF_0$ can often yield valuable insights in both analysis and synthesis of any project. Even relatively simple diagrams can be very useful in clarifying issues and organizing a complex project. On the other hand, this author has seen a number of cases where inappropriate application wasted money and generated much confusion as a result of many illogically intertangled box diagrams. The quote "GIGO" is extremely applicable. Regardless of formatting software, any benefits resulting from this approach depend heavily on the knowledge, experience, and judgment of the modeler.

REFERENCES

1. John C. Williams, private communication.
2. Joseph Harrington, Jr., *Understanding the Manufacturing Process*, Marcel Dekker, New York, 1984.
3. Christopher LeMaistre and Ahmed El-Sawy, *Computer Integrated Manufacturing, A Systems Approach*, UNIPUB/Kraus International Publications, White Plains, NY, 1987.
4. U. Rembold, C. Blume, and R. Dillmann, *Computer Integrated Manufacturing Technology and Systems*, Marcel Dekker, New York, 1985.
5. Joseph Harrington, Jr., *Computer Integrated Manufacturing*, Robert E. Krieger Co., Malabar, Florida, 1973.
6. K. R. Bhote, *World Class Quality*, American Management Association, Saranac Lake, NY, 1988.
7. L. Ealey, *Quality by Design*, ASI Press, Dearborn, MI, 1988
8. E. J. Hay, *The Just-In-Time Breakthrough*, John Wiley & Sons, New York, 1988.
9. John R. Holland, Editor, *Flexible Manufacturing Systems*, SME Publications, Dearborn, MI, 1984.
10. "The Computer: The Tool for Today," *American Machinist*, Special Report 746, New York, 1982.
11. D. W. Karger and G. M. Yaworsky, *Managing Engineering and Research*, Marcel Dekker, New York, 4th edition, 1992.
12. Thomas P. Ryan, *Statistical Methods for Quality Improvement*, John Wiley & Sons, New York, 1989.
13. "Why Plant Automation Fails," an interview with Tracy O'Rourke, *High Technology Business*, November 1988.

14. H. T. Johnson and R. S. Kaplan, *Relevance Lost, The Rise and Fall of Management Accounting*, Harvard Business School Press, Boston, 1987.
15. R. R. Bravoco, "Planning a CIM System Using System Engineering Methods," *A Program Guide for CIM Implementation*, C. M. Savage, editor, CASA/SME Publications, Dearborn, MI, 1985.
16. N. L. Hyer, editor, *Group Technology at Work*, SME Publishing, Dearborn, MI, 1984.
17. Eric G. G. Gerelle and John Stark, *Integrated Manufacturing, Strategy, Planning and Implementation*, McGraw-Hill, New York, 1988.
18. George J. Hess, "Computer Integrated Manufacturing—How to Get Started," *Proceedings of AUTOFACT V Conference*, Society of Manufacturing Engineers, 1983.
19. Raymond F. Veilleux, editor, *Tool and Manufacturing Engineers Handbook, Volume V, Manufacturing Management*, Society of Manufacturing Engineers (SME), Dearborn, MI, 1988.

5

Research on Planning Benefits, an Overview of the Planning Process and the Implementation Procedure to Assure Plan Attainment, plus an Introduction to Measuring Professional Work

The material so far presented should have convinced the reader of the need to plan if an organization is to succeed. Moreover, it should have also been obvious that some must plan merely to survive.

The research findings next presented should inspire readers heading organizations to start their organizational planning as quickly as possible so as to attain the increased performance benefits — meaning creating a successful business. The increased profits can be from 25 percent to as much as 1000 percent in a 10-year period versus comparable non-planning organizations, depending upon the industry classification and the financial measures utilized. But there is a caveat: the planning must be of the variety to be described in this text.

The reader should throughly understand that planning is not just dreaming about what must be done in the future. Actually, it is the hardest work known to man — thinking! Further, if the reader and future planner is the head of an organization (or a person who aspires to such a position), this text will make clear that planning will tend to commit him/her to perform and achieve according to plan. This also applies to sub-unit planners in a non-planning organization. Because of this aspect of planning, such people often become afraid. Therefore it is not surprising that there has been much talk about planning, but very little real planning accomplished and used.

This fear of commitment undoubtly has scared away politicians from *personally* led planning. It also is why they often hire an outside firm to do their planning, since they can always disavow and "wash their hands" of such plans. As will be explained later, such expert-produced plans are virtually worthless since they are not used to determine actions.

One of the primary reasons for inserting this chapter here is to provide some additional and very specific reasons why an organization should plan and to present an overview of planning which every major member of a firm's planning team (all the company's officers and next line of major executives — and sometimes also the directors) should listen to in a presentation of these materials by an expert who would be able to answer questions. In fact, it would likely be best to provide them with a copy of such material before the presentation so they could make notes on it for future reference.

As to the directors, they normally do not *actively* plan with the others, but they certainly should participate in the midpoint and a final review of the plan before publishing it for the internal organization. Actually the company should invite all directors who have available time to attend all major planning sessions — the planning team and the organization would benefit from their presence at these sessions.

The overview of the planning effort describes the steps, procedures, and other parameters of a typical planning effort. This knowledge is necessary for all planning members before the planning starts, else it will require 2 weeks or more before the confusion subsides and the the real work of planning can begin.

Finally, it will be made clear that merely producing a plan will not bring about the benefits. The organization management has to be constrained so as to manage the firm in accordance with the plan. How to do this is presented in detail in Part III of this text. However, the required activities are generally described in the latter portion of this chapter.

I.   RESEARCH FINDINGS

The previous chapters quite clearly show that the current external and internal environments are dangerous to the health and well being of most organizations, especially to profit seeking organizations.

If any rational C.E.O. or management expert has been exposed to material such as shown in Chapters 1–4, he/she should already be convinced that planning is the correct way to proceed. However, even more evidence of the beneficial effects of planning will be presented in this chapter.

It should be indicated before presenting a major and significant research effort by Dr. Z. A. Malik that there has been a substantial number of publicized research projects before and after his research, but almost all of them depended upon the examined organizations to "say" whether they were a long range planning organization. Further, they were seldom, if ever, asked how the plan was actually used, developed, or implemented.

Since most organizations believe they probably should plan or because they perceive people think business and other organizations should plan, they "say" that they are a planning organization and that they use the plans to guide the organization. Naturally research based upon such projects produces flawed results. Some show that planning produces tangible benefits, and some show the opposite.

Two early studies that indicated consistent benefits were by Stanley S. Thune and Robert J. House, and by David M. Herold, who built upon the first study.[1,2] These helped inspire the Malik research. The early study of the combined chemical and drug industries generally approximated the results of Malik's research (1974) on these combined industries.

Noel Capon, John V. Farley, and James M. Hulburt, in *Corporate and Strategic Planning*,[3] included in Chapter 10 a rather complete discussion of planning research. It attempted to draw conclusions on the effect of planning (not at all well defined as to parameters because of research deficiencies by the referenced researchers).

Based upon this author's extensive study of planning and strategic management, library research, and broad planning experience, these ill defined and variable parameters explain the lack of consistent results from efforts defined as "planning" by the various practitioners.

Included in the listing of research projects are the previously referenced Thune and House and the Herold research (1972). Also shown in the studies is a Malik and Karger research project, which is reported on later in this chapter.

The Herold Study had five planners whose performance was compared to five non-planners. All firms were in either the chemical or the drug industries. The span of the planning interval was unknown, as well as who participated in the planning. However, these industries tend to be long term oriented.

The Malik research was shown as containing many of the essential planning details. However, all the facts are shown in the formal research report (later properly identified). This research and the Herold study clearly show a large beneficial impact upon corporate performance from proper planning.

If the reader cares to take the time to carefully examine the somewhat meager data shown in the Capon et al. summary of research, it soon becomes clear that two almost universal weakness were exhibited in most of the cited research. They are:

1. The time span of the planning was generally unknown
2. When the planning time span was stated, it usually was indicated as 3 years. Only the Malik research was indicated as 5 or more years.

More weaknesses in the normal/conventional corporate planning are indicated in the next discussion. Together, the above and the additional factors explain why most plans and planning efforts are seriously flawed.

In spite of the limitations, one could not help but decide, based upon presented data, that properly structured and executed formal planning can have a positive effect upon performance if the firm is operated in accordance with the plan. Beyond the above indication, the authors of the above-referenced text indicate many possible conclusions, but these are based upon very poorly defined data (poorly defined by the various quoted researchers).

II.   THE HALAL RESEARCH[4,5]

Before describing the Malik research and its startling results, a contemporary research project and some observations of the researcher will be presented. The project is of the variety where the corporation (or organization) indicates the status and parameters of its planning, which are then presented for guidance and assistance to other planners.

This project has several kinds of value. First, if one carefully examines the general findings regarding industrial planning one can separate most of the non-planners out of the list of organizations examined by the researcher by comparing their actions with the 10 criteria specified by Malik — presented in the next discussion. If these criteria are not followed, the planning results are almost worthless. The criteria can universally be used as a gauge to separate the planners from the non-planners if enough information is available.

Second, due to the findings of the researcher, Dr. W. E. Halal of George Washington University, several valuable aspects of planning are enumerated. The firms in the research read like a Who's Who of America's largest and best known firms. Some of these latter results will be referenced at appropriate times.[4,5]

Third, in Halal's *The New Capitalism* he discusses the findings of his research on the thrust of planning efforts as well as some more general findings resulting from work experiences, discussions, and library research on planning.

Fourth, this author suggests that *at least* planning directors read his book just to review the wide diversity of ideas and opinions existing in our world, not for information regarding planning. Many practically oriented managers would likely be "turned off" by the book unless they became intrigued with the massive dose of information available. Little help, however, "in a logic sense" is provided to discriminate between the ideas and concepts as to importance. However, it is also true that some of these will likely emerge and become factors significant to planners. If one did all that Halal suggests, this author doubts that any substantial benefit would accrue to a company in the way of increased profits; because, little time could be available for required work.

The planning research (about the length equivalent of one chapter in a book) was really aimed at assessing the *state* of the *art of planning*, and this it does rather well.

One of his data presentation tables from his "Strategic Management" paper[4] is shown in Table 1 of this chapter. It presents some interesting information about how the researched firms go about planning, but in a telephone conversation with Dr. Halal by this author he said that the table did not actually show planning areas. This remark stems from Table 7–1 in *The New Capitalism*[5] which also relates to the thrusts of planning and the similarities and differences in planning between the researched organizations. He uses Table 7–1 to illustrate and discuss matrix management. It is a fact that the displayed planning organizational elements would involve matrix management concepts.

In spite of the above, Table 1 is presented to further illustrate the range of approaches to both the organization of an enterprise or project and the focus of planning on just a few areas of business for the identified organizations.

Table 7–1 in *The New Capitalism* provides some additional helpful data to anyone trying to study planning practices and policies. The companies in the table are the same as those shown in Table 1 of this chapter except for the addition of Comsat.

A quick analysis of one set of Halal's contributions to planning indicates that Marriott has the fewest number of planners (whether these are officers and/or planning department staff directors is not defined) and they report to the chairman. This author is certain that he is an active planner from remarks he has heard him make at annual meetings. Marriott is probably the most successful hotel chain in the U.S.

In contrast Exxon has 40 planners reporting to "Finance"; IBM has 60 planners reporting to its chairman; Dow Chemical has 40 planners re-

Table 1   Organizational Dimensions[a]

No.	Corporation	Years of experience	Primary emphasis	Functional	Product/SBU	Client/market	Regional/geographic
1	Exxon	22	SBU	X			X
2	General Motors	5	Business directions	X	X		X
3	Texaco	13	SBU		X		X
4	IBM	16	Matrix		X		X
5	General Electric	11	SBU/matrix	X	X		X
6	Atlantic Richfield	9	SBU		X		
7	Dow Chemical	9	Product		X		
8	United Technologies	6	SBU	X	X	X	
9	Boeing	10	SBU	X	X		
10	Xerox	4	Matrix		X	X	
11	TRW	7	SBU		X		
12	Texas Instruments	20	SBU		X		
13	Crown-Zellerbach	12	SBU		X		
14	Mead	9	SBU		X		
15	Hewlett-Packard	16	Product		X		
16	Digital Equipment	4	SBU/matrix	X	X	X	X
17	Clark Equipment	8	SBU		X		
18	Rexnord	22	SBU	X	X		X
19	Bankamerica	6	SBU			X	X
20	Citicorp	12	Task force			X	X
21	Sears Roebuck	4	Merchandising	X	X		X
22	Mariott	6	SBU		X		X
23	Walt Disney	16	Project/venture		X		
24	Hoffmann-LaRoche	14	SBU	X	X		
Average		10.6					

[a]Data taken from Dr. William E. Halal's research results as presented and discussed in *The New Capitalism*, copyright 1986 by John Wiley & Sons, Inc. (Reprinted by permission of John Wiley & Sons.)

porting to the executive vice president; and Xerox has 40 planners reporting to its chairman. As an investor and reporter of the business scene, this author could not give these firms high corporate performance marks. This in turn indicates that they likely do not properly plan—meaning that one or more of Malik's 10 required criteria are missing (the criteria are specified under the next subtitle).

The issues or functions indicated as being performed by the planners listed in Table 7–1 are as follows:

Business development (20)   Corporate goals and strategies (20)
Mergers and acquisitions (14)   Issue analysis (23)
SBU consultation (?) (23)   Critique SBU plans (17)
Management training (15)   Resource allocation (6)
                                Environmental analysis (all 25)

All of these functions/tasks are performed by all of these "self professed" planners, except where a number appears after a function in the above list — the number indicates the number of firms performing the function. The reader should also understand that just because some aspect of business has been considered, this does not mean that correct criteria were used in deciding upon "the way to go". For example, look at Chapters 3 and 4 and it should be obvious that the integration of manufacturing, engineering, and marketing has not occurred, even though much evidence indicates that this action is required (General Motors is one of the U.S. firms that is struggling with this lesson and those leading to successful automation).

Just one or two more comments on the above list. The amount of risk taking required to achieve success relates to resource allocation. Has this aspect been properly analyzed? Is management training all that important, except in unusual circumstances? One final comment, the above list is market and finance "driven" as this student of planning "sees" the situation. Nothing is mentioned re engineering/technology or of manufacturing considerations.

Before leaving Halal's research, it is informative to try and analyze or deduce the planning theory in some of these firms. An easy one is GM, and it is intriguing because of the size and prominence of the firm. Its principal emphasis is on "business directions" (a nice broad term) and it does no client/market planning. For an automobile manufacturer to leave out a major consideration such as client/marketing indicates to this writer that its planning is flawed. Also, the planning director reports to Finance, which probably is not at all oriented to marketing, manufacturing, or engineering, and which tends to always "play it safe", which one can not do in strategic planning. Judging from its loss of market share to Ford, Chrysler, and the Japanese, and based upon its having a net profit margin about 2 percent less than Ford, which at times beats GM with its product designs, quality, and marketing, GM obviously is not engaging in proper planning. It also failed to successfully automate. If GM did produce good plans, then it appears they are not using them properly. In recent years it has closed 4 plants and 3 more are scheduled for closing.

Mariott is a planning organization based upon personal observation. Moreover, what it said, as presented in Table 1, "makes sense." Mariott emphasizes project/venture, and eliminates functional from major considerations (Mariott does not have the kind of functions that a manufacturing firm must maintain). It obviously is also concerned with regional/geographic impacts. It is the MOST profitable and successful hotel chain.

Sears says it emphasizes merchandising (per Table 1), and this author based upon personal experience with headquarters can say that the firm is *dominated* by that function. The author's guess is that merchandising is so powerful that it "bends" the planning to suit its desires. The planning is therefore faulty. This is further substantiated by its planners not having anything to do with (per Table 7–1 of *The New Capitalism*) corporate goals and strategies, resource allocations, and no critique of SBU plans (admittedly it would likely have few SBU plans). Moreover, based on the fact that Sears sales and profits are down, the plans obviously do not work. In fact, even its new pricing policy will not work because it has not paid enough attention to providing *both* quality service and quality products. However, it is still possible for Sears to improve and compete with Wal Mart since it still generates some profits.

Boeing probably is a proper planner, even though it says (see Table 1) that regional/geographic concerns are not "big" in its planning. This is easy to explain, since it is the world's largest and most successful airplane company and its planes are used throughout the free world. If a strong competitor develops, then it may need to rethink this aspect — yet, what is regional about an airplane that is used throughout the world? Also bear in mind that Boeing, per *The New Capitalism*, does not include in its planning SBU consultation, management training, or corporate goals and strategies. How many firms can successfully plan and grow by following the plans if corporate goals and strategies are not included? This author would say, very few; however, with its emphasis on products and product line, Boeing may be able to do it. Yet this author would bet that corporate goals and strategies *are* being considered in the planning.

If planners know enough about a firm and its business activities, and have information such as provided by Halal's research (and hopefully that of other researchers), they can usually arrive at correct conclusions in their planning.

Halal in his *The New Capitalism* states the conclusions he reached after his experiences in planning, library research, and after completing his planning research project.

First, most plans are restricted to "hard" business concerns, such as building facilities, marketing programs, and balancing the portfolio of business units (recall the discussion in Chapter 3 of this activity).

Marketing, in this author's opinion (Karger), tends to be overemphasized in the U.S. Moreover, not including manufacturing and engineering is a serious error — Japan has "whipped us" in many areas by paying great attention to the integration of engineering, manufacturing, and marketing (see Chapters 1–4). While buildings can be important at times, they usually are not a major critical issue. Manufacturing equipment (both hardware and software), is usually ignored in planning. Yet these are very important to corporate success — especially if they are properly utilized, as explained in earlier chapters.

Halal's second identified problem with most corporate planning efforts involves the working relations between executives, operating managers, and employees. He further indicates that few firms include lower levels of personnel in the planning and merely impose decisions upon the lower units. Again, as previously mentioned in earlier chapters, the Japanese seem to do a better job in this area.

Halal's third observation is that the planning process is isolated from external groups that can critically affect the company. Examples are labor leaders, consumer advocates, government officials, and other similar group leaders or representatives.

This author of *this* text would NOT include these and similar group represenatives in the planning effort. They would tend to be adversarial and certainly would normally not be overly concerned with maximizing corporate performance — in the sense that the term is usually used. However, the planning should consider such interests if a major issue develops that can affect the organization.

Finally, two general observations made by Halal are important. They are as follows:

1. Successful strategy formulation does not result from simple linear type problem solving. It usually involves a complex and somewhat subjective process that requires many iterations "over the years," since conditions are continiously changing. These in turn require modifications of previous decisions.

2. The above-mentioned decision making process involves a personal, intuitive form of thinking. Moreover, such a strategy is based on abstract beliefs that executives use to interpret or rationalize "messy" problems. Obviously, such decisions will reflect the basic ideals and values of the decision makers. A highly structured and *very formal* planning group that does not permit much informal and candid discussion cannot perform as indicated.

III. THE MALIK RESEARCH[6]

It is now time to discuss Malik's research project. It was a doctoral research project and this author was his senior professor. The researcher contacted 273 firms and 90 replies were eventually secured. Only the chemical and drug industries, when combined, and the electronics and the machinery industries had a meaningful sample size.

Some firms declined to answer the detailed and specific questionnaire as to procedure followed, some provided incomplete response to the questionaire, and some omitted the company name. In addition, if a responding firm did not start planning before the middle year of the 10 year performance measurement period (1964–1973), it too was dropped.

Finally, the number of planners and the non-planners found among the 38 respondents of the industries analyzed are:

Industry	Planners	Non-planners
Chemical and drugs	5	5
Electronics	7	8
Machinery	7	6

The firms were contacted by letter and were asked to complete an enclosed questionnaire. Anonymity was promised and no names were ever released. The performance data cited were based upon Value Line data, which "tells" the reader something about the size of the firms contacted, aside from the dollar limits on sales ($50,000,000 to $300,000,000).

Since this is the place to present Malik's statements defining valid planning, it might be worthwhile for the reader to first look at some other definitions of "planning."

Two very short definitions are the following:

"Planning is the formulation of thoughts and ideas to guide the strategy and tactics of an organization."[7]

"It is the exercise of foresight to adjust the company and its activities in advance of events which will affect them."[8]

A much more complete definition is found in *Industrial Engineering Terminology*, American National Standard's Institute standard ANSI Z94.0 1982.[9] It reads as follows:

Planning, Planning is the process whereby an individual or an organization identifies opportunities, needs, strategies, objectives and policies that are used to guide and manage the organization through future periods. All planning consists of (a) accumulation of information, (b) sorting and relating bits of information and beliefs, (c) establishing premises, (d) forecasting future conditions, (e) establishing needs, (f) identifying opportunities, (g) establishing objectives and policies, (h) structuring alternative courses of action, (i) ranking or selecting total systems of action which will achieve the best balance of ultimate (future) and immediate objectives, (j) establishing criteria and means for measuring adherence to the selected program of action and (k) so managing the organization to achieve the objectives. Some kinds of planning include short and long range planning, product planning, financial planning, etc.

A. A. Milne, author of *Winnie the Pooh*, says something about planning; it is what you do before you do something, so that when you do it, it is not all mixed up.

Malik's study in 1973–1974 cited a list of 10 criteria on which he judged whether an organization engaged in valid planning. Not too surprising is the fact that they are in general accord with the above ANSI definition, but Malik was more specific and definitive in his criteria. If the organization being tested for planning had one or more of the specified elements missing, the organizations were classed as non-planners.

1. The plan is in writing and the time span of the plans looks ahead at least 5 or more years.
2. The plan is the result of all elements of the management team working together.
3. It defines the present and the future business(es) (could have read SBUs) of the organization.
4. It specifically identifies all goals and objectives, stresses the identification of opportunities and the strategies and tactics to be pursued by all business functions so as to achieve goals and objectives.
5. The planning team has identified and determined the extent of all key influences in the external and internal environments. Some will be helpful if properly used, and some must be neutralized to prevent damage. All must be fully taken into account.
6. That the terms used to describe the strategic and tactical goals are stated in measurable terms whenever possible, including the necessary timing of actions and milestone completions.
7. The long range plan (LRP) is translated into the policies and actions of the corporation. The time span must be 5 or more years.
8. The short range plan (SRP) is developed and written immediately *after* the LRP is set and must be consistent with the LRP.
9. The SRP includes the setting of measurable specific objectives for all divisions, functions, and departments. Today this should include

SBUs. A logical extension for maximum performance effect would be MBO objectives to cover individual professional employees.

10.   A control system is established so that the organization can be operated to achieve long and short range organization goals. If the MBO approach is used, then performance of each professional is measured against the goals established for each individual. Departmental goals tend to be somewhat the same, at least with respect to departmental matters, as those for their managers.

Note requirement 9. This process can and should be extended to cover all professional employees — naturally such goals will have varying degrees of connection to the SRP, and some will also have connections to some LRP goals. However, while MBO without such connection to plans has a poor record of success, MBO works very well if it is linked to valid plans, especially the short range plans which are the near term extension of *all* long range strategic and operational plans.

The Malik research report[6] contains considerably more information than the summaries of the records of the planners versus the non-planners and should be reviewed by the serious student/reader/planner.

Table 2 presents the summaries of the results of the comparison between planners and non-planners by industry group. Note that the improvement of the planners is very significantly greater than the non-planners over the 10-year measuring period (1964–1973).

Table 3 is one of three such tables in Malik's research report; there is one for each industry group. The industrial group selected was machinery, since it was between the other two in terms of performance difference. Note that the statistical tests for significance/validity are overwhelmingly strong — the other two industry group tables are similar in every respect.

If the reader examines the 10-year improvement in just sales and earnings per share, there should be no remaining doubts about the need to engage in proper planning. It therefore seems more than reasonable to conclude that planning will have a similar beneficial effect on any company's organizational performance, regardless of the industry group(s) involved.

IV.   OVERVIEW OF REQUIRED LRP AND SRP PLANNING ACTIVITIES[10]

A.   The Steps Involved in Proper Planning

A simplistic view of the steps required are the following:

1.   Select and publicly appoint the planning director and announce the beginning of the planning activity.

Table 2   Quantitative Results of Malik's Research[6] from 1964 through 1973 (a 10-year period)[a]

Index	Electronics, compare means ($\bar{x}_1 > \bar{x}_2$)	Machinery, compare means ($\bar{x}_1 > \bar{x}_2$)	Chemical and drugs, compare means ($\bar{x}_1 > \bar{x}_2$)
Annual rates of change (%): $\bar{x}_1 > \bar{x}_2$ by — %			
1. Sales volume[b]	151%	127%	45%
2. Sales per share[c]	108%	68%	32%
3. Cash flow per share[c]	447%	151%	32%
4. Earnings per share[c]	1009%	321%	64%
5. Book value per share[c]	147%	186%	52%
6. Net income[d]	410%	$\bar{x}_1 = 292; x_1 = 1$	65%
Mean annual rates (%)[e]			
7. Earnings per capital	38%	48%	11%
8. Earnings/net worth	39%	86%	13%
9. Operating margin	26%	55%	32%
10. Dividend/net income	$\bar{x}_2$ is 35% $> \bar{x}_1$	$\bar{x}_2$ is 13% $> \bar{x}_1$	$\bar{x}_2$ is 10% $> \bar{x}_1$
Mean values per year			
11. Capital spending/share ($)	106%	$\bar{x}_1 < \bar{x}_2$	$\bar{x}_1 < \bar{x}_2$
12. Stock price ($)	23%	$\bar{x}_1 < \bar{x}_2$	$\bar{x}_1 = \bar{x}_2$
13. Price/earnings ratio	$\bar{x}_1 < \bar{x}_2$	13%	22%

[a] $\bar{x}_1$ Is the arithmetical mean increase for a group of planners and $\bar{x}_2$ is the arithmetical mean increase for a group of non-planners in the same industry group.

[b] Mean of simple annual rate of change over period 1963–1973 (CBA).

[c] Compounded annual rate of change over the period (Source: Value Line).

[d] Cumulative percentage change during the period (CBA).

[e] Mean of annual rates for the period (CBA).

[f] Mean of annual values for the period (CBA).

CBA, Calculations by author from raw data.

Table 3   Performance of the Research Firms in the Machinery Industry, with Statistical Test Results, 1964–1973

Attribute	Comparison of means (%)	Student t test data, percent accepted at	Rank sum test, data percent accepted at
Rate of change (%)			
Sales volume	127%	5%(95%)[b]	1.1%(99%)[b]
Sales volume/share	68%	6.5%(93%)	6%(94%)
Cash flow/share	151%	−(95%)	3.7%(96.3%)
Earnings/share	321%	11%(89%)	12%(88%)
Book value/share	186%	4%(96%)	3.2%(97%)
Net income	NMF	2.5%	0.7%
Mean rate (%)			
Earnings/capital	48%	1% (99%)	1.1% (99%)
Earnings/com. equity	86%	<0.5%(99.6%)	0.7%(99.3%)
Operating margin	55%	6.5%(93.5%)	9%(91%)
Dividend/net income	13%	−	5%
Mean value ($ or number)			
Capital spending/share	$x_1 < x_2$	−	−
Stock price	$x_1 < x_2$	−	−
Price/earnings	13%	5%(85%)	14.7%(85%)

2. Educate the planners regarding the planning process, the usage of the plans, and the expected results. Especially make them well acquainted with the subject matter and the parameters of strategic planning.
3. Create a standard view of the organization so that everyone plans for the same perceived company.
4. Define future horizons, both external and internal, for the length of the long range planning period (must be 5 or more years).
5. Select the planning site.
6. Define present business(es).
7. Define future business(es).
8. Establish the long term strategic and tactical objectives.
9. Expand the near term portion of the long range plan into the short range plans. The SRP naturally will also include items that are not part of the strategic plans.
10. Operate the business(es) per the plan and measure performace against plan goals and objectives.
11. Revise plans yearly (the usual time frame for revisions) and when really important new data appears.

B.   The Planning Director

It is of great importance to have an excellent planning director. This should not be a training ground assignment except possibly for C.O.O. or C.E.O. The immediate and long term fate of the organization depends on the director providing excellent and proper leadership. His/her actions will have great influence upon the development of the plans.

In theory, he/she could be the C.E.O., but usually such men and women are too busy to handle the many details of this position and to guide and assure proper preparation of the plans. Ideally the planning director is a high level manager (vice president in most cases). But if a company has never before planned and does not have an experienced planner of the proper stature, it is recommended that for the first *long range* planning effort an expert from the outside be brought in to lead and help the person who will act as the future planning director.

The director must have the stature, "presence," and strength to control the planning group so that everyone's views are properly exposed — this at times may require restraining a strong C.E.O. from dominating the meeting and forcing incorrect conclusions. Read this paragraph carefully.

Some management consulting organizations can supply the kind of planning director indicated above. Some university professors in the School of Business or Management can also have the required qualifications often provide personal consulting service. However, do *NOT* hire a firm and/or individual unless the individual who will do the work has previously worked in the job involved. If you consider the lack of proper planning in U.S. industries, you will begin to understand why few people have the required qualifications.

There always must be a first time for anyone desiring to perform such a task, but do not let them gain their experience by practicing on you — unless you are aware of the situation and have agreed to the arrangement. However, remember you are possibly adversely affecting the future performance of your organization.

One other comment. If the firm is lucky enough to have a major executive who also has substantial proper planning experience, do NOT make that person the planning director and expect him/her to more or less personally produce a set of plans. *No* planning director should ever take such action.

Representative tasks that must be performed by the planning director are now given to aid in selecting an excellent director:

1.   Does not do the planning, but takes actions so as to make sure that the right things get done at the right time by the right people. Just one real life example of this requirement is provided. The newly

planning firm was a regional supermarket. It was known that some such firms were going to 24 hour operation and that others were experimenting with pricing policy. The firm needed to know what conditions made 24 hour operation successful and what pricing policies seemed to work best and why. An expert was needed to present data and information on these subjects. The director identified the need and secured the services of an expert to provide the data and advice. The resulting decisions greatly helped make the firm outstandingly successful.

2. Acts as chairman of all planning sessions.
3. When a planning impasse occurs or it becomes obvious that some "expert business commentary" is required, he personally "fills the gap" if he possesses the necessary knowledge and then returns to acting as chairman of the meeting.
4. Arranges for data acquisition, both internal and external. At times the external variety may require bringing in one or more experts on various subjects.
5. If he/she sees that an incorrect (from a business view) conclusion is developing, the director job requires the director to state the facts as he/she sees them — with no "strings pulled."
6. Plays a lead role in identifying strengths and weaknesses since incumbent managers do not like to identify weaknesses and they overemphasize strengths.
7. Sets schedules and meeting dates and makes all arrangements.
8. Publishes (for the planners) the results, discussions, and other such information resulting from a planning session.
9. Helps develop statements of objectives used as measurement of performance of the plans which affect managers and some professional workers.
10. Reviews what historical financial data is available and then arranges for the accounting/financial functions to produce the data needed to begin planning — the director usually needs to identify many of the classes of material needed.

This is a very important position and its occupant can very substantially affect the performance of the company.

V. THE PLANNING MANUAL

The planning activity generates a considerable amount of paperwork, and such material must be properly organized for each of the planning group if it is to be of practical use. One way to help accomplish this is to provide a planning manual for each planner. Usually this is a large three-ring binder properly identified as a planning manual. Each such manual has its own serial number and is assigned to a specific person. All recipients should be advised that all its contents are company confidential and should never be exposed to anyone except those who have a "need to know."

Typical dividers in the manual for the first year are as follows:

1. Correspondence.
2. The basics of planning (something similar to this chapter; however, the reader should note that it is copyrighted material).
3. Environmental appraisals and forecasts of the future. Normally one might think that this would also be the proper place for a statement of corporate strengths and weaknesses. However this set of material is so sensitive that portions of it often need to be handled verbally and with great sensitivity.
4. Corporate (overall) and functional background material (other than financial).
5. Financial background
6. Business(es) and their definitions as well as the strategy being pursued.
7. Long range corporate plan.
8. Short range corporate plan.

Both 7 and 8 are extremely important documents for the company and must not be exposed to any person who might "leak" such information to others!

In parallel with the planning effort, someone on the staff of the planning director or the function responsible for "Systems and Procedures" should prepare a standard system and procedure covering all elements of the planning process so that everyone in the future will know what is to be done, when it is to be done, by whom, etc. Naturally, it will become a part of the planning manual provided to future planners.

VI.   CREATE A STANDARD VIEW OF THE ORGANIZATION

Each member of an organization has a somewhat different view or concept of the organization for which he/she works. Different people see different strengths and weaknesses. They also see the company pursuing differing objectives. Any existing statement of policies is also likely to be somewhat confused in the minds of the planners. Hence, each such planner will be planning for a somewhat different organization unless steps are taken to build or create a common view of the organization in the minds of the planners.

These divergences become of great importance since planners must plan achievements and business directions, goals, etc. to take advantage of company strengths and minimize and/or correct weaknesses. A company is at war, for all practical purposes. Further, no war was ever won in the short term (1–3 years) correcting weaknesses. A war can only be won by taking advantage of strengths and trying to minimize the effects of weaknesses. Therefore the above planning requires the careful identification of strengths, assessing their magnitude or importance with respect to problems and opportunities, and then determining how to take advantage of the strengths. The importance of a strength usually varies with the problem or opportunity involved.

The discussion of strengths and weaknesses brings to the fore other aspects of these characteristics. No one and no organization likes to admit to any weakness, especially if the weakness is in an organizational subunit or function in which they work. Further, strengths tend to be exaggerated by insiders. Therefore, someone from the outside, like a consultant, often must perform the identification task the first time.

The areas that must be defined, especially as to strengths and weaknesses, before real planning can begin are the following:

1. Corporate board.
2. Executive talent.
3. Product lines and products, including an assessment of quality for each product (if possible use "outside" assessments).
4. Manpower (quality, quantity), general and professional and broken down to kinds and types.
5. Financial position and capability.
6. Facilities.
7. Markets and marketing positions.
8. Corporate image and reputation.

The corporate board must determine the ground rules for risk taking and for "betting the company" — and in the final analysis, board members must make all decisions of this type. Is the experience of the board collectively broad enough to handle the above and to guide the development and marketing of new product lines or the entry of the company into a completely new field? How experienced and knowledgeable are they in the area of finance with respect to seeking and securing any required new equity capital and/or corporate loans? Do any have international experience? Do any have substantial knowledge regarding the areas of technology involved? How about knowledge regarding computer integrated manufacturing? These are just a few of the items that must be examined in evaluating the present composition of the board.

With respect to manpower evaluation there are many sources of help.

In fact the company's personnel department should be able to indicate these categories and skill/knowledge items:

Managerial personnel: depth of talent.

Engineering and Scientific: professional talent other than engineering talent; supporting personnel by type.

Skilled, semi-skilled, and unskilled workers: geographical dispersion of activities.

Compensation practices: morale and loyalty of employees.

The evaluation of facilities must include a consideration of items such as the following for each plant, warehouse and office.

1. Size, location, type, layout, condition, modernness.
2. Types, kinds, condition, modernness, adaptability, etc. of manufacturing and material handling equipment.
3. Accessibility to transportation, raw material, suppliers, markets, etc.
4. Operating and maintenance costs.
5. Ownership and/or leasing arrangements.
6. Excess capacities by classifications.
7. Availability of adequate amounts of water, power, and other required utilities.
8. Whether any facilities polute and what actions and costs are involved in correcting improper conditions.

The marketing evaluation is going to be extremely important, and here the considerations are lengthy and difficult. The following should be considered as a partial or represenative list of topics. The actual list should be created to best meet corporate needs and expose corporate problems and opportunities.[8]

1. Total available market for present product lines and products based upon current quality, service, and product features. If possible, try to arrive at a second set of market figures based upon optimum changes in service, quality, and product features.
2. Fraction of total market secured for each product.
3. Reasons why a larger market share of the products has not been secured.
4. Market structure. Do this by product line. Indicate customer characteristics, geographic locations of markets, price-volume relationships, product substitutes, and anticipated life of each product in the market.
5. Replacement parts market for each product line and/or product. Is this market being properly exploited?

6.   Seasonal and cyclical factors by product line.
7.   Competitive position by product and product line.
8.   Channels of distribution (types, numbers, and strengths).
9.   Service policies, facilities, and organizations. Can changes be made that will make this a major asset?
10. Market research capabilities based upon prior performance.
11. Brand recognition. If possible, assess importance of this attribute on sales for each brand.
12. Types, cost, and effectiveness of each variety of advertising and/or sales promotion by product line, and possibly by product.
13. Price and discount structures by markets and/or products.
14. Patent position by product and outlook for future.
15. Scope of corporate charter and identify opportunities and limitations.

A considerable portion of the material shown for manpower evaluation, facility evaluation, and marketing evaluation is discussed in *New Product Venture Management*[8] and other such books.

It should be somewhat obvious that the strengths and weaknesses in the financial area are of equal importance. These must be made available to all planners.

The financial data should include a 10-year financial history (profit and loss statements and balance statements), if possible broken down to products and division. Future *projections* should also be provided. If a *forecast* is possible, provide it and explain the basis of the forecast.

Things to worry about and include in the development of strengths and weaknesses are capital structure, liquidity, equity, cash flow, lines of credit, currency variations, liabilities, etc. Some other possibilities to think about are policies and procedures, standards, definitions, computerization, financial measurements, and budgeting.

One final comment: Any new plans should certainly take into account possible future changes in cash flow caused by the various planning objectives.

VII.   DEFINING FUTURE HORIZONS, EXTERNAL AND INTERNAL

First, a comment on the general planning time horizon: All indications point to making it a minimum of 5 years. However, most experts also say that it really should reflect the expected longest product life — this is why chemical and drug firms generally plan for significantly more than 5 years.

As to variety of horizons, these probably should include for the average industrial firm economic, technological, social, demographic, ecological, political, legal, and competitive factors.

Economic forecasts are available from governments, large banks, investment advisors, financial journals, universities, etc. Do not ever depend on one such forecast, and look at all of them with some suspicion.

Technological forecasts tend to be created by experts and are often exposed in technical journals. Trade associations are also often a source. Talk to university people in the engineering schools.

Product life cycle analysis should be used as part of the product planning process.

A practice that should be followed is to request each major executive and board members to read broadly and to identify new information that may have value to the firm. When such items are identified, they should make photocopies and send them to the planning director to record for future reference and to pass on if they are relevant to the company.

VIII.   THE PLANNING SITE

Generally planning sessions should not be attempted at "home base," especially the first few times through the process. Get away from telephones and the possibility of other intrusions. Possibilities include resorts, American Management Association facilities, and hotels.

A room used for planning should be quiet and contain sound-deadening material. It should be quiet, be tastefully decorated, contain a projection screen, and have projection facilities, chart pads, blackboard, etc. Bring along a really good secretary, a recording system, and make sure photocopy reproduction equipment will be available to the planners. Think carefully and determine what your planners will need and see that it is supplied. Personally, this planner prefers to have the planners around a table unless their number is too great—then go to an arrangement that provides a table surface for each planner.

IX.   COMPONENTS OF STRATEGY

Before the planning starts make sure that everyone knows the difference between strategies and tactics. Strategy is a plan of action to be implemented by the firm/organization that will provide significant or major benefits if accomplished and if it works as planned. Strategy and strategic actions usually are a response to external (to the firm) environments, although sometimes they are either wholly or partially based upon internal factors. The factors requiring the development and implementation of a strategy very often are detrimental to the firm unless neutralized by the strategic actions. However, at times a strategy is conceived that takes advantage of envirormental factors to further the interests of the firm.

Tactics do not represent "grand strategies," but they are important. The dictionaries, virtually all of them, define strategy and tactics in terms of military organizations. Editors and writers seeem to not recognize the importance of these terms in everyday life. Tactics in the non-military world, especially in the business world, are concerned with the details or a deployment or action. In the case of planning, tactics can apply to both strategic and operational plans, but they usually are focused upon internal operational plans. Strategic plans involve major actions. If the exact method of doing it is important to success, then tactics will specify the detail as to actions, the sequence in which they are to be accomplished, who and/or what organizational element is to do it, when the actions are to be accomplished, and any other similar required detail.

Segment the strategic considerations for ease of handling whenever possible. Some of the more obvious components of an overall strategy are as follows:

1. Definition and scope of business(es).
2. Competitive edge; probably must be for firm and by product and/or product line.
3. Risk level.

As to defining a firm's business(es), it might be instructive to read Peter Drucker's *Management*.[11] The first time this subject is discussed, many will be amazed at the thinking of many of the planners.

Competitive edge has to do with those attributes of the firm that provide a competitive advantage over competing firms. It must include a consideration of the total organization as well as with products and/or services. It is extensively discussed in Chapter 10. A company's competitve edge can be made up of a number of attributes, some of which are likely to come from the following list of typical possibilities:

Product features versus competition.	Product reliability.
Favorable price/quality ratio.	Integrity of the company.
Financial position.	Industry leadership.
Market share.	Modern plants & facilities.
Skillful marketing.	Excellence of management information system.
Low L.T.D./equity.	Large net profit margin.

Low overall costs per quality unit versus those of competitors.
Low labor content in product.

When thinking about competitive edge the reader must understand that the purchasers' views are likely to be different and must also be fully taken into consideration—in many cases their views are the most important. Examples of elements found in a purchaser's view are as follows:

Utility of product function to the customer.
Price versus that of competing products.
Absolute quality of product from all views (features, workmanship, appearance, etc.).
Realiability (i.e., mean time between failure).
Ease and expense of repair.
Total life operating and maintenance costs versus competing products.
Delivery versus competition and in absolute terms.
Status of product ownership for consumer products.
Personal relationships with company personnel.
Service.

Risks accompany every profit making opportunity and must be taken into account in planning. One so-called axiom generally cited about risk is that "the greater the possibility of gain, the greater the risk"—usually this is an absolute truth in most kinds of situations.

For both profit seeking organizations and non-profit organizations, there are internal risks and external risks—just the components are usually different.

Some of the more obviously important internal risk areas (when thinking of them versus competition) are the following:

Desirability of portfolio of products and/or services.
Product/service innovation process.
The level of commitment of resources.
Debt/equity ratio.
Gross and net profit margin.
Head-on versus competitive edge competition.
Expediency management versus proper strategic and tactical planning.
Operating on the edge of legality versus trying to conform to all laws.
Investment in talent.
Financial practices.

External risk areas are equally important, perhaps more so since these surprises often are not at all anticipated. Here is a representative list:

Rapid or unexpected change in technology.
Change in customer desires due to new classes of customers or due to pure change—such as in life style.

Geographic market shifts causing problems regarding product demand
   changes and/or distribution system.
Inflation and/or recession.
Change in resource availability.
Environmental problems.
Change in competition.
New legal restrictions.

In Chapters 1–3, we discussed expansion or growth via internal growth,
acquisitions, and mergers, as well as divestments. Any one or all of these
may enter into the planning.

Planners must take into account the effects of "organizational learning," in their own organization and in competitor organizations. This
effect shows that in virtually all properly managed organizations costs go
down 15–20 percent every time production experience doubles (the product produced is twice as great as at the reference or starting measurement).
Naturally, a large question is whether the planning organization is as far
or farther "down the learning curve" than its competitors. If not, how
can it learn faster, i.e., do better at cost reduction in the factory? Make
no mistake, the rate of learning can be affected substantially by corporate
actions.

The quality of management is the key ingredient, and this must involve
all functions of the business.

Another possible view of the products and product lines involves classifying each in terms of the following:

1. A cash eater that has low market share but high growth potential.
2. A cash eater that has high market share and high growth potential —
   class 1 products should move into this class.
3. A cash generator (high market share and low growth potential is the
   usual situation). These products tend to die and require replacement,
   an action which usually requires the investment of resources.
4. Cash generated is low for the size of the market (low net profit
   margin). These products should be divested unless one can replace
   them with products that will make a reasonable profit and have potential for growth.

There is a host of additional things that could be mentioned, but many
of these will be identified in later chapters. However, do keep in mind
that the world is rapidly changing, in terms of governments, geographic
areas, management knowledge, technological knowledge, etc. These are
the things that the planning firm must *continually* monitor.

X. MEASUREMENT OF PLAN ACHIEVEMENT AND
ASSURING CORRECTIVE ACTION

This subject will be extensively discussed in Part III of this text. Here will only be mentioned what must happen in general.

Naturally, the milestones (major and more minor steps or actions that must be accomplished) of the strategic amd operational plans need to be measured as to progress toward achievement. For strategic plans this usually must be done at least every 3–6 months so that needed corrective actions can be initiated at the correct time if they are required. Operational plans need monitoring every 2–3 months for the same reason.

This author suggests paying for good to excellent performance. With this thought emphasized, the measurements and payoff for achievement must occur within a 1-year period. The effect of a payoff for performance diminishes rapidly if the payoff occurs farther out than 12 months.

Any such payoff needs to be carefully designed and should take into account the size of the employee's salary and provide a bonus award comensurate with performance and the effect upon the company. Further, any such reward system must be clearly stated and be well understood by all participants. Especially should it be viewed as fair to all parties involved.

The organization's progress in attaining the objectives of the long range and short range plans obviously needs to be measured, at least every year. Actually more frequent measurement should be made, and this is discussed in Chapter 12. The only measurements that will have any effect upon personnel and their performance are results measured during the current year — in most organizations such measurements are made every 6 months. Naturally, once the current year passes and the new plans are issued, a new set of standards for the year ahead should be established. A new progress measurement is started.

It will become obvious from the mentioned measurements who is maintaining or achieving their portion of scheduled plan achievements. Not only should corrective actions be started if a failure to properly perform occurs, but also bonus payment amounts to executives can depend upon the degree of achievement of plan objectives.

MBO, in part based upon the corporate plan, can be used to motivate all professional personnel; this can bring about a 20 percent increase in performance. How to do this is covered in Part III.

Since the popularity and usage of MBO have decreased in recent years, a few words should be said about the reasons for the poor current repute of such plans. First, the MBO plans were not based upon strategic and operational plans (long and short range), so there was little reality addressed by the objectives. Second, they were not organization-relevant objectives expressed in measurable terms. Third, many were initiated by persons who did not realize that meaningful and measurable objectives were an absolute necessity. Fourth, many did not realize that the objectives had to be attainable in the specified time with the expenditure of a reasonable amount of energy. Fifth, in some of these plans the personnel were encouraged set their own goals — a procedure never intended in MBO plan development. This often resulted in non-relevant goals and/or goals that were too easy to achieve. All that sounds simple to correct, and the mistakes should have been few and far between? Right!

Unfortunately, the simple is often difficult, and the mentioned deficiencies of MBO *did* exist. Moreover, the managers applying them had not acquired the discipline and habits resulting from the development of the overall LRP and SRP mentioned above. In fact, this writer doubts that the designers of many MBO plans were expert enough in business and management to understand the need for planning and stating valid goals in measurable terms. This makes it all the more reasonable that the the early MBO plans failed.

The existence of the LRP and SRP organizational plans makes possible the extension of the plan objectives to those upper level managers involved in their achievement. Different managers will be involved with different objectives. Moreover, some of these objectives apply to lower level managers — those objectives of the department that are derived from the organizational LRP and SRP. Further, if the whole organization plans, the departments will also be expected to develop plans leading to still further improvements, and these objectives also should be used in the MBO system.

This and much more is further explained in Chapter 12.

The fact is that the development and existence of plans create an opportunity to establish a management by objectives (MBO) program that has *real* and very important performance objectives; moreover, the plan achievement requires a measurement program such as MBO. Since many managers and professionals will have not many goals closely related to planning goals, it means that additional *meaningful* objectives need to be established for each individual manager and professional employee if the measurement system is to have a significant beneficial effect.

While some benefits in performance, such as a 5–10 percent improvement in individual performance, can be obtained with this kind of MBO, it is possible to achieve 10–20 percent in improved additional overall performance if financial incentives are attached to the MBO program.

A word of caution to the reader who wants to hurry and establish such a scheme. It will fail, and it will cost the firm money (in increased salary expense and by weakening the control of the LRP and SRP), if the reader does not proceed as specified in Part III. It is a difficult and delicate program to design and establish, but well worth the trouble since it could add another 10 percent or more to the planning benefits.

It also means that the organization must first have an overall organizational strategic plan and a SRP. Finally, there must be related departmental plans produced during the development of the LRP and SRP.

REFERENCES

1. Stanley S. Thune and Robert J. House, "Where Long Range Planning Pays Off," *Business Horizons*, August 1978.
2. David M. Herold, "Long Range Planning and Organizational Performance, A Cross Valuation Study," *Academy of Management Journal*, March 1972.
3. Noel Capon, John V. Farley, and James M. Hulburt, *Corporate and Strategic Planning*, Columbia University Press, New York, 1987.
4. William E. Halal, "Strategic Management: The State-of-the-Art and Beyond," Working Paper of Dr. Halal, George Washington University, Washington, D.C.
5. Reference 4 taken from William E. Halal, *The New Capitalism*, Wiley, New York, 1986.
6. Zafar A. Malik, *Formal Long Range Planning and Organizational Performance*, doctoral research and dissertation, Rensselaer Polytechnic Institute, Troy, NY, December 1974.
7. D. W. Karger and R. G. Murdick, *Managing Engineering and Research*, The Industrial Press, New York, 1969, 1980.
8. D. W. Karger and R. G. Murdick, *New Product Venture Management*, Gordon and Breach Science Publishers, New York, 1972.
9. *Industrial Engineering Terminology*, American National Standard, ANSI Z94.0, Industrial Engineering and Management Press, Norcross, GA, 1983 (see Standard Z94.9).
10. D. W. Karger, "What Effective Planning Is All About," *Industrial Management*, July–August 1970.
11. Peter F. Drucker, *Management*, Harper & Row, New York, 1974.

II

THE STRATEGIC AND TACTICAL PLANNING PROCESSES, INCLUDING DISCUSSIONS OF ALL MAJOR AND RELATED ASPECTS

Special Note to Readers. While the material to be referenced in this "Special Note to Readers" is provided for planners in sub-units of non-planning organizations and for planners in non-business type organizations, much of the material would also be valuable to all other kinds of planners. Therefore, unless the reader is very knowledgeable or has no interest in the messages (some of which apply to all planners), it is recommended that all readers of this text read this special material before continuing with Part II. It is presented in Appendix I at the rear of the book, entitled Planning Guidance for Sub-Unit Department or Division Planners in a Non-Long Term Planning Organization and Non-Business Type Organizational Planners.

INTRODUCTION TO PART II

As noted in the table of contents, Part II consists of Chapters 6–12. While it primarily deals with the "how to" procedures, it offers much additional direct and indirect information about planning. The "how to do it" material is based upon much personal experience of the author, observations of planning efforts, and much library research.

The chapter titles essentially represent major "milestones" in the planning process and appear in the normal sequence of starting each of these steps. More on the sequencing of the steps in planning will be presented in Chapter 6.

6

How to Introduce an Organization to Planning

I. INTRODUCTION

It is seldom possible to produce a successful plan if the organization's introduction to the process is a mere announcement of the fact that the executive group and their professional staff are to develop a long range strategic plan and a companion short range operational/tactical plan under the guidance of a specified member of the executive group. This statement is true, even where quite competent officers and managers are involved.

Range and term are used interchangeably in this book. Moreover, in order to save space, long range/long term planning will often be abbreviated by LRP.

There will be resistance to long range planning because few managers have participated in such planning. Moreover, there often will be resistance to such planning because officers and managers perceive that their performance will be measured against plan objectives and they feel threatened. Others think long term planning makes it impossible or impractical to properly cope with unplanned "happenings" or emergencies.

Still others will argue that since it is impossible to forecast the future, 5 or more years ahead, that it is a waste of time to plan for the long term.

Finally, others may have heard about using LRP objectives in a management by objectives (MBO) program and want no part of such performance measurements and therefore try to discourage LRP. They do not want to have their performance measured.

Moving to LRP from short range planning (1–3 years) may somewhat ease a few of the fears mentioned, but it will not eliminate all of them. Neither will it generate automatic acceptance of a long range corporate or strategic plan and its associated operational/tactical plans (short term and long term).

The chief executive officer (C.E.O.) therefore has a major challenge in how to accomplish the required task of getting the executive team to embrace LRP and SRP. First, he/she must understand that the C.E.O.'s role in starting the planning activities is primarily that of evangelist, educator, and monitor. Second, he obviously will need key people to help with the introduction and with the direction of the planning activities.

Finally, the C.E.O. should not forget that he/she is to also function as one of the planners—but must always be careful not to so dominate the planning that the other planning team members are "turned off."

Essentially, the key executives (all the officers, and in smaller companies all the upper level managers) must be exposed to the kind and type of material contained in Part I, and the planning director must be certain that they understand the content and meaning of the material before they are likely to be "sold" on the idea of developing a proper set of plans.

The first time the kind of planning espoused in this text is accomplished, it is best to seek the help of an experienced expert unless one exists within the organization. By "experienced" it is meant that the individual chosen/appointed to direct the planning actually has previously directed the successful development of one or more acceptable LRPs and SRPs.

II. UNDERSTANDING SOME CONFUSING ACTIONS THAT ARE ANCILLARY, BUT ARE A NECESSARY PART OF LONG RANGE STRATEGIC PLANNING

It has been previously stated that the strategic long range planning activities are aimed at producing a strategic plan for the entire organization or corporation. Such planning activities must also include long range and short range tactical planning. This kind of planning must be accomplished toward the end of the corporate overall planning activities since they (first) represent an expansion of the near term portion of the LRP.

Another reason why short range plans must be an integral part of overall corporate planning is that the corporate LRP often must deal with functional/departmental matters—especially is this true regarding the correction of weaknesses (sometimes departmental in nature) and regarding the taking advantage of corporate strengths. These latter are also often functional and/or departmental in nature.

It is prudent and necessary for the functions or departments to also plan if they are to improve and assist in meeting corporate objectives. Therefore, they too must be moved into a planning mode—if they are not already there. In some cases such planning greatly affects overall company strategic planning, another reason why it must be accomplished. This kind of planning activity is *not* to be a direct concern of the corporate planners. Such planning is mostly performed by department/functional planners whose heads usually report to a member of the corporate LRP team—meaning that each corporate planner may be a head of one or more operational/tactical planning teams.

As to planning schedules and the sometimes execution of sections of the LRP, the departmental planners should be responsible to the overall planning director. However, the titular head does much of the directing activity under the guidance of the corporate planning director. Examples of such plans include the following:

1. Financial plans
    (a) Longer range financial plans, but not nearly as detailed as budgets. Often this plan will also contain components of the corporate LRP.
    (b) Budgets for the year ahead.
2. Facility plans (these sometimes contain components of the corporate LRP).
3. Manpower/human relations plans.
4. Manufacturing plans (usually broken down to plans for each of the functions such as industrial engineering, inspection, production management areas of responsibility, plant engineering, janitorial and yard maintenance, etc. Sometimes these can be plans for the year ahead and others often must consider a longer term, especially when a component of the strategic plan is involved.
5. Marketing plans.
    (a) The longer term plans (these often have longer term strategic components mentioned in the LRP).
    (b) The year ahead.
6. Technical function plans.
    (a) The longer term plans (these may have some strategic components identified in the LRP).
    (b) The year ahead.

Long range strategic or corporate planning focuses on overall organizational planning, *not* on facilities planning, financial planning, manpower
planning, market planning, production planning, or technical function
planning, etc. Yet it must also be said that while the corporate LRP
activity mainly examines overall concerns, the execution of many to most
of the resulting plans has functional components. This is why it is a
mistake to completely divorce corporate planning from functional or departmental planning.

Once the corporate planning indicates that an action is required of a
function, the action becomes an overall corporate objective and it must
also become an objective of the functional plans. Usually such a situation
requires coordination by the top executive organization, including that of
the planning director.

The overall corporate planning team members must not let themselves
get deeply involved in *detailed* functional planning. Should they do so,
they will get so bogged down with detail that the strategic plan will likely
have little beneficial effect upon organizational performance—long or
short term.

Having mentioned the beneficial effects of corporate LRP, a few additional thoughts should be expressed to help the reader understand the
initial and the continuing focus of the plans. Malick, cited in Chapter 5,
indicated that companies reaped great benefits each year as a result of
proper planning.

Some writers say that the early planning research of the 1960—1970s
indicated sizeable benefits because the organizations had never before
planned. True, they almost never had planned. In fact, this is largely
still largely true today when one is looking for planning as described in
this text.

A more important observation about the results of proper organizational planning is that such organizations have significantly superior performance (year after year) than similar firms (those in the same industry
group) who do not properly plan. There are a small number of identifiable
firms that can boast about such a continuing record. Examples are IBM
(in the past, but they are now too large and mature to sport a record
equaling their early days—for the last few years they have stumbled,
probably due to poor planning, attempting to control a market which is
no longer easily controllable by one firm, and because their technology
has been outpaced at times by their competitors), Mariott, Gannett, Automatic Data Processing, Bandag, Bard, Comdisco (stumbled for a couple of
years when they tried some "fancy" trading tactics), ConAGRA, Federal
Express, Flight Safety, Rubbermaid, Safety Klean, McDonald's Corp.,
etc.—virtually all of those named are first in their industry or sub-field of

their industry and the consistency of their performance indicates that they *likely* are acceptable planners.

The first time an organization does this kind of planning, they likely will discover many opportunities for new and better business opportunities, ways to improve profit margins (gross and net), reduce the interest burden of long term debt, discover new classes of customers, identify new product opportunities, etc.

The reader may decide that once this has been accomplished there is no need to replan for the next year. WRONG! The next year, the planners must examine whether their strategies were correct and proper and if they were executed. Then they must do everything else (as to planning activities) all over again because new data will surface and must be taken into account.

Remember that the focus in the corporate LRP is 5 or more years ahead and in 1 year some of the factors affecting the 5 or more year period may well have changed direction or emphasis. Moreover, the first effort may have identified some business units that had too low net profit margins or had a shrinking market, and in this effort they may need to consider disposal of the poorly performing business units. Moreover, they will again have to examine how to further increase sales and profits. IT IS A CONTINUING BATTLE TO INCREASE SALES AND PROFIT-ABILITY. It is exactly what a long range strategic planning firm does *every* year for the years ahead.

One other, often misunderstood, aspect of this kind of planning is that it seldom requires the use of highly complex modeling or other such planning techniques. Most of these, if used, will be used in the functional planning. Seldom are they needed or used in strategic planning.

Finally, most firms know enough about planning to handle the functional planning chores, hence these will not be discussed in this text. Moreover, they will not be significantly different from the procedures to be further described.

III. SELLING THE LRP AND SRP PROCESS AND MOTIVATING THE EXECUTIVES/MANAGERS

The more typical reasons why considerable opposition to long range planning will likely be encountered were mentioned in the Introduction. Many times resisting executives and managers will say very little, even though they are opposed to using the process. This will usually cause them to espouse weak objectives. Therefore, a second look at some of these reasons may be instructive to the reader.

As to fear of threats to existing jobs and/or jobholders, this area of concern must always be considered. There are no tangible reasons why planning is a threat to the existence of a job, unless the job (work involved) is no longer required. If this is true, and the person doing it is an effective and knowledgeable manager or professional employee, it is just as likely that new jobs may be identified that require accomplishment and will be opportunities for either promotion and/or expansion of an employee's knowledge and skills. LRP seldom has any significant negative impact on the continuing existence of jobs, but planning *does* tend to expose someone who is not doing an adequate job.

As to not being able to precisely forecast the future, this is not the sole or most important task that gets accomplished in the process of predicting future environments. The planner does, however, need to acquire knowledge as to future environmental changes that will adversely and/or helpfully affect the organization.

Most of the time identifying and defining the kind of changes and the direction of movement for each kind will be 75 percent of what is needed. Actually, if one can accomplish this, he/she also can likely guess at the magnitude of the environmental factor. Examine Chapters 1–4. These are examples of what can be discovered. More such examples will be mentioned in other chapters.

By attempting to determine "the future" one usually discovers one or more of the following:

1. That existing factors in the environment are adversely affecting the organization and/or that existing factors could help the organization's performance if the factors were only taken into account in the daily operations of the organization. These existing factors sometimes are in the early stages of existence and increasing in their effect, and in other cases they are fully developed and have stablized their impact. They can also be receding. If the effect of a factor is negative (adverse) then the stronger the trend, the worse the effect, and when it begins to recede things begin to improve. If the firm can take advantage of a factor and it grows, things can get better—just the opposite of the previously described situation.
2. That events are such that a new definable factor is about to appear which must therefore be considered in long range planning.
3. That forecast technological developments seem to have no applications to the activities of the firm—remember that forecast technology is not the same as innovation, especially new product innovation. This is a common occurrence unless the firm is strong enough to become a pioneer in a new kind of technology and/or business.

4. A forecast technological development looks like an area of business to consider for the future. In this kind of situation remember that before these kinds of businesses become money-makers they usually require 5–10 years. During this period of developing product and market they will lose money for the firm.

Another of the fears mentioned by executives exposed to planning relates to the future establishment of general overall organizational objectives that could measure managerial performance by MBO type objectives that *are* definitive performance measures. This is true because they are tied to the strategies and/or operational/tactical plans, which makes possible the creation of significantly important performance standards.

The excellent performers in their jobs and those who really want the company to succeed (so they can better succeed) will tend to climb on the LRP and SRP "bandwagon" early in the process, especially if they sense that good performance will be rewarded—and this is exactly what is described in Part III.

Second, somewhere in the "selling and motivating" required to properly start LRP (both types) and SRP, it should be emphasized that planning will help the managers and workers do a better job because it provides correct advice and guidance.

Regardless of whether the planning director is an insider or a consultant (outsider), it is important that the C.E.O. open the initial planning session. He can leave no doubts in the minds of the planners about his/her agreement on the importance of planning and on its proper implementation. The C.E.O. must also must participate in all other major planning sessions.

The C.E.O. needs to basically describe what is to be expected in this first and introductory planning session. Further, the C.E.O. needs to reassure the group (for the benefit of the people who are apprehensive) that the plan is for his benefit and for their benefit—all should benefit substantially if the planning is properly accomplished.

Both the C.E.O. and the planning director must share the selling and motivational aspects of the first real planning session. However, the primary selling thrust should come from the C.E.O., and some of this will need to be continued in one-on-one meetings.

The rest of the session is primarily of an educational nature and is the prime responsibility of the planning director. If a consultant is used as the first director, the continuing director (in this case the author is assuming that the director is already on the payroll) should be working with him and should make some of the presentations. If next year's director is not yet "on board," it then will likely be necessary to again hire the consultant unless the company is able to find a person with experience — not an easy task to accomplish.

The first session will likely be an all day affair since there will need to be time allowed to discuss not only the need for planning, but also the details of the plan achievement monitoring system. Even more time consuming is the proper introduction and explanation of any associated performance appraisal system and how this will be used to affect pay and/or bonus payment. Further, keep in mind that considerable discussion will ensue if some of the important trends to the industry involved are clearly exposed.

It is at this first meeting that a planning manual should be given to each attendee. If possible it should have an approximate identification of the major events in the process and an approximate time for their achievement.

The attendees need to be able to refer, in the future, to much of the information provided in the first meeting, hence the director of such a planning effort needs to consider whether copies of the speeches are to be provided and/or whether copies of this or a similar text be provided.

IV. ORGANIZING THE PLANNING PROCESS AND GENERATING A "STANDARD PROCEDURE"

Integrated formal long and short range planning must be a joint cooperative effort of people in all areas of the business, as well as those of top management—which at various times should include the board of directors. No such plan should be promulgated before it has been approved by the corporate board (where such board exists).

The possible need for hiring a consultant or some other person as a planning director the first time through the process has been mentioned in Chapter 5 and earlier in this chapter. The president of the company, if the firm has 100 or more employees, is too busy and too involved with everyday problems to lead and organize the planning. The continuing planning director should help the director of the first effort at every stage and in the accomplishment of almost every task.

One aspect of the initial planning effort is the production of a "standard procedure". It probably would be a good idea to have the continuing director write it. A *representation* of the procedure can be developed using a format such as that shown in Figure 1, which will be helpful, but a procedure in the standard format of such a document should also be produced.[1]

Figure 2 presents a sort of event/action flow chart, which illustrates a

Major steps	Person responsible	Schedule		Actual completion
		Start	Complete	
1.				
2.				
Etc.				

Figure 1   Format for planning procedure.

possible procedure for getting the plan through the organization the first time.[2] Actually, such a scheme needs to be tailored to the needs and facts surrounding the organization. The illustrated chart indicates that almost one full year is required. Actually, it is possible to beat that chart substantially, even the first time through the planning process. Certainly, after the first such effort, it should be possible to cut the time by 50 percent. This author completed a very successful plan (from the viewpoint of performance improvement) in about 3 months in a firm then doing about $125,000,000 per year.

Part of the organizing for planning involves a considerable amount of not so exciting work. For example, it is necessary to develop a preliminary schedule (rest assured that it will be modified). Assignments and schedules for all activities must be prepared, at least for the first third of the sessions and/or events.

The financial data and plan format need to be established prior to planning. This is because the financial activity must have the specified 5 year financial data sheets, mentioned in Chapter 5, completed and ready for distribution at the first planning session.

The procedure for reconciling functional plans must be agreed upon before the first meeting.

Why is all this needed prior to the first meeting? Simple. The planners will be asking questions about all this and more. The people running the process can not afford to overlook the need for such material.

In fact, a draft of the material that goes into Figure 1 for at least the first third of the planning process should be presented at the first meeting. Also, the flow of events and actions illustrated in Figure 2 should be modified for the first session, especially as to dates.

Before leaving this somewhat general discussion of the required first actions of starting a LRP and SRP planning activity, a bit more needs to be said about first steps.

One of the first things that obviously needs to be done is to describe the uses and benefits of long range planning and short range planning in order to convince the planners that it is a necessary and desirable activity. Originally, this author thought that citing the research results was enough.

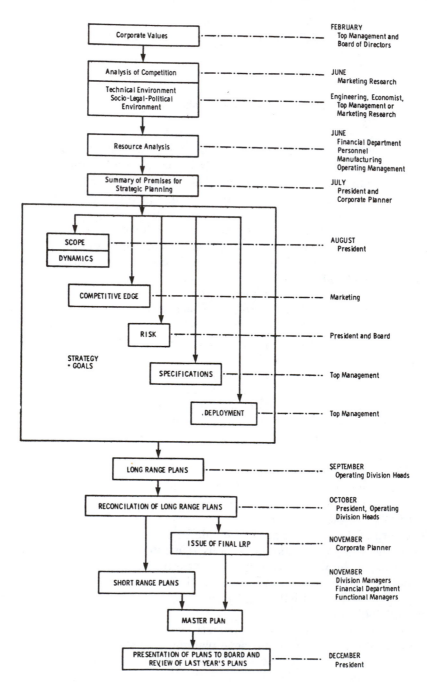

Figure 2   Development of corporate master plan.

However, it soon became obvious that much more was required since the inherent resistance to planning is of significant magnitude.

It is really a major part of the motivation for writing and including Chapters 1–4 in Part I of this text. However, it also accomplishes more than merely citing reasons for planning. It also provides an up-to-date example of typical and existing external and internal environments, as well as disclosing some very important internal weaknesses in many U.S. industrial firms.

The above material is why the first session needs to involve presentations of the material found in Chapters 1–5. Asking the planners to read the material would help, but having an expert make the presentations who would would be able to answer questions posed by the audience will cause a much greater and more desirable impact upon the planners.

Included in the presentations should be the following additional items:

1. The actual steps in the planning process.
2. The sequences in which the planning actions must occur.
3. The role of the planning director.
4. The reasons why consultants are sometimes used.
5. Why the organization's strengths and weaknesses must be identified and a strategy must be developed.
6. The data requirements of LRP and SRP.
7. How the plans are actively created.
8. How the plans should be stated and used.

Some readers will wonder whether the functional department heads should attend this meeting since they too must engage in SRP and LRP activities that at times will contain components of the corporate LRP. In general, the proper answer is yes. However, keep in mind that the organization may want to spend some time in defining the firm's businesses as discussed under the next subtitle. There are both pro and con reasons that pertain to this situation.

The planning director and next year's director should meet with the chief planners, dividing the planners randomly between them for such one-on-one meetings. Without the meetings, many of the planners will merely skim the material without trying to develop a thorough understanding of its contents.

In addition, a letter from the C.E.O. which reminds the planners of the importance to be attached to the planning process would be appropriate and would be substantially helpful.

V. THE NEED FOR CREATING A STANDARD VIEW OF THE ORGANIZATION

In virtually all initial planning sessions it will become quite apparent, if the leader gives the audience a little encouragement, that almost each member present sees the organization as having a different mission or purpose. One of the most frequent variations will concern the kinds of businesses in which it should engage.

Other variations will include such factors as the proper role of debt versus equity, whether the firm should contract or expand its business area, etc. Further, different people see different strengths and weaknesses. It is because of all this that a common view of the organization must be developed before meaningful planning can commence—although developing the standard view is an integral part of planning. The creation of a standard view of the firm is important because the planners must determine objectives regarding every aspect of the organization.

One portion of the standard view can be determined in part before the first session and in the session itself. The other part must be accomplished *after* the first session—that of determining strengths and weaknesses.

As to defining the business(es), this author has accomplished it successfully by using two different approaches. One method has the planning director, the chief officers, and the board meeting separately before the planning meeting to explore the aspects of a standard view that does not concern the matter of defining strengths and weaknesses. Even in this close and powerful group, there will initially exist considerable differences in opinion. It is interesting to observe how a consensus (of most of the group) develops.

Then, in the first session, assuming the board is not present, at an appropriate point, the statement developed by the board and officers is provided; its source is indicated; and the director should indicate that the "floor" is open to suggestions, revisions, and/or statements about the definition. Naturally, they need to understand that their ideas will be brought before the board.

If a reconciliation is needed, this will be the first order of business at the next planning session. Be sure to discuss this situation with the board before any reconciliation meeting.

If the board is to attend the first planning session, in this author's opinion a very suitable way to proceed is to bring the topic of defining the business(es) of the firm forward to all members at the same time. Expect considerable variation in opinions *and* expect to reopen the subject at the next planning meeting. It usually takes two or more sessions to settle the various possibilities. There is more on this general subject in Chapter 7.

The actual determination and discussion of strengths and weaknesses of the firm (the other component of "A Standard View of the Organization") are discussed in Chapter 9.

VI. DEVELOPMENT AND USE OF PLANNING MATERIALS

Before leaving this chapter, it seemed best to say a few things on the above subjects.

As an organization acquires experience with planning, it should develop policies, manuals, training materials, and forms for the guidance and support of the planners. The planning manuals and materials, including the final plans, will likely be contained in one or more loose leaf binders that are properly identified as to content.

The essentially descriptive portions of the LRP and SRP should be made available to all professional employees. This does not mean distributing a copy to all employees, but it does mean they should have an opportunity to read it—but be sure they cannot get to a photocopy machine and copy it.

This author recommends providing copies only to the main planning group. These copies should be serially numbered.

The planning of an organization, including its planning procedures, is of vital importance to the success of an organization. Moreover, if the actual plans fall into the hands of a competitor or become common knowledge in the business community, the firm has sustained a major loss. All of the planning material should be considered proprietary information.

What actually goes into the planning documents will vary with the organization. Binders have been mentioned. There should be dividers indicating the way the material should be classified. If the material contains many documents, there should also be an index for each class of documents.

The documentation would likely include most of the following classes of material:

1. Correspondence (scheduling and specific procedure/planning assignments can be established via letter or by a separate procedure). For the first planning endeavor, assignments are probably best handled by letter, thereafter by procedure.
2. Environmental appraisal and forecasts (or summaries of same).
3. Special studies such as competition, identification of customer classifications, foreign developments, etc.
4. Corporate and functional background material.
5. Product/service background material.
6. Financial background.

7. Strategies.
8. Long range plan.
9. Short range plan.

A discussion of content for most of the above will be provided later in the book—for the more important and complex categories.

REFERENCES

1. D. W. Karger, *Long Range Planning and Corporate Strategy*, D. W. Karger, DeFuniak Springs, FL, 1978.
2. D. W. Karger and R. G. Murdick, *Long Range Planning and Corporate Strategy*, Karger and Murdick, Troy, NY, 1975.
3. John Argenti, *Practical Corporate Planning*, George Allen & Unwin Ltd, 40 Museum Street, London WCIA ILU.

7

Establishing Corporate Values and Image

I. INTRODUCTION

Common sense indicates that the organization in which top executives hold widely diverging value systems is very likely to be a trouble prone organization. It will be difficult to agree on important basic policies such as the "value" to be provided the customer, whether "short cuts" in terms of quality will be tolerated, whether "fair dealing" is held in high regard, whether the customer is to be fleeced or "well served," and a host of other similar value oriented goals or policies. It will also affect the ability of the organization to hold to a unified sense of direction and whether it will take the short term or long term view of business plans and operations.

The corporate image, which in a large part is shaped by the corporate culture (composite of views held by the executives) as viewed by the various corporate publics, will naturally tend to be blurred and seem to shift positions. Examples of the "publics" include customers, vendors, financial institutions, governmental agencies, service clubs, unions, professional societies, etc.

Clarification of the values of the individual managers should be "helped" toward the desired orientation (sometimes it can be done and sometimes it can't) prior to long range planning if maximum benefits are to be secured. In some cases it may mean the failure or endangerment of such planning if rogue views cannot be changed or neutralized by a vast majority of acceptable views.

What is an acceptable view depends upon the person or persons making the judgement. However, we are here treading very close to what can be done legally. Most readers would agree that certain actions triggered by rogue beliefs will likely lose the firm some customers, superior executives, and unleash a host of other negatives. These are the views that must be considered important from a business view.

Fortunately, some of this establishment of a corporate culture occurs as a natural process. Bosses tend to surround themselves with men and women holding similar value systems. In a similar manner, employees like to be "around" employees holding views similar to theirs.

II. THE VALUE SYSTEM OF INDIVIDUALS

All individuals possess their own system of values. Values are preferences based upon beliefs that some things are "good" and others are "bad." For example, one person might have numerous sets of values, such as the following:

1.   Theoretical—the manner in which one searches for truth.
2.   Economic—one's belief or disbelief of stated factors in our economic system. Often the importance to individuals of certain precepts is heavily influenced by any penalties and rewards associated with them.
3.   Aesthetic—preferences in the creative and/or artistic aspects of life.
4.   Social—belief as to a person's role in society, including the degree to which they "love people," the perceived importance of status, etc.
5.   Political—the extent of a person's desire for power and the degree to which the individual believes that power differentiation is desirable and/or needed.
6.   Religious—belief in a unified set of religious precepts and the mysticism underlying religion.

All of the above will be heavily influenced by their childhold and early life experiences. As to the last classification of values, in the modern world (especially in the United States), we have so mixed the ethnic and religious orientations of the various populaces found in many countries that what has resulted in some areas is a composite of many views, beliefs, and values. This mixing has largely been caused by poor economic performance, ethnic persecution, religious persecution, wars, etc. However, intermarriage and changing work locations also have played a role.

Because of all these factors, plus existing laws, any goal stated in religious or ethnic terms is usually illegal. This merely means that these issues must be approached on the basis of expressing the basic values desired.

III.   THE VALUE SYSTEM OF ORGANIZATIONS

An organization of human beings will, at best, have a sort of composite value system or culture. It is a reflection of the majority of values, especially of the top managers. Moreover, it might be interesting to some to note that what is referenced here is not a concensus arrived at in a conscious manner.

If one person or group having strong opinions dominates the company, it is often expressed as a creed or a set of policies that then appears in annual reports, speeches of executives, advertising, product warranties, etc. What is spoken of in this paragraph is created because the C.E.O. or the managerial group wanted it created.

This chapter is mainly directed at the firm that has not arrived at a statement such as mentioned in the above paragraph and which realizes that a statement of "values" can help the firm succeed.

These organizational values, as distinguished from the individual values previously mentioned, relate to factors such as the following:

1.   Concept of leadership—stated assumptions and/or beliefs about the proper behavior of people and the role(s) of the leader.
2.   Philosophy of "right" and "wrong"—the creation of ethical standards for conducting the business and for personal conduct within the organization.
3.   Nature or mission of the organization—normally the primary concerns are the desired varieties and kinds of products, services, the quality and value aspects of products and services, marketing efforts, and other related actions of the firm. Yet some firms have a mission that involves the customer, like Maytag and its trouble free products.
4.   Risk considered acceptable to the organization—it should be defined in terms of measures that automatically take into account the size and profitability of the company.
5.   Innovation—should the firm emphasize new product conceptions and renewal of old products, and the associated development and engineering, manufacturing, and marketing of a stream of new products, or should the firm try to be a "fast follower"? This is a good strategy and tactic for a firm possessing a major market share in its product line(s). If a major market share is not possessed, then the next

acceptable strategy is to be a fast follower if that ability can be developed. Otherwise, the prospects are dim.

6. Organization development—concerns the development and growth of people within in the organization and the continuing improvment of the organization/management system so as to assure the achievement of goals and objectives (often involves organizational structure).

7. Communications and secrecy—the extent to which open communications are encouraged and the degree to which secrecy is deliberately pursued and preserved in specified areas of the business.

8. Economic and social responsibilities—to the owners, the public, customers, and society.

It seems appropriate to briefly discuss some of the above topics, whereas others are believed to be so generally understood by managers that not much need be said beyond having indicated their presence and importance in developing the value system of an organization. From what has been said regarding business oriented organizations, it should not be difficult to create a similar list for non-profit and governmental organizations—some will be the same or very similar with respect to the "thrust" of the issues.

The implications of the statement concerning "organizational risk taking" implied that the only kind to consider was financial and that these should not be stated in terms of a simple dollar amount. Rather, the risk should be expressed in terms of the net worth of the organization, of its free cash flow, of its net profit margin versus that of competitors, of its debt/equity ratio, or in terms of two or more such measurement bases similar to these.

However, there are many other risks, and whether these should be addressed depends upon the organization and its susceptibility to being adversely affected by one or more of these. Involved are such things as (1) patent protection, (2) "trade secrets" such as manufacturing processes that cannot be patented or other such "secrets" important to the company, (3) the chance that products can be superceded by new technology, etc. The entire gamut of such possibilities should be explored.

In Part I of this book, a union election was mentioned that occurred in a Nissan plant in Tennessee. The union was soundly beaten by those who wanted no part of a union. Why? Because of fair treatment of the workers, including suitable wage rates and job security. Does not this indicate that it might be important to pay attention to values, organizational development, communications, and social responsibilities?

IV. THE DEVELOPMENT OF A SET OF VALUES

The development of a set of values by a majority of an organization's executives could be a difficult matter to resolve because of the sensitive nature of the matter involved. Often an outsider may be called in to chair a series of top executive meetings to clarify feelings and to develop common ground for written expressions. The author has had only one such experience.

Organizational creed or culture statements usually are one or two page documents and often are prepared so as to express the generally perceived values. Many critics claim that such creeds are so general as to be worthless. However, they can, even then, serve as a reminder to executives who are in doubt about some proposed actions. Moreover, it might serve a useful purpose in the event of a legal action bearing upon corporate conduct.

A value system or creed will often be directly translated into policies, and when this occurs the policies will be much more explicit. Such policies can and often do concern the public, customers, vendors, financing, product quality, etc. The creed will tend to lead to the development of a clear image of the organization.

When such a set of values is to be discussed it is best not to distribute a topic list prior to the meeting. In fact, by letting values "surface" from the participants in a setting, interesting sources as well as concepts will arise from the executives.

Do not give them a lot of time to think about "acceptable" values. Make a list, similar to the following, and use the questions one at a time to generate remarks and discussions after the audience has "run out of ideas to discuss":

1. What "value" do you place on the reputation of your organization?
2. What should be the company's attitude(s) toward customers?
3. What examples of conflict of interest should the organization explicitly identify for executives?
4. (a) Should employees try to influence customers, vendors, competitors, goverment officials, etc.?
    (b) Obviously, some forms of influence are a part of business actions and considered acceptable. However, some actions are not considered acceptable. What acts need to be defined?
5. What are the bounds of industry cooperation versus collusion in restraint of trade?
6. (a) Does our business have any social responsibilities other than to make a profit?

     (b)   If so, what are they and what limits need to be associated with some of them?

7. (a)   What do we owe our employees?

     (b)   Do we measure up to our standards and should they be expressed in writing?

8. (a)   What efforts should be made regarding minority groups (ethnic, color, sex, etc.)?

     (b)   What about handicapped persons and older people?

     (c)   Relate the above to regular employees. What should we say and how should it be expressed?

9.   Should the firm have special policies and/or programs for alcoholics, drug addicts, persons with criminal records? (Special note: This is a "touchy" subject, and you may want to first discuss this in a small group. Moreover, remember that you may have to institute random drug and alcohol testing as mentioned in Part I.)

10. What traits in a person do you like to see before you trust them completely? Should the company exhibit the same traits of behavior in its dealings?

11. What, if any, social actions should the firm support?

The topics are not in any important order for discussion, so if someone opens one of the topics (or even opens the consideration of some other appropriate subject) go ahead and discuss it. However, the leader should at least bring up the questions in the list that have not been covered.

After working through these topics, the leader might try to develop a set of principles which would serve executives as a guide in most any situation. These should be limited to a reasonable number, which means that they need to be powerful and "clear-cut" statements.

A "creed" or a set of corporate values is not an absolutely essential element of planning, but in the longer term, most good and successful corporations and other organizations will find it worthwhile to define such a set of values. A more common expression of these values will be found in policy manuals—often it is referenced at a number of points.

V. DEFINITION OF THE BUSINESS(ES)

In Chapter 6 it was mentioned that the planners should define their organization's business(es) (activities and/or purposes for non-profit and governmental organizations) before beginning active planning. Otherwise, different planners will be planning for different business(es).

The obvious approach to defining such things as creeds and values (as previous discussed) is to hold one or more meetings on the subjects. It is possible to also discuss the "definition of the business(es)" of the firm at such a meeting—assuming the presence of the board of directors. All planning organizations do not try to define creeds and values, but it is a logical and potentially valuable action. If the decision is to do both, it probably would be logical, in most such situations, to first discuss the "definition of the business(es)" and then take up the matter of creeds and values.

A definition of the business engaged in by the organization involves defining the nature of its business in the broadest acceptable sense—its products/services, its markets, its customers, geographical area of operations, and any other factors deemed important to the success of the organization.

First an example of what not properly defining your business can cause is illustrated by the following actual case example. It was a small ($100,000,000–150,000,000) regional supermarket chain that had never thought about such a definition. Also, there was no public stock, it was all privately held. As a direct result of no such definition they operated under three different store names and each had a different discount structure (discount had no relationship to locale). Out of 30+ tractor-trailer units owned and operated by the firm, only 3 carried advertising and the name shown was the parent firm, which had no real meaning since the buyers did not make a connection to the supermarkets because no one realized that they were the owners and operators. The owners were not stupid, they were merely doing what happens in many such firms.

After a number of planning sessions, the company decided that its primary business was to operate deep discount full service supermarkets in the larger cities in their geographic area. They gathered all the markets under one name and moved the whole chain to 24 hour operation—the first chain to do this in their area. All property, including the tractor-trailer units, carried the store name. In about 6 months they moved from a loss position to a firm and significant profit position and today sales are in the $300,000,000 plus range.

For large companies, it is as important to say what businesses the organization will not engage in as well as defining what it will do. For example, GE at one time said it would not (or be apt to) enter the retailing industry, the clothing design business, or enter into mineral extraction except as a producer of equipment.

In the case of conglomerates, there may be a common thread of technology, product, marketing, production, or customers served among the companies acquired. Or the policy may be to treat companies like an investment portfolio by selling off the least profitable and acquiring more profitable companies.

"Looking at the firm's 'companies' like an investment portfolio" is foolish. Such an examination is almost entirely financially oriented. Financial performance is an important decision determinant, but it is likely not the main or proper major determinant regarding operation versus disposition.

This is substantiated by research conducted by G. A. Jarrell and R. Comment of the University of Rochester's William Simon Business School.[1] There are other reports of a similar nature, and an earlier example was cited in Part I. These men studied 120 publicly held firms that restructured from the start of 1984 through 1987. They used sales to measure the degree to which such restructuring moved the firm to greater concentration on core business. Based upon the referenced discussion, the use of sales was by business category. They therefore could determine if there was greater or less concentration in core business and to what degree. The 30 companies with the largest increase in concentration ratios produced (on the average) 10 percent higher annual returns to shareholders (dividends plus capital gains) than the 30 companies with the lowest rise in concentration ratios. It also appeared that this also likely included a consideration of what the stock market did "as a whole"— presumably this meant what a market index did during the time period. Moreover, this is similar to what was experienced by the company described by the author in Part I as mentioned above. The reader should recall that the owner wanted to grow his firm by a factor of more than 100 times. The message shouted by the results is clear, stick to what the firm knows best.

Conglomeration in terms of the modern world also needs to be examined in planning if the firm is a conglomerate or is considering such an action. If it is accquiring a successful company making the same product as the firm's core product, the remark does not apply. In the action just mentioned, one can almost assume that the firm wishes to increase its market share and make more money. One more thing needs to be mentioned regarding conglomerates. When there is an LBO of a conglomerate, or of a firm with a number of businesses, the first action is to unconglomerate by disposing of poorly performing units and using the money to pay off debt.

A new factor has entered into acquiring a firm. It used to be that product designs *changed slowly* and manufacturing processes crept or crawled forward—ever so slowly. Therefore, if a firm had a product that was highly successful, one could expect to have considerable time to improve the product and to further modernize manufacturing. Today, one needs to examine firms being considered for acquisition much more carefully than in the past since change in these areas is *very rapid*.

Today, if one buys a successful and profitable firm, one may be buying a WWII plant and designs that can only be produced in a WWII plant. This author consulted for one such company in their home plant. Soon afterward it was acquired by another firm in the same business, in 1987 or 1988. Neither firm at the time of the purchase was ready to compete in the world's markets. The acquired firm had no automated facilities and the acquiring firm (a larger firm) had only one small automated line.

In this kind of situation, if the purchasing firm does not immediately recognize its position AT ONCE, the Japanese, or the Koreans, or the Taiwanese, or some other country's manufacturers will put the entire firm out of business.

In Chapter 3, growing the company via acquisitions and mergers was discussed. Again, it was obvious that this kind of action required much thought and very careful planning.

The railroads a decade or two in the past said that their business was railroading—no more, no less. Moreover, they consciously, in most cases, excluded the hauling of any passengers anywhere under the definition of railroading.

Part of the error was by the government. The car lobby was all for killing off the railroad passenger travel, and the government helped them do it. Our country spent uncounted billions in road and bridge building, and today the roads and bridges are falling apart because no one spent money on maintaining them.

The railroads did make money, once they fixed their tracks so the trains would not wreck. Now the tracks are good enough to carry passenger trains and there is modern and excellent passenger equipment available for purchase in several countries (other than the U.S.), but no one is buying.

However, it is also true that Amtrak is running more trains and some places are considering the installation of new high speed lines. Amtrak is handicapped since it does not own the tracks it uses. Here is a first class example of what happens when government does not properly plan.

The airlines once espoused SERVICE and it was a pleasure to fly. Today, they see themselves as providing transportation from runway to runway. In many respects they are following the railroad actions of about two decades ago. This author now avoids them when he can.

The problem in defining the business is not to make it so restrictive as to rule out taking advantage of logical future opportunities, yet the specified boundaries should be specific enough to hold up "the stop sign" when management wants to start in a direction that appears to be illogical or highly risky. If an opportunity is big enough, you can always decide to "run the stop sign." Yet, when this is deliberately done it means that even greater caution will be exercised than normally, and this is what is wanted from such definitions.

Large companies with many businesses may need to develop a number of subsidiary definitions, one for each business and one for the overall corporation.

Defining the firm's business will not substitute for planning—it merely facilitates and greatly aids in the planning effort. It also helps the planning by guiding the business(es) in the right directions in the future by its effect upon the development of the plans.

There are a number of good discussions on defining one's business(es), and this author prefers Peter Drucker's thoughts, including those in *Management* (cited in earlier chapters).

VI.   THE ORGANIZATION'S IMAGE

The image of a corporation or of any organization consists of the total set of beliefs, feelings, and attitudes as conjured up in the minds of a particular set of people regarding the company. The image held by the organization's bankers will likely be quite different than the image held by a firm's customers. Other images are those in the minds of employees, vendors, stockholders, investment bankers, etc.

Corporate image and/or brand recognition is of more importance than the average person thinks. For example, Lippincott and Margules, a market survey and product/package design firm that also was a leader in image and logo design, was asked to discover (quite some time ago, but the example is still valid) whether S. C. Johnson and Sons' "image" could serve as a vehicle to successfully market shoe polish.

They said to prospective respondents that they were setting out to discover the most popular and best thought of shoe polish. They mentioned several manufacturers, including the name of S. C. Johnson. While their survey placed Esquire in the number one position, in second place was S. C. Johnson & Sons' shoe polish. Believe it or not, at that time S. C. Johnson & Sons did not manufacture or sell a shoe polish! This made it a reasonable and safe bet that they would be successful in introducing a shoe polish if it was of acceptable quality.

Most successful corporations and many non-profit organizations try to present a single well-defined image to all groups doing business or having meaningful contacts with them. The overall image should be viewed as a long time/long duration concept. Therefore, this too must be taken into account in planning activities.

The image is also multi-faceted and consists of various images to the

organizations various constituents. Examples of possible image components are:

1. Great financial strength.
2. Progressive.
3. Innovative.
4. Fair dealer with all.
5. High quality service.
6. High, low or medium
   prices.
7. Steadily profitable.
8. Effective marketer.
9. Conglomerate, automaker,
   etc.
10. Growth company.
11. Friendly
12. Social minded.
13. Aggressive.
14. High quality products.
15. Fair pricing policy.
16. Excellent customer service.
17. Tight credit policies.
18. Liberal dividends.
19. Corn product company.
20. Multinational giant.

Advertising, policies, and the actions of all employees must be consistent (reasonably so) in order to either build a desired corporate image or
to maintain an image. This requires continued communication of image
objectives to employees, and follow-up evaluations.

Once the various components of the corporate image and their descriptions have been prepared, the implementation must be integrated into the
long and short range plans.

The establishment of a corporate image is not achieved by a few quick
actions. It requires a *consistent long term action* that very likely will cost
a significant amount of money, but the return on investment is excellent.

A favorable image affects sales and earnings. Batten, Barton, Durstine
& Osborne, Inc., made a 2 year study of two companies in each of four
industries. Each pair consisted of a company with a high price/earnings
ratio for stock and one with a low price/earnings ratio. In-home interviews
with men and women earning over $10,000/year (1969–1970) showed that,
without exception, the higher price/earnings companies rated higher on:

1. Always improving products or introducing new ones.
2. Very profitable.
3. Public would believe management in a labor dispute.
4. Public would prefer to buy the company's products over competitors'
   products.
5. Public would be willing to pay a higher price for the product.
6. Company is well known to the public.
7. Company cares about the public interest.[2]

In order to project and reinforce a clear image, company executives must be induced to act consistently with respect to the image. Further, support for the image is achieved through:

Advertising.	Institutional literature.
Packaging.	Company logotype.
Signage.	Participation in community affairs.
Stationery and forms.	

VII. SOME REINFORCEMENT MATERIAL

At various places in this text, the reader will find reference to the Strategic Planning Institute (SPI) of Cambridge, Massachusetts and its PIMS (Profit Impact of Market Strategy) program. Originally the program originated as an internal research project of General Electric.

From 1972 to 1974 the PIMS program was established as a developmental project at the Harvard Business School. The researchers revised the computer program and the project began to operate on a multi-company basis. Much of the current computer software package from the viewpoint of system and accessibility was developed at that time.

In February 1975, to facilitate the evolution of the program to an operating system, PIMS program was organized as an autonomous institute [The Strategic Planning Institute (SPI), Cambridge, Mass.], and focused explicitly on the analysis of strategic business plans. It is a non-profit corporation, governed by its member companies, with a charter permitting not only academic research, but also application activities of various kinds.[3]

Any corporation can be a member. This author once sat on the board (among others) of the Bunker Ramo Corp. (NYSE listed), which became a member at his suggestion. The board later sold the firm to Allied Signal. Member companies, in this author's opinion, derive many significant benefits.

Many of the research findings are distributed to corporate members in the form of small booklets called PIMSLETTERS. In 1987 the findings of many of the PIMSLETTERS to that date were gathered and synthesized in the book *The PIMS Principles* by Buzzell and Gale.[4] Since these findings can be important to planners, some of them will be referenced at various points in this text with the permission of the Strategic Planning Institute.

In planning one needs to take into account the reasons for the above relationship mentioned in PIMSLETTER number 24[5]—the reasons should be obviously true with a little thinking about the matter. The main reasons are listed below:

1. High-share businesses benefit from the economies of "scale."
2. High-share businesses benefit from "the learning curve"—costs go down in a given firm by approximately a fixed percentage every time production experience is doubled. The last portion of the sentence is talking about group/organizational learning, with also depends upon individual human learning. There is much data on this subject, both from SPI and in many text and referencebooks.[6,7,8]
3. High-share businesses have bargaining power.

The above discussion shows both the importance of all these concepts and findings, but it also shows the extreme complexity of dealing with the subject matter in planning. Planning *is* hard work and requires "the best" from the planning team.

After thinking about the above, it should be obvious that the corporate objective should be to increase awareness of the company and its product, since this translates into increased market share, which translates into greater profitability.

Except for SPI and its data bank, plus a *few* research reports on planning such as the Malik research referenced in Chapter 5, there has been a lack of data describing the performance impacts of proper planning (especially from SPI) and the strategies that businesses have followed which can be used to achieve long term benefits.

Bradley T. Gale and Donald J. Swire (both members of the SPI organization) especially expressed most of the above thoughts, plus others, in "Business Strategies That Create Wealth" in *Engineering Management Review* in March 1989.[9,10]

It also is a fact that through the use of the SPI data bank and its Profit Impact of Marketing Strategies (PIMS) program that winning strategies have been identified. While these can be very important to a firm's operational success, they do not substitute for the strategic planning goals primarily concerned with the exterior environment. PIMS findings, however, do make it possible to "fine tune" operational factors—in this author's opinion it represents the major source of such information. Most of the material which follows is taken from *The PIMS Program.*[3]

The SPI program will supply feedback to member/participating companies by the following:

1. Reports on the general principles of business strategy as discovered by analyses of the data base are issued when any such research and/or analysis project has been completed.
2. The member company will receive specific reports on each business/SBU from which a data contribution has been made by the member firm.

3. The member company will have access to computer models in which the general strategic principles are incorporated. These are designed to be useful for planning strategy and for simulation. Additionally, members have available instruction and counsel relative to the interpretation and use of these resources.

The specific reports mentioned in 2 concern an individual SBU and make use of all research findings to the date of such a report. The results include evaluate statements about the concerned business and specific strategy advice for the business. They are computer generated and use the above-mentioned empirical models.

The major reports supplied are:

1. The par report. It specifies the ROI (return on investment) that is normal (par) for the business (SBU).
2. The strategy analysis report. It presents the pre-testing of possibly valid strategic moves as well as specific action recommendation in areas such as quality, ratio of marketing expense to sales, etc.
3. The optimum strategy report. This report nominates a combination of several strategic moves.
4. Report on "look alikes" (businesses) in the data bank.

Additionally, there are many other available services and reports. In this author's opinion any larger firm interested in successful strategic planning as described in this text should seriously consider becoming a member of the Strategic Planning Institute.

While the PIMS program and membership in SPI can help develop a winning strategy, such membership will not automatically produce a winning strategy. Moreover, it tends to focus on "fine tuning" policies, strategies, and tactics—which would be the obvious result from the use of the data bases.

The final strategy *must* be a product of the people who "manage the company." Therefore, their intelligence, knowledge, expertise, and dedication and application really are the final determinants of a successful strategy and its execution.

Small firms *can* develop a successful strategy, but the same determinants enunciated above will ultimately set the limits to a successful effort at planning and its execution.

REFERENCES

1. "Going Back To Basics Seems To Be A Smart Move," *Business Week*, Nov. 20, 1989

2. Harold H. Marquis, *The Changing Corporate Image*, American Management Association, New York, NY, 1970 (page 21).
3. *The PIMS Program*, The Strategic Planning Institute, 1030 Massachusetts Avenue, Cambridge, MA 02139, 1980.
4. Robert D. Buzzell and Bradley T. Gale, *The PIMS Principles: Linking Strategy to Performance*, The Free Press, New York, 1987.
5. *The PIMSLETTER on Business Strategy*, No. 24, Brand Awareness and Profitability, The Strategic Planning Institute, Cambridge, MA, 1980.
6. Delmar W. Karger and Walton M. Hancock, Advanced Work Measurement, "Chpt. 3, The Learning Curve Methodologies," Industrial Press, New York, NY, 1982.
7. *Experience Curves as a Planning Tool*, The Boston Consulting Group, One Boston Place, Boston, MA, 1970
8. *Perspectives on Experience*, The Boston Consulting Group, Boston, MA, 1968, 1970, 1972.
9. Bradley T. Gale and Donald T. Swire, "Business Strategies that Create Wealth" (Reprinted from *Planning Review*), *Engineering Management Review*, Institute of Electrical and Electronic Engineers, Inc., March 1989 (Spring Edition).
10. Bradley T. Gale and Donald T. Swire, "Business Strategies that Create Wealth", *Planning Review*, March/April 1988.

8

External Environmental Analysis

To dream the impossible may give a person a great feeling, but in business one should dream the possible. Environmental analysis requires a form of dreaming, really thinking and defining for self and associated planners the present and likely future factors that could affect their organization's plans—factors that both help and hinder the organization.

Remember that in this chapter the discussion centers upon environments external to the organization. Chapters 1–3 and, to a degree, Chapter 4 clearly illustrated that such factors are usually identified by reading (possibly scanning if a speed reader) publications and relating them to personal observations and experiences. Then the planner must decide which of the items/factors that were identified are important, and how they are important.

None of the referenced material in the chapters or the personal observations were pure forecasts. In fact, almost none of the factors were originally identified as trends. They were mostly the description of and the identification of events and effects that had already taken place or were in the process of happening. In essence, however, they could be identified as trends—some stronger than others.

Next, go back to the first part of Chapter 1 and reread the observations of Peter Drucker. What he was presenting as thoughts about the future were essentially items similar to the items that *followed* in Chapter 1. However, the trends in his source material upon which he based his deductions were not as obvious as those in Chapter 1. His material required wide ranging critical thinking about what was going on in the world and what was likely to occur. However, in the final analysis both varieties involved the identification of *faint*, yet identifiable trends! This is the essence of how one identifies exterior environmental factors.

The reader will not find many "pure" *forecasts* that identify possible factors that will have much application to the practical planning of management actions required in an organization's Strategic Planning. However, from time to time, one can find comments related to technology that have application to technical plans. The same is true for business in general. However, this does not mean a recommendation to ignore any kind of forecasts. Examine them carefully. Some may be of great value.

All of the above is saying that in this aspect of the planning activity, the planner will be involved in the analysis of facts, trends, predictions by others, newspaper and magazine stories and articles, speaches by various kinds of experts, conversations with experts at professional meetings, and any other possibly useful bits of information.

For example, the *Fortune* September 25, 1989, issue contained the cover story "Where Japan Will Strike Next."[1] *Fortune* said that Japan was embarking on another export "push," is loaded with cash (true), and is readying a wide variety of new products—many are high-tech. This is an eight page article so the reader should look at it directly since it involves a very broad effort concerning a wide variety of products that the Japanese will next introduce and try to capture a major market share.

The above article said that a *Newsweek* poll[2] showed 54 percent of the respondents believed Japan was a greater threat than the U.S.S.R. (because of economic strength). Yet another poll[2] indicated that 70 percent of American senior executives believed the Japanese were not the greatest threat, but rather that domestic competition was the largest threat. This expression of the thinking of the average American business executive clearly shows why the Japanese beat U.S. business firms. Do not be misled by polls, Japan is a threat. If you doubt it, reread Chapter 1.

A story similar to the one previously mentioned that appeared in *Fortune* is "How Do You Shut The Darn Thing Off?," *Forbes*, November 13, 1989.[3] Japan's rate of corporate investment in plant and equipment is about 14 percent higher than ours. Capacity to produce is growing faster than their domestic consumption, so they will have to increase exports. A related article that can help uninformed readers understand how Japan functions is "Understanding How Japan Works" by Carla Rapoport, which appeared in *Fortune*.[4]

The conclusion one must reach is that we will face further competition from them. They are investing about 2.4 times what the U.S. is when measured as a percent of GNP. Almost all their industries are spending on new plants and equipment. They obviously are planning to win, especially in the long term—and the reader may recall what this meant for involved U.S. firms.

Moreover, people can not ignore the fact that the Japanese government helps their industry. They have cheap financing and their real cost of money is about 40 percent less than ours. This, however, does not change the fact that they are outspending our companies on internal improvement.

One final comment about the *Forbes* article: Japan's real boom in investment is aimed at reducing production costs and developing new products and new technologies. All of these will give us serious trouble, but the last two could be the eventual major problem. The U.S. lags far behind in solving its product design and manufacturing problems, as mentioned in Chapters 3 and 4.

Before strategic goals (or operational goals) can be set, an evaluation of both the present and future internal and external environments of an organization must be made (and of its subunits for organizational/tactical planning). This is *required* in order to be able to define strengths and weaknesses—a subject previously mentioned several times.

This chapter is associated with the problem of defining the organization's external environments. The next chapter will be concerned with defining internal environments and the strengths and weaknesses in the organization.

An organization's strategic goals are its survival plan and its conclusions on how it expects to grow and be successful. This relates to a common similarity between an army and a company with regard to planning.

Who would want to be a part of an army going into battle whose general and staff had not beforehand developed a plan of action that they believed would lead to success? Such a plan must take into account the strengths and weaknesses of each side. An army's chances of winning would be low without a plan, unless they had an overwhelming superiority in men and armament—and this is seldom the case.

Do NOT think from the above statement that the Pentagon properly plans. It may plan properly when in a battle situation, but it does not do so in civilian life settings. The strategic advisors develop plans and, believe it or not, the budget arm completes plans showing an entirely different spending pattern. The top officers in each service plan for their service without reconciling the plans with each other or with the strategic advisors. Likely there are still other such plans. None are reconciled within the Pentagon and they certainly are not reconciled with Congress. Part of this "mess" is described in "Teach the Pentagon to Think Before It Spends" by Franklin Spinney, who is a permanent Pentagon official.

A condensation of his essay appeared in the *Wall Street Journal*[5] and the complete version will appear in the *Naval Institute Proceedings*.[6]

It is essentially the same kind of a situation when a company enters into a competitive battle with competing firms as for an an army going into battle with another army. The chances of winning are very slim unless one has a superior strategy that takes into account the strengths and weaknesses of all competing units.

Do not misunderstand what strategy represents. It is not some clever ruse that expects to win by using "smoke and mirrors"—which politicians are often said to use to fool the public. It represents the strategic (intelligent) use of actual strengths to overcome the enemy, while avoiding the fatal exposure of weaknesses. Some of the strengths may include so-called soft factors like company image, commonly *perceived* attributes, etc. However, such soft factors will never bring victory on their own.

This development of a strategy can not be done in a realistic manner without information and intelligence about all aspects of the world and the firm that could affect the success of the strategic plan. Remember that companies often do not perceive their weaknesses, and if they do, they usually underestimate the magnitude of their weaknesses and overestimate the magnitude of perceived strengths.

Some readers may think or say "under their breath" that such analogies explaining why planning is necessary are easy to generate. Take the next 10 to 30 minutes to see whether you, the reader, can generate a significant number of *plausible* analogies why planning is not necessary or is pure foolishness—other than those based upon earlier statements of why executives do not plan. A typical faulty attempt at presenting the advantages of the short term view, in this author's opinion, is "Managing For Results, Don't Waste Time Planning—Act" (no matter what action?), *New York Times*, Business Section, Sunday, Oct. 29, 1989.[7] It never once alludes to the vast amount of published logic stating why America is failing because of its short term view.

Of great importance to strategy are the strengths and weaknesses of the organization. Never forget that one can only create a winning strategy by taking full advantage of strengths—and this must be done at once (short term and long term). The weaknesses must be assessed and corrected, but do so on the basis of the real importance of each weakness—correct the most important before lesser weaknesses.

Correcting a weakness takes 1 to 2 years; seldom can it be accomplished in much less than 1 year. Correcting weaknesses is important, but not as important as taking advantage of strengths.

In developing strategic and operational plans, it is necessary to to *identify* environmental factors, external and internal, that can affect the firm's (organization's) future. Do not try to discover the future of a factor by pure extrapolation. Usually, but not always, this procedure will lead to an incorrect conclusion.

The life/development/diminishment of a factor is dynamic and the things affecting it are changing at varying rates—some very fast and some very slow. This is the reason that forecasting by the use of intellectual trend analysis is probably the one most important way to proceed.

However, one usually learns some additional things by comparing a forecast from intellectually examining evidence of a trend to an attempt to actually project a trend into the future—when such a projection can be made in a practical manner. If an actual projection of a factor is attempted, the projection should start about 5 years previous to the time the projection is attempted—otherwise the result is likely flawed.

Finally, once the environmental forecast is produced, the real work begins. The planners have to segregate the factors that can help in building a winning strategy and those that must be avoided so as to not weaken the strategy. It is also likely that some trends will be perceived as having little importance to the organization's future performance.

The limits and range of strategy are often called the opportunity and capability of the company. The opportunity is in a large measure what the external environment provides. Capability is a function of the company's resources including the expertise, performance, and creativity of the management. The successful strategy is one which matches capabilities to opportunities in the most profitable manner. It involves the establishment of practical time tables and involves the consideration of an adequate number of alternatives—even future reversals should be considered in the planning, since this is a likely event.

I. FORCES OF THE ENVIRONMENT

The more general components/forces/factors (whatever you wish to call them) which often are significant to the health and/or success of an organization (almost any kind of organization) are:

1. Economic.
2. Technological and scientific (general and specific products).
3. Social.
4. Demographic.
5. Political.
6. Business law.
7. Patent and trademark law.
8. Taxes.

9.   Import/export law.
10.   Competition.

The factors must be examined not only from the view of the home country, but also in terms of countries that are host to competitors of the organization. Moreover, the only safe way is to also examine the remainder of the world. Do not think of the above as a comprehensive and complete list. However, it is a good starting point.

Before looking at specific source possibilities, it would be well for the reader to remember that many very important factors to the life of organizations were identified without ever consulting an article or other writing identified as predicting the future of anything.

Basically, most of the material was extracted from reading "the press," business and general news publications, and a few professional journals. One has to read broadly and voluminously. There will be many things read that will be perceived as possibly being important. But usually the material in one publication does not contain enough information to assure the reader that the item is really a good or bad trend.

It is therefore important and necessary to keep a clipping file so that it can be matched with confirming information in another publication. More will be said on this matter just a little later. Be observant enough to detect the emergence of new factors and to also detect the death of older factors.

Many organizations correctly believe that there is a need to develop and maintain information on their environment, the action recommended above. It can be of vital importance to the success of the planning effort and it is not a task that can be accomplished easily and quickly.

The fact is that much of the information needed is never quite exposed to the public as data on the future, neither is it identified as predicting an aspect of the future. It is usually presented as an event or events that more or less "just took place." This is exactly why it is important to encourage every member of the corporate planning team to bring important material to the attention of the other members and check it against information identified in the past.

How is it possible to do this? If there is no company standard procedure on this matter, the C.E.O. and the planning director should jointly begin creating one and quickly instruct the other planners as to what they are to do and how the information is to be sent to the planning director. Be sure to include in the instructions to send a "clipping" or photocopy of the article or news story to the planning director.

This also means that since functions, divisions, and departments also will produce plans, they also should have have key people "on the look-out" for information. These planning divisions and/or departments should keep one copy or set of any identified possibly important information in their file and they also should send a copy to the planning director. Have key people in each organizational unit who will be involved in planning activities instructed to continuously look for new information. Make sure they understand that they are expected to report on this activity from time to time to the corporate planning director. Naturally, the latter should also check with and/or remind such individuals from time to time so as to make sure the matter is not forgotten.

All this partially bears upon an activity that some firms prefer to ignore or else try to hide because it could get them into trouble—the matter of industrial spying. Unfortunately, not engaging in this practice can also get the organization into deep trouble.

Any firm that must overcome competitors (part of what business success is all about) must know what competitors are doing that might have an effect upon the firm. Not only is it advisable to know what known competitors are doing, but it is just as important to know what potential competitors are doing that might affect the firm. Be assured that industrial spying (often referred to as "surveillance," actually a more correct term—but it does not grab attention) is not illegal so long as no illegal acts are used to acquire the information. It is fairly prevalent and it "makes sense" to engage in this activity.

One Japanese firm is so strongly convinced about the importance of this activity that it has any gathered intelligence transmitted by the fastest means possible. It especially watches for changes in pricing policy, credit terms, product introductions, factory force level changes, financing actions, executive changes, etc.

If this activity is started, then it should likely be a multifaceted activity. One part of the activity must be aimed at gathering information on a very broad variety of subjects. Often, some of the individual bits of information will not be perceived to have much, if any, relevance to the activities of the organization until they are combined with other bits of information in the file.

Basically, this portion of the search, scan, and study operation is a broad effort to gather both competitive information and information on subjects such as the nine general factors listed directly under the sub-title "Forces of the Environment." This is the kind of search activity that was discussed earlier in this chapter and in Chapter 5 under "Defining Future Horizons, External and Internal."

The second part of the activity deals with comparing products of competitors with the company's products through a *broad* engineering study (usually a continuing project in a large product oriented firm where such an activity exists).

By broad is meant not only to have product engineering perform the study, but also to include other engineering functions such as industrial engineering and quality engineering, as well as the non-engineering functions of purchasing, financial, and marketing. The studies should look not only at pure product engineering, but also at manufacturability, design for high quality, design for repairability, customer features, esthetic design, price, credit to customers, and the marketability of the product.

Pricing was mentioned: this requires a cost study. In order to estimate the manufacturing cost of a competitor's product, the firm will first have to perform a "make versus buy" analysis since one does not know what the competitor does and the cost should be on the basis of how the firm doing the analysis would do it, unless the team members are reasonably sure of what the other firm would do based upon knowledge of its degree of mechanization, its capabilities, etc.

The cost estimating function (often located in industrial engineering) must estimate "make" labor and add all the other cost estimates and have the purchasing function secure vendor prices for all purchased parts. Then with the help of the accounting department the two functions (cost estimating and accounting) must arrive at a likely factory cost of the product. Required equipment for this needs to be identified, but there is no standard way to "handle" it; the decision is usually a practical one that permits arriving at a reasonably valid comparable cost. From this, marketing and the accounting department can arrive at a sales price. The latter price is compared with the market price of the product.

This process is commonly known as "benchmark spying"—*and it is all legal* if accomplished as described. There should be no collaboration between the two involved companies. Moreover, if two companies band together to make such a study, the effort will likely be declared illegal if discovered and a lawsuit will be instituted.

There is nothing wrong with buying a product on the open market and then examining how it is made. Just do not bribe competitive employees to spy for you or perform any other illegal act. Incidently, do not blindly copy a product, this *is* legal.

Many organizations believe the need to develop and maintain information on their environment is of vital importance to their planning success. This not a task that can be accomplished easily or quickly. Maintaining detailed files on appropriate data regarding environmental factors is the way large companies develop such data.

It can be a manually maintained filing system, with a separate folder (or set of folders) for each subject, factor, or item. A likely more practical route to handle classification, listing, and key information is to utilize a computer.

The subjects can be computer listed and filed by alphabet with the data in each folder indicated by standardized data codes whose definitions are also in the computer. The computer file probably should also contain summaries of each important piece of data and/or environmental factor. This sounds complicated, but is relatively simple once the codes required are developed. All this can easily be handled on an ordinary modern personal computer (PC)—but it should have a hard disk, at least a megabyte of random access memory (RAM) (with a possibility of expanding it by 1 or 2 more megabytes), and a Norton S.I. rating above 15. This author's advice is to utilize an IBM or IBM compatible, unless your main computer is of another make, in this case the reader must decide what action would be appropriate.

Do ignore data items that have no relevance to the business or purpose of the organization. Many data subjects may require collection of data by country involved and then require its summary by subdivisions—such as by product line, kind of service provided, etc.

Copies of articles will be involved. Incidently, in this modern day and age, the fax machine will see a lot of use instead of photocopying everything. These copies obviously need to be placed in file folders. Moreover, these will likely be augmented by correspondence.

This means you likely will not push everything into a computer unless your operation is big enough to put a very intelligent and broadly educated and experienced person on the job of summarizing and commenting in a manner similar to what was done in the early chapters.

Some topics/categories are competitive, demographic, economic, governments, international, technological, public attitudes, social and cultural, product lines, products and/or services, worker skills, raw materials, etc. It is an almost unending list. However, through practical judgement one can keep the data within reasonable bounds.

Occasionally a major publication produces a helpful study for accomplishing the above. For example, the Peter Drucker forecast in Chapter 1 indicated that the business world was moving toward regional "trading blocks," and one of these is obviously the Pacific Rim countries. An example is "A Strategic Guide To The Rim" (a part of a major study of the Pacific Rim countries), in *Fortune*, November 13, 1989.[8]

Another source of such information is to use a consultant who works with firms in your industry classification(s). The author knows of consultants who hire consultants to gain access to special information, in fact this author has done exactly that when helping a firm to plan. The author did not possess the required expertise.

One could even "dream" that the Department of Commerce or some other government entity would help U.S. industry by attempting the search, storage, and analysis functions and thereby try to help U.S. industrial firms by detecting and exposing general factors like many of those exposed in chapters one and two. This author also wonders whether MITI of the Japanese government does any of this kind of activity for favored industries? His guess is that they do exactly that for companies and for their own decision making.

Data Sources

Financial Services aimed at investors are an excellent source for many firms. If a competitor is listed and described, for example, in Value Line, you can immediately review 10 years of key financial data such as:

Sales/Share Cash Flow/Share Earnings/Share;
Dividends/Share Dividend Yld./Share %Div. Yld.;
Cap. Spending/Sh. Book Val./Share Cur'nt P.E. & Av.P.E.;
Sales/Year Operating Margin Net Profit Margin;
Depreciation Net Profit Tax Ratio;
Working Capital Long Term Debt Net Worth;
%Ern'd on Capital %Ern'd on Net Worth %Retained to Comm Eq.;
%Dividends/Net Profit

Further, Value Line provides data, ratings, and/or forecasts on capital structure, current financial data; annual percentage rates of change for sales, cash flow, earnings, dividends, and book value for the past 10 years, the past five years, and an estimate for the next five years.

Further, discussions of important current operating factors as well as actual past history and forecasts for about a year or more ahead are provided. Most such discussions are concerned with factors that will affect earnings, dividends, and sales.

The company data sheets are presented in groups by industry classification. Beginning each of these sections is an analysis of the industry.

Standard and Poor produces similar, but not as detailed, data (in this author's opinion). Both Value Line and Standard and Poor data sheets can be found in various brokerage offices, university libraries, and some public libraries. In fact, stock brokers can often provide company and industry studies.

Economic forces are indicated by government produced data such as gross national product, gross domestic product, personal income, disposable personal income, employment statistics, capital investment planning, housing starts, business failures, productivity, price indexes or indices, output of electrical power, railroad car loadings, and many other such indexes.

The company should identify the indexes and sources of such data since it will help forecast the business trends associated with their business. One does not have to start from "scratch." Industry associations may already have the forecasts needed.

A few related government publications are:

Annual Survey of Manufacturers
Business Cycle Developments
Census of Business
Economic Indicators
Economic Report of the President
Monthly Labor Review
Survey of Current Business
Statistical Abstract of the U.S.

Top management should at least scan (preferably speed read) the following:

Business Week	*Industry Publs.*	*The Economist*
The Financial Weekly	*Forbes*	*Fortune*
The New York Times (Sunday)	*Science*	*Time*
The Wall St. Journal	One or two major general newspaper(s)	

An information source not often mentioned, but which executives should monitor by personally listening and viewing is, the following TV programs:

The Nightly Business Report (Mon.–Fri., Public TV)
Wall Street Week (Fri., Public TV)
Washington Week in Review (Fri., Public TV)
This Week With David Brinkley (Sun. noon)

There are many CNN business oriented programs. Also, there are other programs similar to "This Week With David Brinkley" that are also worth watching. An example is "Meet The Press." If you are going to miss an important program because of your personal schedule of activities, tape it on your VCR.

II. TECHNOLOGICAL ENVIRONMENT

The firm's technical function should perform this job and a very capable member of the team should brief management from time to time. Moreover, if something unusual or otherwise important is noted, that person should immediatly send a note on the matter to the key individuals who should be notified.

It hardly seems worthwhile listing publications, since these are well known by engineers and scientists who keep themselves well informed. However, a somewhat general publication on the frontiers of science and which is very readable by almost anyone with a technical background is *Science*—even those without that background will be able to fathom and enjoy much of this publication. Naturally, the various professional journals applying to the areas of science and engineering in which the organization is engaged should be perused/scanned.

Books providing technological assessments and forecasts do get published from time to time. The first way to assess whether such a publication is worth reading is to examine the qualifications of those who produced the assessment.

It also is probably worthwhile to read a book of this sort that is at least a decade old based upon copyright date and note that many forecasts are not "on the mark." This does not mean ignore forecasts, merely that the reader should take such forecasts with a "grain of salt" and adjust decision making to dealing with considerable uncertainty.

There are some journals covering the future aspects of technology. Examples are:

Futures
The Futurist
Social, Demographic and Ecological Changes
Technological Forecasting and Social Change

There are journals that deal with the role of business in a changing society. While the information from a general business view is often valuable, its value as a forecast applying to the reader's planning efforts is not likely to be present in many articles. However, what is different about that? It is exactly the way the situation is with every publication mentioned. Some examples of these journals are:

Business and Society
Business and Society Review
California Management Review
Harvard Business Review

Political and Legal Environment
Sloan Management Review

Special legal news services are helpful in keeping up with court decisions and legislation affecting business. *The Journal of Marketing* has an excellent section, "Legal Developments in Marketing," that is subdivided by categories.

If you seek help in properly classifying "your industry," the place to initially go is the SIC Classifications of the Department of Commerce.

III. THE INDUSTRY STUDY

If a firm is operating within a recognized industry classification that contains firms of a significant size, then there is a fair likelihood that studies containing some prognostications of that industry can be found among investment advisors and/or brokerage houses, industry associations, major business/management journals, etc. One sure place to look and obtain some likely useful information (but seldom breakthrough or highly controversial information) is the most recent (published yearly) *U.S. Industrial Outlook*, International Trade Administration, Department of Commerce. The 1987 book contained data on 350 industries and was about 1300–1500 pages thick.

Advisory service firms quite often produce forecasts that are available to subscribers (which often include libraries). An example is *America In The Global '90s; The Shape of the Future—How You Can Profit From It*, by Austin H. Kiplinger and Knight A. Kiplinger with the staff of *The Kiplinger Washington Letter*, published by The Kiplinger Washington Editors, Inc., Washington, D.C.

Also remember the previously suggested Value Line investor advisory service as a good possibility. Further, there are commercial research firms that provide such information, but it will be somewhat costly in most cases.

There are significant advantages in developing your own industry study if a major firm is involved. It is too much of an effort, in this author's opinion, for a small firm to attempt it. For those who do want to attempt an endustry study, Table 1 provides an an outline of what is needed to develop the basic information. However, in acquiring that amount of detailed information, it should be obvious that some big advantages as well as big disadvantages will likely be identified. This kind of information needs to also be shown with the environmental forcast study, since both are forecasting the future.

The reader or planners will have to decide whether to put the findings

Table 1   Industry Study Outline[9]

1. History of the industry

   a. Origins of need for products
   b. Technological developments and key innovations
   c. Growth of companies within the industry
   d. Development of marketing channels
   e. Geographical location of companies in the past
   f. Development of legislation impacting on the industry
   g. Pricing practices and trends in the past

2. Products

   a. Functions of products
   b. Limitations of products
   c. Ecological impact of the production and use of the products
   d. Growth in complexity
   e. Quality (if possible an assessment by competitor)
   f. Serviceability and service (by competitor would be desirable)
   g. Rate of innovation
   h. Competitive products or systems which may be obsolete the industry

3. Technology

   a. R & D as a percent of sales for industry [and of principal competitors if at all possible (see Value Line Data)]
   b. Trends in technology which impact the industry
   c. Technological opportunities
   d. Technological leaders in the industry
   e. Equipment developments affecting manufacturing costs and, if possible, indicate how costs can be reduced by proper design, automation, labor standards, etc.
   f. Patent positions of companies in the industry
   g. Government rulings and legislation affecting the direction of development within the industry
   h. Identify growing scarcity of any required natural resources

4. Sales and profitability

   a. Past and forecast (as well as projected) sales trends
   b. Current market and market potential
   c. Approximate share of market by the firm and principal competitors
   d. Past and future cost trends and their implications
   e. Past and future profit trends of industry and firm
   f. Profit in relation to life cycles of involved products
   g. Average value-added by companies in the industry

Table 1   Continued

5. Investment

    a. Cost and entry into the industry
    b. New firms and failed firms (by year) and as a percent of total
    c. Capital renewal requirements for capital assets
    d. Working capital requirements for various levels of operation
    e. Future trends for the above items

6. Employment

    a. Total industry employment and trends
    b. Type of workers required (current and future), wage levels, and
        availability
    c. Productivity, if possible break down to labor classifications
    d. Labor cost per dollar of sales, by competitor if possible
    e. Degree of industry automation, and state of company's automation
        effort
    f. Unions and union-management relations in general

7. Marketing

    a. Market structure, include identification of companies in the industry
    b. Methods of selling and distributing the product, trends in the industry,
        and relative cost and effectiveness of all alternatives
    c. Advertising and promotion, provide similar details to above
    d. Pricing, warranties, and service, details on all players
    e. Financing
    f. Innovations in marketing, past and anticipated
    g. Trends and changes in consumer tastes and desires
    h. Industry associations

8. Political-legal-social influences

    a. Legislation and trends
    b. Political posture toward the industry
    c. Strength of industry lobbying
    d. Ecology movements and their expected effects
    e. Cultural changes and changing mores and taboos
    f. Shifting quantity and/or location of people in various age and skill
        groups over time and how this will affect firm

referenced in the above paragraph at the front or the rear of the study.
The "politics" of the players (top planners) enter into this decision, as
well as other practical considerations involving other "forces" that may
become involved.

In making your own study, it is important to define the players (competitors). For example, competitors are not just the firms which make similar products, but they are also firms whose products are substitutable. A simple example is a can manufacturer. Often they find themselves facing a big competitor who manufactures glass containers or plastic containers. Box manufacturers sometimes find themselves competing with a plastics manufacturer.

The assessment of an organization's external environment is a major task, but it is far from being impossible of achievement. However, it should also be clear from all that has been said in this text that such a study can be very important to the life of the company—so do the best possible job.

REFERENCES

1. Gene Bylinsky, "Where Japan Will Strike Next," *Fortune*, September 25, 1989.
2. Casper W. Weinberger, Publisher, "Commentary on Events at Home and Abroad," *Forbes*, November 13, 1989
3. Andrew Tanzer, "How Do You Shut The Darn Thing Off," *Forbes*, November 13, 1989.
4. Carla Rapaport, "Understanding How Japan Works," *Fortune*, November 13, 1989.
5. Franklin Spinney, "Teach the Pentagon to Think Before It Spends" (a condensation), *The Wall Street Journal*, Monday, October 30, 1989
6. Franklin Spinney, "Teach the Pentagon to Think Before It Spends," *Naval Institute Proceedings*.
7. Robert H. Schaffer, "Managing For Results; Don't Waste Time Planning— Act," *The New York Times*, Sunday, October 29, 1989.
8. "A Strategic Guide To The Rim," *Fortune*, November 13, 1989.
9. Delmar W. Karger and Robert G. Murdick, *Long Range Planning and Corporate Strategy*, Karger & Murdick, Troy, NY, 1977.

9

Internal Evaluations

I. INTRODUCTION

It is obviously about time to develop a general sense of corporate direction, the tasks that must be accomplished in the near term and the long term. However, we have not yet delved deeply into the organization's operations, resources, facilities, and the capabilities of its personnel and organizational units. This means that the planning effort must now be directed inwardly, so that the corporate (organization) strengths and weaknesses can be identified. Strategy cannot be established on a rational basis until this task is accomplished.

Always remember to focus on the goal in all the tasks to be mentioned, which is to sharply and definitively identify every major strength and weaknesses. Moreover, identify the minor strengths and weaknesses, because these may represent opportunities to greatly improve the organization with a relatively low level of effort.

The evaluation of internal resources should not be started without first developing a check list of organizational units, including sub-units, that should be examined. A start at this task is to accumulate a complete set of the firm's organization charts—which need to be supplemented by lists of important individual professionals where appropriate.

This inventory process becomes extremely complicated when a large organization with various divisions and multiple plants starts the planning process for the first time. The second time through the process will be significantly easier.

For general guidance, each division should eventually have a divisional set of strengths and weaknesses resulting from the internal examination. Such evaluations must include product line(s) and individual product evaluations, organizational unit evaluations, personnel policies evaluations, evaluations of services, facilities, resources, and any other sensible measurements—almost nothing is to be excluded. Moreover, the product evaluations must take into account (and specify) each product's position on *its* life cycle curve. Using these as a base it might be worthwhile to try to develop a composite life cycle curve for each product line.

If portions of the firm are organized by function, there naturally needs to be a similar examination of such functional units and their sub-functions in a manner that will result in a determination of strengths and weaknesses. Again these must not only be for the people aspects, but also for all the other kinds of measurements mentioned in the previous paragraph.

Except in very small firms, it would be foolish to expect the C.E.O. to identify the strengths and weaknesses. It is a formidable task and he will not have the time or the detailed knowledge necessary to do this. Neither can one expect his managers to talk to him openly about these things. If the C.E.O. in a small firm has allowed weaknesses to develop and/or has not taken advantage of strengths, he/she will not want to face these facts.

Neither can the larger firm expect each functional or departmental head to perform this task. What manager would tell "his corporate world" that his function/department has serious weaknesses? Of course he/she will identify strengths, if he perceives them, but such a manager will also likely exaggerate them.

Another handicap regarding this problem is that the planning director cannot ask a functional head to evaluate someone else's department. Neither can it be done by an insider without creating a great deal of animosity toward the insider: the firm cannot condone this and the insider would be foolish to accept such an assignment—and this includes an insider planning director, especially the first time a serious attempt is made to accomplish this task.

The first time through the process it is recommended that either a skillful outside planning director perform the strength and weakness evaluations (not the inventory and general evaluation of each function or department), or that it be done by a skillful outside management consultant. Either of these approaches will work satisfactorily.

In many respects, the first time through the process a competent consultant who has previously led such projects would be the best candidate both to lead the planning and to work with the firm's managers to identify the weaknesses. Often the weaknesses in one department are identified by another department when a consultant is doing the probing.

Some general guidelines on how to tackle this complex task will be given. However, most of these guidelines will concern what needs examination. The specifics of how to go about identifying each strength and weakness are almost impossible to cite since they must be created to match the organization to be studied.

Still, it can be said that when *that* aspect of the internal evaluation is performed (usually by the people in the function or department), the departments should be requested to identify strengths and specify the degree of such an attribute. This will make it easier and faster for the outsider evaluations to be completed. Remember, these outsider evaluations must be accomplished with great skill and tact, since the concerned organizational units must not be "turned off" or wounded in the process.

II. EVALUATION OF RESOURCES FOR STRENGTHS AND WEAKNESSES

The general classes of resources to be evaluated for *strengths and weaknesses*, as well as for other mentioned factors, that most organizations may use as a starting point for deciding what should be carefully examined are:

1. Board of directors—details discussed in next subtitle.
2. Management performance and competency—evaluate by function and/or organizational unit, for the company as a whole and for all of the existing organizational units.
3. Professional and craft skills—do by profession and craft, and indicate degree of availability of replacements or additions—it may also need sub-dividing by divisions and/or by other organizational units.
4. Financial position—examine current and potential financial performance; (LTD/equity, percent earnings growth per year, etc.) for the firm, including all organizational units SBUs.
5. Financial function—examine for compentency and experience of personnel, breadth and depth of experience (identify all important areas). For example, are foreign currency problems properly handled? Has self insurance been considered in very large firms? Has debt versus equity financing been properly analyzed?
6. Marketing—consider overall, by product line and products, and for SBUs if at all possible. The various facets to examine here are many, but fortunately much help is available in modern texts.

7. Technical and engineering—evaluate by technical and engineering fields and by overall company and organizational divisions (possibly even by SBUs). Have the design team concepts mentioned in Part I been recognized and utilized? If not, why not?

8. Manufacturing/production—people with a solid industrial engineering background should lead in this task. However, because of the increased attention being paid to manufacturing, such people do not necessarily have to have a formal industrial engineering education.

    Often the most capable manufacturing specialists have a technical degree in computer systems, science, or other engineering disciplines as well as having industrial engineering knowledge. Such people tend to be more prone to integrate the activity as described in Chapter 4. More than conventional manufacturing needs to be recognized as necessary in most all cases.

    Such integration is vital since it is increasingly evident that a manufacturing person with some knowledge of standard engineering, information systems, quality, and material handling techniques and methodologies can contribute a great deal in an enterprise. Finally, do not attempt to go from a WWII type facility to a fully integrated and automated facility in one step.

    The evaluations must consider the overall company and its subdivisions; at times it may be necessary to also do it by location. Such evaluations must include a consideration of the degree and kinds of automation per organizational unit if manufacturing is conducted in several places and/or for different products; material handling; warehousing; location of facilities; the facilites themselves; past, present, and expected future productivity; manufacturing costs for all major products vs those of competitors; etc.

9. Information systems—including computer hardware, software, and data communication; CIM is a major need.

10. Purchasing, for company and its subdivisions (a very important function since it can materially affect product cost, product quality, and even product service—it is a function that is sometimes ignored)— this evaluation must include an examination of sources of materials and vendor relationships as well as examining the use of the "just in time" delivery concept and control of vendor quality.

11. Quality of products and/or services—is a very important attribute. The evaluation must be by product and service lines and then by products and/or services—also for SBUs. Not only traditional statistical quality control, but more up-to-date approaches utilizing experimental design should be considered. Eventually one must also look

at plants and/or offices. Are computers being properly used in the function? This likely will require special software.

12. Material control and distribution by product oriented organizational units—is it technologically up-to-date and are "just in time" material concepts utilized? This requires joint and cooperative actions by purchasing, engineering, industrial engineering, and quality control. In turn, it also usually means that special methods of parts distribution are needed.

13. Plant engineering, for company and sub-units—an excellent function of this kind can again save large and medium sized firms considerable money. Is the function staffed so employees can recognize and take advantage of new technology? Are environmental concerns properly recognized and handled?

14. Personnel and industrial relations—for the company and sub-units. Further, as was identified in Part I, the training portion of this function may have zoomed into importance. Is it staffed and capable of handling the obviously increased responsibilities in this area? Is the overall function doing useful things to bring management and the company's workers closer together?

15. Legal skills and legal positions.

16. Company policies.

17. Corporate image.

18. Competitive advantages and disadvantages, from both the company and customer viewpoints, for all product lines and the important products (current and future)—this concept will be further treated in Chapter 10.

Discussions of the kinds of actions and work involved will be provided for many of the above categories. However, one could almost write a book on many of the subjects, and therefore some of the details involving the more conventional factors will not be discussed. These tasks will be left for the reader/planner to decide on how to accomplish.

III. BOARD OF DIRECTORS

The board of directors represents an important resource of the company if it is properly structured as to composition and if it is properly used. One important use of such a body is that of a sounding board for the thinking and ideas of the inside members. This in turn requires the chairman and/or president to bring all major questions before the board for an open discussion. Therefore it should be obvious that the board members (primarily the outside members) should represent a very broad spectrum of knowledge and experience so that their thoughts will be of significant value.

So members know major physical assets and executives, board meetings should be scheduled at all major activity centers—perhaps on an established schedule. The greater their knowledge, the more valuable their contributions. If the board members are made to fully understand that suggestions will be welcomed and appreciated, they will provide valuable guidance.

The cost of maintaining a well structured board composed mostly of outsiders is still a bargain for U.S. industry. If the board is composed mostly of insiders, the company management is essentially talking to itself, which usually accomplishes little. However, the internal members, especially of small firms, seldom discuss overall business problems, even though they should do so. A retired insider appointed to the board is still an insider. Such members do not help the management of the company, the shareholders, or any of the other corporate constituents.

The ideal board is composed of men and women who have broad specialized knowledge and expertise in a wide variety of fields. Usually one should attempt to have as much diversity as possible, so as to expand the knowledge and experience of both the board and the that of the company as a whole.

Do not worry about having too powerful a board—such a problem virtually never exists. Neither will a powerful board tend to create unnecessary "waves." This author has sat on nine main corporate boards and on the boards of many other kinds of organizations and never has seen a problem caused because by having powerful board members—further, no such a problem was ever mentioned in discussion with other directors who also sat on other corporate boards. To be classed as a powerful board member, he/she would have to either be on the board because of a wealth of related knowledge (why this author was elected to boards) or because the member was a top executive of a major firm who possessed a number of areas of expertise—equating to knowledge.

If the owner/chairman of a small firm intends to have it grow and tries to make it do so with an insider board that might include the firm's bank president, its lawyer, and possibly even relatives, then he/she is very foolish. When the firm is small, one whould restrict the selection of board members to people located within about a 150 mile radius so that travel is no problem. Naturally, the people selected will usually not have the stature of those in major NYSE listed corporations, simply because the choice of people will be more limited. However, it is not unusual to find some very talented people. The board's stature and experience should be greater than those of the insiders. Surprisingly, most of the people approached will agree unless there are some unpleasant aspects to the firm. Being sued by shareholders or others because one is on the firm's board can be very expensive for a board member—and corporate insurance to cover this aspect can be expensive. However, if the individual board member behaves in a prudent and knowledgeable businesslike manner, the odds of being sued greatly decrease, especially if such a board member makes his/her business views (sound ones that the outside world would approve of) evident in the board meeting and gets them recorded in the minutes. If the firm goes ahead with what is deemed imprudent, the board member should resign and see his/her lawyer. Also, the firm can take some actions that might reduce insurance cost.

The real problem with the small firm is that the C.E.O. and any other large shareholders will not ask any top outsiders to join the board. They are afraid that they will be misled or "taken"—this author has never seen this happen, neither has he been told of such an occurrence. However, it is true that sometimes a board member decides that the company would be a good acquisition for his firm. Most of the time this is settled in a friendly manner between the involved C.E.O.s, but sometimes it has evolved into an unfriendly acquisition attempt. If the attempt is successful, it usually costs the acquiring firm a hefty price.

As to putting a firm's banker on the board, it often occurs that the firm finds it does not want anyone in the bank to know what the firm is doing or what it wants to do in the future. Possibly, the firm even decides at some point that it wants a new or another banking connection. Do not put your banker on the board.

If the firm has a strong and experienced (*in corporate matters*) attorney, he/she should be considered for board membership. However, do not use a personal general attorney as a member of the board of directors.

The evaluation of a board can only be accomplished by the C.E.O. and board chairman, either working alone or with the help of a very senior consultant. Most of the top 5–10 consulting firms have such people) also, some top business school deans tend to act as part-time consultants and could easily handle this kind of job.

Never doubt the fact that there are plenty of experienced and capable people who would be willing to serve on the firm's board—assuming that it is not a "sick" corporation. However, throughly investigate any individual considered before making any contact with him or her—again, a consultant can rather easily perform the investigation without ever disclosing what firm is interested. In fact, the consultant can identify excellent prospects and bring two or three to the firm for evaluation and investigation. Generally, they turn in a very adequate performance on such a task.

Other possible additional considerations are the following:

1. Size of board—a simple matter is to check with other C.E.O.s/chairmen heading a similar sized firm. However, a board of over a dozen begins to be unwieldy. A small firm ($5,000,000–25,000,000 annual sales) can be well served by a board of 5 to 8 people (total number). One problem observed with C.E.O.s who own much of the company and are board chairmen is that they "do not listen very well" to their board members—they do what they want to do, in spite of warnings (usually proven to be correct by what happens subsequently).
2. Directors' age usually is no problem *unless* an older member begins to exhibit loss of mental power. One must admit that this would be a problem. A relatively easy way to handle this is to make the membership of people over 65–70 on a year-to-year basis, which should be specified in the corporate bylaws. Firms usually have age clauses in their corporate bylaws which exclude people at age 65–70 years. However, this author believes that these generally need revising upward since people now live longer and "elder statesmen," having lived longer, have therefore acquired much more valuable experience and knowledge than young people—and such people are active and can easily contribute to a board. Moreover, they can be removed fairly easily; this writer has seen it happen.
3. Do any of the members represent negatives? If so, who and why and how? Can they be removed? If not, such members can often be neutralized by one or more specific individuals.

IV. MANAGERS, PROFESSIONALS, AND CRAFTSPEOPLE

The subject of employee evaluation is rather common, and many personnel departments have experts on the subject. Many consultants can also offer expertise in this area.

At this point, a detailed discussion of the evaluation factors to be listed is not believed to be warranted. However, it should be obvious that the depth of management talent can be of great importance. For example, should the firm embark upon an aggressive new product or acquisition program, the firm should have available managerial people to assign to such an activity. If the backup personnel are not available, they should be acquired before the actual need develops. The new people should learn "the company" before tackling a new assignment of the variety mentioned. It is generally impossible to handle learning the company and the new job at the same time and still turn in an excellent performance during the first 6 months of such an assignment.

The following can serve as a checklist of what kinds of tasks must be accomplished:

1. Managerial personnel. Job classifications must be developed and qualifications on the basis of experience, ability, special talents, and potential growth as well as availability of such people need to be recorded. If there is no inventory of skills and qualifications such as these, one should be developed. If there is none, why hasn't one previously been developed? Does the lack of an inventory signify that personnel in the function do not perform properly?
2. Depth of management talent or backup for present managers.
3. Scientific and technical talent—evaluate and record data according to fields, specialties, technical strengths, and locations. Do not forget industrial engineers, quality engineers, manufacturing engineers, tool and equipment engineers, etc.
4. Professional talent other than engineers and scientists. Examples of these would be accountants, finance specialists, marketing and sales specialists, attorneys, etc.
5. Technical and professional supporting personnel.
6. Dispersion of the above personnel to subsidiaries, divisions, departments, geographical areas.
7. Language capabilities and fluency must not be forgotten for almost any category of employee. More and more professionals are foreigners who studied in the U.S. and stayed. Today's craftspeople and workers, even people who are "helpers" need to be able to read, write, and compute. Close to 40 percent of those coming out of our grade and high schools are *functional* illiterates. More and more firms will need to start educating workers who can not read, write, and compute at the 12th grade level of two to three decades ago, not the level of graduates receiving social promotions through grade and high school. No, this is not a category of employee, but basic education must be considered in each category since graduation from high school no longer indicates reading, writing, and computing ability. There is one other problem associated with the "other end" of the problem, which is, are there people literate in the languages of the countries in which the firm operates? Firms must use some U.S. people abroad.
8. For factory employees, is there an adequate supply of workers having 12th grade reading, writing, and calculating ability? Try to quantify this factor by location.

V. PERSONNEL POLICIES, MORALE, INTERNAL WORKING CLIMATE, AND EMPLOYEE PERFORMANCE CHARACTERISTICS

Most C.E.O.s and top managers think that they are excellent communicators and that the firm's employees fully understand what the company is trying to do, and how much consideration is being given to employee welfare. If one of these executives has read the above message and really wants to know what the employees think, he should have a consultant conduct a survey. The firm's personnel department might even try to conduct a survey by providing "evaluation boxes" at numerous places in each plant. The department should ask the employees for anonymous answers to a set of questions on readily available forms at each "evaluation box." Be sure to define factors being examined and also clearly indicate who is being referenced by the word "management" (be very specific)—there is a big difference between departmental managers and the C.E.O. and top management. The result will likely be startlingly different from that which the executives believe to exist.

If the reader thinks that "the workers" trust "the bosses," read Alan Farnham's "The Trust Gap" in *Fortune*, December 4, 1989.[1] Surveys show employee confidence eroding. Further, a Lou Harris & Associates poll shows that it is not necessarily job security and pay that are of paramount importance. Ranked above these things are respect, a higher standard of management ethics, and increased recognition of employee contributions.

Companies tinker with medical benefits and try to reduce their contribution. They try to raid any surplus in the pension fund. This writer has found that even in the academic world, a surplus of many millions tempted the board of trustees of a major university to try to capture the surplus.

The top brass think that they are sending messages to the workers, but much of the time these messages never reach the workers. Towers Perrin concluded that the "open doors" of corporations were only "slightly ajar." The Hay Group found that statements from the boardroom are met with increasing disbelief by all employees below the vice president level.

Eighty-two percent of Fortune 500 executives believe that their corporate strategy is understood by "everyone who needs to know." Yet, less than a third of the employees say management provides clear goals and directions—which is important and is not even corporate strategy.

One final "wake up" statement. The C.E.O.'s compensation has risen about 280 percent since 1979, versus only about 155 percent for the hourly production worker. Both of these figures are far more than what would result from the inflation rate. Further, after the compounding effect of the hourly workers' rise, the C.E.O.'s compensation has almost risen "out of sight." Peter Drucker has a suggestion, which also is supported by J. P. Morgan—it is that the C.E.O. to be paid about 20 times the average worker pay. Herman Miller Inc. (a successful firm) does this.

Read the referenced article and some related pieces such as Graef S. Crystal's "At the Top: An Explosion of Pay Packages," *New York Times Magazine*, December 3, 1989.[2] Then find out what *really* exists in the way of beliefs about the company and it top bosses. This should substantially help develop goals and actions that will pave the road to better relations between the workers (all kinds) and the bosses.

This may appear to have been a superficial treatment of the topics in the subtitle, but if the message the author tried to convey is received, the solutions can be developed to the problem defined and to any other problems discovered relevant to the subtitle.

If the reader wants a few suggestions, here are a few to illustrate some possibilities:

1. Morale and loyalty of employees, by subsidiary, division, and/or department—as well as by geographic area.
2. Compensation practices—are they uniform within each country? Is there a written policy that is enforced?
3. Performance of employees. Are they measured against realistic standards? If performance is tied to specified rewards there is a significant increase. For what classes of employees does this condition exist? The Japanese did not have financial incentives for ordinary workers, but they are now beginning to install them. The beneficial impact upon performance is too great to ignore.

Performance does *jump* upward and stays up if pay plans provide tangible rewards. Doubters should read Nancy J. Perry's "Here Come Richer, Riskier Pay Plans" in *Fortune*, December 19, 1988.[3] Moreover, talk with any "work measurement expert" (this writer is acknowledged as having expertise in the area) and he/she will tell you that standards with an associated reward plan for performance will produce a gain of at least 15 to 20 percent in productivity. Look at Chapters 2 and 15 of *Advanced Work Measurement*.[4] The last chapter discusses "Work Measurement Applicable to Professional Employees." Reward schemes based upon performance will raise worker performance. Why not take advantage of this factor? The C.E.O. gets a bonus that presumably is based upon performance.

VI. FINANCIAL CONSIDERATIONS AND POTENTIAL

The financial analysis of an organization is most important since it will certainly set the initial limits on the strategic plan and the long range operational plan. It should start with 10 year spread sheet data of both the profit and loss (P & L) statement and the balance sheet statements by company total. In addition, one of each of such sets of three should be prepared for each subsidiary and, if possible, for each product line and SBU (product or narrow class of products).

In simple terms the minimum requirement for the P & L statement should be similar to that shown on a typical Value Line data sheet. It should show the following: per share data for sales, cash flow, earnings, dividends, and capital spending. Additionally, it should indicate shares outstanding (common), average annual P/E (price/earnings), sales, operating margin, working capital, long-term debt, net worth, percent earned on total capital, percent earned on net worth, percent retained to common equity, percent all dividends to net profit.

In addition, the P & L should really contain such additional data as the following: (LTD (long term debt)/NW (net worth) or LTD/equity (usually very similar), average net profit margin, average 5 year P/E, percent 5 year price change of common stock, industry median P/E (several data sources exist for this), Value Line's price growth persistence, some recognized rating of financial strength for the company, and other possibilities. These should also be shown for the subsidiary and product statements except for those involving stock price.

These data tend to be useful in evaluating company and product performance. For example, if the firm has a net profit margin (NPM) greater than 4.8 percent, its earnings and stock performance is greater (on average) than firms having a lower profit margin.[5] Moreover, while looking at this measurement, how does the firm's NPM compare with other firms in the industry—the firm with a higher NMP has a distinct advantage.

McDonald's Corp. had an NPM in 1988 and 1989 of about 11.65 percent. This is anywhere from about 8 to 2 percent higher than any other firm in its classification. If one jumps to hotels, Mariott is essentially a pure hotel/motel operator (except for its services division, some of which is being sold at the time of this writing) and its NPM at 3+ percent is better than its competition when one "weeds out" casino operators and those in restructuring/buyout situations. Its earning growth for the past 5 years has been about 18 percent and its predicted growth for the next five years is 16.5 percent—yet this firm's NPM is less than the benchmark of 4.8 percent. *Note that the industry involved makes a big difference.*

This last discussion illustrates the admonition of showing, where possible, performance measures as mentioned in the second paragraph above for the firm's major competitors. It will provide considerable help to the the planners in trying to decide upon the important factors and issues.

LTD/NW (or LTD/equity) can signal a possible weakness. Those firms with an LTD/NW of less than 52 percent (25 percent is even better) exhibit stronger performance characteristics than those with a higher ratio. Both of the last two measures or gauges were identified by the Strategic Planning Institute, some of whose additional findings will be discussed in a later chapter.[5]

However, the industry classification again makes a difference. For example leasing companies like Comdisco normally run a high LTD/NW ratio.

A question that should be asked by the C.E.O. and the Board is, has the finance/accounting function ever discussed such matters as the above? If not, why not?

The financial data and operating procedures should include the analysis not only of the main firm, but also of subsidiaries (sometimes even by division and/or SBU), and readable practical guidance standards should be presented to management (when possible) regarding data and expenditures such as the following:

1. Capital structure. In addition to LTD/NW or LTD/equity, examine long term versus short term borrowings—depending upon interest rates, the near term future of the economy, and the financial strength of the company this ratio may be of importance.
2. Liquidity. Are the cash reserves adequate? What of "lines of credit"? Are they adequate, and will they be honored when needed?
3. Return on equity, total capital, and working capital. Are the returns adequate? How do do these factors compare to the firm's major competitors? Even if you can't get competitor's figures on this or any other performance measure, determine an industry classification that is fairly similar as to firm characteristics, and that is listed in Value Line or some other data service. Compare such data to the measures used by the firm doing the planning—it might be an "eye opener." Just like some of the previously mentioned performance measures, if a competitor or competitors exceed the performance of the firm doing the planning, such firms have greater freedom to cause even more "pain" to those with lower performance. There are great differences in this factor relating to the industry classification.
4. Cash flow. Is it large enough to provide support to the long and short range plans—how much dare the firm use without substantially damaging future earnings since other normal uses of the cash flow have to be deferred? SPI, mentioned in Chapter 5, has an interesting booklet on cash flow.

5. Lines of credit. These analyses should not only be for the overall firm, but also for subsidiaries, and/or plants—and possibly by geographic area and/or country.

6. Currency. Since most large and many small firms operate in more than one country, there is a necessity to deal with more than one currency. Are the firm's money management policies, intelligence gathering procedures, and pricing actions preventing significant losses? Does the firm engage in hedging currency positions? Some firms even make money in this area of activity. Has the handling and transfer of money from one curreny to another been standardized? Make sure that currency does not confuse the financial measurement of subsidiaries in a foreign country.

7. Contingent liabilities. Often these are not recognized until it is too late to protect the firm. Are these subjected to a formal yearly review$^{2}_{*/}$ What part of the total amount is covered by insurance, if any? Is there a proper division between insured coverage and self coverage?

8. Financial policies and procedures. Are they in writing for virtually all possibly involved areas and have they been promulgated to all concerned personnel? Does this include all subsidiaries and all plants in all countries? What about revisions and upkeep? Must any of these be adjusted for foreign country laws and regulations? Is proper use being made of electronic communication via computers and satellites?

9. Standards. Has the firm established practical and up-to-date financial performance standards? Are accounting/costing standards on a current basis or are many outdated and no longer realistic? It is a fact that many cost systems do not reflect the proper allocations of cost to a product, especially in the manufacturing or standard cost of the product, especially where "allocated" costs are involved. Has this problem been specifically addressed and needed corrective action been taken? This problem existed in most firms 40 years ago, and it is still true for many firms in 1990.

10. Definitions. Is there an up-to-date "chart of account"? What about agreed upon definitions of key terms? Have they been translated into all pertinent languages? Have the U.S. definitions been modified, where necessary, to be in accord with the laws and regulations in other countries? Has the problem of translating data from one country's system to the U.S. system been solved? How are these and other such problems being handled from a "software view"?

11. Computerization. This is an important factor in all sizes of firms, but the larger the firm and the more scattered the operations the

more critical this becomes. Do not try to handle this without having "on-board" expertise. Do keep to the fore that a firm's computers must be able to communicate with each other.

VII.   MARKETING

So much has been written about marketing that it does not seem reasonable to try to produce a very comprehensive list of factors to examine. However, it is also true that this is one of the very most important areas to consider. Therefore, plan on devoting a major effort in this area.
    Here are some of the more important areas to examine:

1. Available market *and* the fraction held by the company. The total available market should be based upon present and anticipated products and product lines if possible. Usually this ideal is not possible to achieve. Are there any hidden projects that will generate products? Forecast future changes in the involved markets and clearly show growth or decline in the firm's market share.
2. Competitive position, by product and for total firm. Identify strengths and weaknesses of important competitors and estimate of their importance.
3. Reasons why a larger share of the market has not been secured by product and by product line.
4. Competitive edge. What is seen as the firm's competitive edge? The same question applies to each product line? Further, what holds true in the U.S. likely is not true in other countries in which products are sold. Was this factor previously defined?
5. Market structure by product line. Include such items as demographic distributions, price-volume relationships, position in product life cycle, possible new competition, and a forecast of the future for each.
6. New products. Identify by product line and forecast effect upon the product line. New product introductions tend to depress ROI in the short term, especially if market share is weak. Has this been taken into account? Indicate probabilities of success (generally and for major new products scheduled for near term introduction) and provide the basis of such predictions.
7. Replacement parts market for each product line—this includes standard parts that are purchased by the company. What is the firm's market share in each product line? Is it profitable? What can be done to increase profits and market share? Perhaps more importantly, what are the possibilities for service centers? Will better

repair service build additional sales? Will poor service cause loss of
sales? If so, these facts must be taken into account.
8. Brand recognition.
9. Patent position. Do by product and/or product line.
10. Market research abilities. If no internal resources exist, how is this
    task accomplished?
11. Advertising and sales promotion. Is this all handled internally? If
    not, why not? How is sales literature written and produced? Could
    not this be accomplished internally to a large degree?

VIII. ENGINEERING AND RESEARCH

American industry requires twice as long as the Japanese to translate
designs into a finished product ready for customer shipment—much of this
problem centers in the structure and composition of the product design
team. See Chapters 3 and 4 and the reference material in these chapters
for a more comprehensive look at this problem.

Second, the engineering design functions do not know how to design
for ease of manufacturing a product (producibility). They need to know
how to design for the above in a flexible manufacturing environment.
Carried to its logical conclusion, this flexibility involves modular design,
since it and the right kind of equipment make it possible to switch production from one variety of product to another or even to switch from one
product to another with relative ease.

Another task of the engineering design team is to design quality into
the product (discussed earlier in this book as previously mentioned). Most
engineering departments either do not know how to do this, or else they
are not allowed to do so by their managements because of the unfounded
fear of significantly increasing product cost.

Still another problem is that most engineering departments seldom are
able to take advantage of older existing designs that could be used with
only minor revisions. They cannot use these older designs because they
cannot be identified and located. This subject too was also initially discussed in Chapter 3.

Substantially more information will be available in the fourth edition
of *Managing Engineering and Research*.[6] In fact, if this subject is a
problem in the planning firm, it is recommended that the referenced text
and other similar books be consulted.

The evaluation of the engineering and research department should be
under the direction and guidance of the chief engineer or the technical
vice president. A few of the things that need doing will be listed just to

provide the reader with an idea of what may be needed. The real difficulty is that each of the factors listed below could be expanded into many pages. They are as follows:

1. Areas of expertise. What areas of expertise exist within the technical area (research, development, and engineering in the larger firm)? What is the degree of competence in each of the fields involved? Which fields need strengthening and why? What fields can be utilized better so as to generate more new products *that can be made and sold at a profit*? Where further expertise is needed, is adequate use made of consultants? Usually, when new expertise is needed, it can be secured faster by using consultants, and they are no longer an expense once the job is completed.
2. Engineering facilities. If additional items are needed, indicate the reason, and the likely tangible benefits.
3. Foreign based facilities. The same data mentioned in 1 and 2 will be required for these. Also, how well are these integrated into the firm's technical activity? Are jobs exchanged between the foreign based technical department(s) and the U.S.? If not, why not? Is technical know-how and discovery shared between the various engineering departments?
4. Patents. Do any issued patents or those soon to be issued provide any income opportunities through licensing? Have licencing opportunities been called to the attention of the patent department or patent attorney? Is the company paying royalties in order to use someone else's patents? Why? Can the company design "around" such patents? Are any trade secrets used in manufacturing patentable? How are patents written and submitted? How much income is generated by patent royalties? These are just some of the questions. Are the "right" things beings patented? Often ideas are patented "just because they can be patented." This is a wrong action. Only patent if it protects the firm, gives it an advantage, or can produce royalty income.
5. How many of the engineering department design team weaknesses mentioned in this text exist in the planning firm? What steps are being taken to remedy the situation? If none, why not?
6. Are products designed for ease of maintenance? How can this be proven?
7. Is the model shop adequate? If not, what is needed? Why?
8. Are computer terminals located in all needed positions? Is a CAD/CAM software system installed in the main frame, or are the computers stand-alone PC type computers? In the latter case, is AUTO-

CAD or some similar software available? What about a plotter? What other enabling software is available (like the Group Technology based system mentioned in Chapter 3)? Do design teams have software to assist in designing product for ease of production and for low cost? (Software for the latter factor is available and mentioned in *Managing Engineering and Research.*[6] Moreover, this and other related software is mentioned in Chapter 19 of *Engineered Work Measurement, 4th edition.*[7]) Are the computers interconnected in any manner? What is really needed in this area?

9. Are costing, material control, and other systems installed and properly operating? What is the weakest area?

10. How cordial are operating relationships with other organizational units of the company?

Top management, engineering management, and industrial/manufacturing engineering all need to be cognizant that the undiscounted return on process R & D is about $1.75 per dollar invested whereas the undiscounted return on product R & D for the same industrial sample was $1.67 per dollar invested. Moreover, process R&D not only has a slightly higher payoff, but it also pays off at a faster rate.[8]

This is just one more reason why (1) the design team and other integration concepts mentioned in Chapters 3 and 4 should be implemented (if they have not already been implemented) and (2) the engineering department responsible for process R&D (usually industrial and tool engineering) should be provided the financial resources to adequately build the required departmental strength. In fact the above-referenced SPI data also support the concept that integrating industrial engineering, quality engineering, and marketing into to the design team will not only reduce the time lag between product conception and product introduction, but it will also reduce the time lag experienced with payoff on product R&D.

Spending more and more on product R&D is not necessarily the best "way to go." To fully discuss this subject would require many pages, so only some pertinent facts will be mentioned, and more information can be obtained from "Non-Technical Considerations in Applied Research, Development, and Engineering Project Selection," ASME paper 85-WA/Mgt-1,[9] to a large degree based upon further SPI findings.[10] Overspenders (above normal) will depress ROI, but market share has a great effect upon the results. Generally, the higher the market share, the greater the impact on spending policy.

The ASME paper also shows that product quality has a tremendous beneficial impact upon ROI, with an additional beneficial impact coming from market share.[11,12] On this same subject, quality, SPI findings indicate that relative price and relative quality determine value and product position. Moreover, high and rising value increases the odds for gaining market share (Exhibit 3 of PIMSLETTER).[13]

IX.   MANUFACTURING

As mentioned earlier in this chapter, industrial engineering (I.E.) is probably the logical leader in producing this portion of the internal study and analysis. This is true since I.E., usually includes manufacturing/production engineering, tool and equipment design, processing, work standards, and plant engineering. In addition, other functions are sometimes the responsibility of this department. However, it should report frequently to the vice president of manufacturing regarding progress, and this person should be the final arbiter of the study's content. Naturally, he and the Director of Planning should brief the manufacturing study team regarding the planning needs of the firm before the project is started.

Obviously, one of the primary areas of concern must be the necessary degree of automation/mechanization and integration. To achieve best results in this area, it will require that I.E., quality control (Q.C.), purchasing, and marketing are fully accredited members of product design teams. This also will be required in order to implement "just in time" material deliveries, make possible the production of quality products, reduce the time between product conception and product placement on the market to a minimum, and make possible the successful implementation of modular manufacturing techniques (requires modular designs). Much of this was mentioned in Chapters 3 and 4. More information will be found in *Managing Engineering and Research*, 4th edition.[6]

Labor standards are another important area. Have they been created and has an incentive pay system been installed? These can raise productivity by about 25 percent. It should be understood that such standards can also be used for routine office jobs throughout the plant. Paying workers on the basis of performance has many benefits.

Since the central project is long range planning, it naturally should be reported as to whether manufacturing and engineering oriented activities have long range plans. If not, why not? They certainly should now develop a set or else revise existing plans where required. Manufacturing and product engineering plans often contain strategic components.

X. INFORMATION SYSTEMS

The makeup, organization, equipment, and links now in existence between major computers and other such matters are too important to leave to technicians. For example, should one purchase or lease equipment from a firm such as Comdisco? Comdisco can provide back-up in case of a major failure.

The most important benefits relate to better planning, control, and decision making—not in automating clerical procedures. Moreover, further major benefits really stem from providing prompt, reliable, and appropriate information. This is a very major subject area that affects virtually every facet of the firm.

Engineering's use of computers was mentioned under the previous subtitle. In the modern firm computers are found in stockrooms, and on the desks of secretaries, professionals throughout the firm, managers, accountants, etc. If the firm is small, do not let this area get out of line. It involves big money, not only for the equipment and for specialized people to operate large units, but also for time and talent wasted by not having the correct equipment, providing the proper linkages, and having the correct software (*possibly more important than the hardware*). Really big money can be lost in these areas of content.

XI. MATERIALS SOURCES AND VENDOR RELATIONSHIPS

Probably the most important question at this point is—has the just in time (JIT) material and parts supply concept been fully implemented in all plants? If not, this is the place to save major money. For those not yet using this philosophy there are books on the subject and consultants who are specialists. It will not work with low quality and/or poorly designed products or poor suppliers. It involves very close relationships with vendors, including their manufacturing and quality assurance systems. A firm not using such an approach probably cannot successfully compete with a firm that does!

There are a host of other rather obvious areas to examine, such as the following:

1. Cost of shipping. This examination should include a look at whether the cost for each reasonably significant part adds appreciably to the cost of the material. If it does, can it be reduced by changing the routing or by changing vendors to firms nearer to the planning firm's plant?

2. Has the possibility of using substitute materials that could raise product quality and reliability and/or reduce cost and provide equal service to the product been examined recently?
3. Are those plants requiring raw materials located near the source of the materials?
4. Are substitute materials readily available? If not, has a long term legal agreement been reached with the supplier?

XII.   ORGANIZATIONAL CHANGE AND ORGANIZATIONAL DYNAMICS

Some aspects of this subject have already been covered earlier in this chapter. However, there are a few additional items noted below that probably should be examined:

1. Teamwork. Does good to excellent teamwork exist among the entire management team? If there are problems, where are they and how can they be corrected?
2. Do virtually all the employees feel proud to work for the organization?
3. Initiative. Does the organization structure and policies encourage individual initiative? If this is not a characteristic of the organization, what changes are needed?
4. Entrepreneurial attitude. Is such an attitude encouraged? If not, why not?
5. Does management provide equal support for all classes of employees? This is a desirable attribute, and should be encouraged.
6. Do organization policies and actions provide for broadening employees' knowledge, experience, and skills? In any growing organization this is a very valuable attribute. To a large degree it is accomplished by transferring employees to new and more senior situations. Is this a characteristic of the planning organization? If not, why not?

XIII.   MORE ON THE PLANNING DIRECTOR'S ACTIVITIES REGARDING THE INTERNAL STUDY

Whether the planning director is an insider or outsider, and to a large degree whether it is the first time through the process (or even if the organization is experienced in planning), the first thing the director should normally do after determining the strengths and weaknesses is to discuss the findings with the C.E.O. He will not want to surprise the C.E.O. in front of the main planning session. The C.E.O. may also want the C.O.O. (if one exists) and the internal planning director if a consultant is acting in that role for the concerned round of planning. These should at least be suggested for the described activity.

This should follow the acting planning director's review of the individual study reports submitted by the various organizational sub-units. It should also come after the Director's conversation with the heads of the major sub-units, and possibly even a physical review of some of the facilities and equipments involved in strengths and weaknesses.

If this is the first time through the process, the outsider/consultant planning director should personally lead the future internal planning director though the review process. Both should make their own evaluations and certainly should be free to comment on any of this activity. Naturally, this should occur before bringing the material before the C.E.O. If the Chairman of the Board is not an insider, then the C.E.O. may or may not want him present at his private review session.

Sometimes a similar review session is also held with the C.E.O. for the external environmental factors, but this separate session is usually not necessary. However, the C.E.O. may want to know about these before a major planning session.

The full planning session should determine the ultimate importance of each strength and weakness before beginning the determination of Strategies. The planning director and his organization should have presented a rating for each of these before the full planning session starts its job.

REFERENCES

1. Alan Farnham, "The Trust Gap," *Fortune*, December 4, 1989.
2. Graef S. Crystal, "At the Top: An Explosion of Pay Packages," *The New York Times Magazine*, December 3, 1989.
3. Nancy J. Perry, "Here Come the Riskier Pay Plans," *Fortune*, December 19, 1988.
4. Delmar W. Karger and Walton M. Hancock, *Advanced Work Measurement*, Industrial Press, New York, 1982.
5. Sidney Schoeffler, *Impacts of Business Strategy on Stock Prices*, PIMSLETTER No. 20, Strategic Planning Institute, Cambridge, MA, 1980.
6. Delmar W. Karger and George M. Yaworsky, *Managing Engineering and Research*, 4th edition, Marcel Dekker, New York, (in press).
7. Delmar W. Karger and Franklin H. Bayha, *Engineered Work Measurement*, 4th edition, Industrial Press, New York, 1987.
8. David Ravenscraft and F.M. Scherer, *Is R & D Profitable?*, PIMSLETTER No. 29, Strategic Planning Institute, Cambridge, MA, 1982.

9. Delmar W. Karger, "Non-Technical Considerations in Applied Research, Development, and Engineering Project Selection," Presented at Winter Annual Meeting (invited presentation), November 17–21, 1985, American Society of Mechanical Engineers, New York, Paper 85-WA/Mgt-1, 1985.

10. Mark J. Chussil, *How Much To Spend on R & D*, PIMSLETTER No. 13, Strategic Planning Institute, Cambridge, MA, 1978.

11. Robert D. Buzzell, *Product Quality*, PIMSLETTER No. 4, Strategic Planning Institute, Cambridge, MA, 1978.

12. Mark Chussil and Sidney Schoeffler, *Pricing High-Quality Products*, PIMSLETTER No. 5, Strategic Planning Institute, Cambridge, MA, 1978.

13. Bradley T. Gale and Richard Klavans, Formulating Product Improvement Strategy, PIMSLETTER No. 31, Strategic Planning Institute, Cambridge, MA, 1985

10

How to Develop a Strategy

I. INTRODUCTION

A good to excellent strategy is the only known means by which a company can survive and flourish in its environments. This strategy results in a statement of strategic objectives that are to be achieved, and the actions required to attain each of the objectives. It should evolve or result from a planning effort that has been accomplished as specified in this text since there is no other logical way to develop strategic objectives.

One needs to understand the above, and also the fact that strategy consists of various elements, each having a somewhat different degree of importance. For example, if one or more external environmental factors present significant or major dangers to an organization, a way should be found or devised to neutralize or overcome them before proceeding to develop other strategic objectives. One should do the most important things first in the planning effort.

Of course, if one has a great new or replacement product that can "blast away" all competition, *maybe* that ought to be given equal attention. However, this is a seldom to never type of event.

Why act as suggested? Simply because if a firm is competing with opponents who are beating it because of *how* they operate their businesses, they will obviously continue to beat the firm until it too utilizes the same operating factors as the competitors, or until it creates new strategic operating procedures that are obviously better and implements them. However, think carefully before attempting the latter course. Your competition, in the above example, obviously has successful procedures—so think two or three times before trying to beat it with an unproven procedure.

This can be made even more clear. Go back to Chapters 1, 2, 3, and 4. Review a few of the things disclosed that are of extreme importance to business success, and how foreign competitors (especially the Japanese) are beating our firms (often driving them out of entire lines of business that they originally developed) because of the manner in which they operate and how they design, manufacture, and sell their products. The following factors are mainly why they beat U.S. firms:

1. Recognizing the importance of quality products.
2. Recognizing the importance of quality service.
3. Realizing the need to match product features to the desires of prospective customers.
4. Capitalizing on the advantage they gained by learning how to reduce the time required from product conception to market introduction by 30 to 40 percent (for the ordinary or average Japanese firm successfully competing in the U.S. market).
5. Taking full advantage of the "just in time" inventory management philosophy or approach.
6. Introducing and using the proper kinds and amounts of automation. This is necessary to compete with both LDCs and with the best of the firm's competitors.

In order for U.S. firms to accomplish most of the above, they need to understand that items 1, 2, 3, 4, and 6 require the use of the design team composition mentioned in Chapters 3 and 4. There are other such items, but they will be mentioned later.

The Japanese design products with better features, possessing higher delivered quality, take products from conception to marketing in about half the time required for U.S. firms, produce them at highly competitive prices with equal or higher wage rates (at present time, they also have proved they can do it in the U.S.), etc. U.S. firms obviously have to counter or neutralize these advantages or they will fail. Yes, the Japanese once had lower wage rates, but if we had done the above things and automated successfully as described in the first four chapters, we could have largely held them off—rather than letting them acquire 100 percent of certain product lines as well as a large percentage of others.

Most of our firms still can not match the Japanese because they have not adopted proven successful techniques. They have not learned from the Japanese experience. Like many others, they suffer from the "not invented here" syndrome. Also a big roadblock is a deeply embedded bureaucracy. Such U.S. firms are destined to lose still more customers, market share, and profits until they change—change by using the Japanese ideas, most of which the Japanese borrowed from the practices of the best U.S. firms and the thoughts of some experts. This action would minimally neutralize the Japanese. Likely, with just a little more creativity, U.S. firms could beat them.

Most readers will likely conclude, if they are honest in their thinking, that most American firms competing with the Japanese should be using the identified successful techniques and those of other enlightened competitors. This should be accomplished as quickly as possible. It likely would represent the most *urgent* elements or factors that should result from strategic planning based upon a study of the external environments. However, in virtually all cases, there are many other needed external and internally oriented objectives. Furthermore, merely designing, producing, and selling somewhat "me too" products will not solve the major problems of most U.S. manufacturers.

All this is not to say that other strategies associated with *other external and internal concerns* are not important. However, it would be unusual to be able to negate the very high importance of the above conclusions. Those factors are likely to be important thoughout the nineteen nineties.

Many firms that claim to be planners somewhat arbitrarily set generalized goals and label them long range strategic planning goals. They then proceed to somewhat mechanically develop the actual "how to achieve them" objectives. Such goals are *not* the equivalent of strategic objectives.

Strategic objectives must specify the directions, goals, and specific objectives that must be attained if there is to be successful competition with rival firms which can effectively cope with other external forces.

Finally, the results from a firm's planning effort is not the result of just what has been recommended, but how well all the ideas and concepts needed for correct planning have been used (put into practice) by the planning team. It is important to use the proper theories and knowledge, but their use is dependent upon the specifics of the firm. The ultimate results will be a test of the excellence of the firm's management, especially its strategic planning team, and the management's implemention of its objectives.

Before proceeding to the next sub-title, this author would be remiss if he did not discuss the different major items that might affect the strategy selected by non-manufacturing business firms. First let us examine the problem of small merchandising firms in the smaller cities. Small department stores, dress shops, neighborhood groceries, and even small hardware stores are facing likely extinction when the big chains enter the town—but there always are some exceptions. Usually one or two grocery chains are the first to enter such markets. Then something like Family Dollar or a larger chain offering a wide variety of goods enters. Finally, the likes of Wal Mart or K Mart enter.

Local larger grocery markets can survive by offering quality goods, at reasonable prices, excellent meat and butcher service, and friendly quality service. In fact they not only survive, but can actually succeed in a very substantial manner. This author has personally observed such actions and also the further described effects of modern competition.

Dress and clothing shops catering to reasonable sized segments of the local market can survive (but they will be hurt) when chain competition enters. A Wal Mart or K Mart WILL drive out (cause the close down) any local small department store type establishment and all but a few dress shops catering to the low cost market.

Local hardware stores seem to survive if they are a full line establishment. These are run by local residents and offer friendly and quality service.

Is it possible to prevent such damage? This author doubts it. The only solutions he can devise require either moving to another location (and even that may be temporary) or changing the line of business.

If one merchandising chain is trying to compete with other such chains, there are some actions that can help overcome the competion—several of these were mentioned in Chapters 1, 2, 3, and 4. One is to provide excellent, friendly, and quality service. The prize example of such success is Nordstrom. Also, believe it or not, Wal Mart offers friendly and helpful service, as well as very competitive prices of standard brand merchandise.

It should become clear that there are no universal cures, remedies, or strategies. Each set of problems usually requires a somewhat unique set of strategies—although there will be much borrowing from those used by firms in other kinds of situations.

The next series of sub-titles will identify some strategic and operational components of strategies.

II. COMPONENTS OF STRATEGY

The definition of strategy requires the development of the following components:

1. Scope of the business.
2. Competitive edge.

3. Risk level.
4. Specifications.
5. Deployment of resources.
6. Dynamics, the timing, monitoring, and adjustment of milestones speci-
    fied in the long range strategic and operational plans.

In order to develop a strategy, the organization must first establish a
"base line," that is, determine where it is, what it has been doing, and
what has caused any failures to cope with competition—and what has
worked to overcome competiton. This was *one* of the purposes behind
the recommended or specified inventory of external and internal environments and how these related to the business results of the firm. It will
become a "point of departure" for the development of strategic and new
long range operational objectives.

Moreover, in developing strategic objectives, it will also be necessary
to keep in focus the definition of the business(es) of the firm. Many
firms find it necessary to modifiy some of the original definitions of the
business(es) as they proceed through the planning process. This is a
natural event in the planning process, so planners should not be surprised
when it happens.

III. SCOPE OF THE BUSINESS

This is a part of the action to establish a base line for the planning activity.
The scope of the business defines the limits of the business in terms of:

1. Products/services—types, models, characteristics, and any other sig-
    nificant attributes. Relates to the effort of defining "what business(es)
    one is trying to conduct."
2. Markets served and channels of distribution.
3. Price/quality ratio for each of the products.
4. Users/purchasers of the products/services as to class, location, and
    any other significant attribute.
5. Location of offices, plants, and warehouses.
6. Information channels and capabilities as to types and kinds of infor-
    mation—and which are accessible at each facility. More and more
    companies will require very sophisticated communication networks
    (remember the insurance company which sent data to Ireland to be
    processed?).

The scope of a business is directed at product-market opportunities.
Defining the scope is the starting point for defining strategy, since it

establishes the limits for all other components of strategy. As the other components are defined, the scope will be further developed and refined.

Although an environmental analysis and internal resource analysis will have pointed the way for product opportunities, relationships among present and future products, channels of distribution, sources of somewhat common materials, processes, and customers will need to be considered. These relationships are concerned with synergy—the reinforcement of each product on other products. Some considerations for synergy are:

1. Breadth of line to satisfy full-line demands.
2. Product overlap to utilize common marketing resources. If this is possible, has advantage been taken of the fact? If not, why not?
3. Are there common parts (or can they be created?) so that production experience is enhanced?
4. Are modular design and maufacturing techniques used for any products? Is this readily transferable to other products being manufactured or to be designed and manufactured? What is the general level of flexibility? This pertains to volume, product mix, design, and routing of parts. Can this level be increased?
5. Can service departments be combined so as to handle other company products?
6. To what degree is the company integrated with respect to communications, design, manufacturing, any automation, inventory systems, warehousing, and quality? How many of the "parts" "talk to each other" to make a larger whole?

IV. PRODUCT PORTFOLIO

The company needs to consider its businesses and products/services as an investment portfolio, which should be constantly monitored. From a strategic viewpoint, the commitment to continue basic product areas should be reviewed, and their established status should be reaffirmed if appropriate. Naturally, products should be developed and added, retained, or pruned from the portfolio as strategy dictates.

New products and services are so important to the success of most companies that they must be given special attention and treatment. If the reader is not well informed in this area, review what the Japanese have done with transistor and microchip applications—each product line that they establish they rapidly expand so that the competition is either overwhelmed or "locked out" by products which they rapidly bring to the market.

Safety Kleen, a U.S. firm, has done well in the area of services by introducing new services. Gannett has also done well in expanding its lines in the newspaper publishing area. So has Dow Jones (moved from almost complete concentration on *The Wall Street Journal* into additional areas, especially electronic services for the investment and business communities). Other firms are Lubrizol (additives) and Ethyl (has added enough new products to virtually neutralize the decline in the use of "ethyl"). Learning by example is often the best way to find out how to do what needs to be done. Some relevant material can be found in *New Product Venture Management*[1] and other such books.

Companies have grown large by continually developing and adding new products. A few examples are 3M, Federal Express, GE, and many others. Unfortunately, it is also true that many companies have stagnated, failed, or been absorbed, because they did not develop and pursue proper strategies in this area.

Up to now, the meaning of "product" has been discussed as a physical entity. A product can be anything that satisfies a bundle of needs of the buyer. This can be functional, psychological, social, and/or cultural. Each such aspect influences the buying decision of prospective customers.

When considering products and/or services, keep in mind that there are three major classes of purchasers:

1. Consumers who use the product for personal satisfaction.
2. Industrial purchasers who use products in the production of other products. In a sense there are two main divisions in this class. First, there are firms that incorporate a product into one of their products. Second, there are firms that utilize machinery and equipment in the production and distribution of products/services.
3. Governments and governmental bodies that purchase products to fill operating or social needs.

Various time cycles also influence market characteristics. Essentially, products may be characterized by four types of time cycles:

1. Long cycles of cultural swings, such as fashion cycles. Examples are skirt lengths, the brevity of swim suits, cuffs or no cuffs on men's trousers, high or low waists, amount of decolletage, beards or no beards for men, healthful versus unhealthful foods, etc.
2. Product life cycles. These may be as short as a few days or as long as decades—the Swiss made Atmos clock has been around for over 50 years.[2]
3. Planned obsolescence cycles. The automobile is probably the most cited example of this kind of cycle.
4. Sudden death cycles, often caused by government laws or require-

ments. Roniacol was used for years as a vaso-dillator, yet the government said it had no beneficial purpose. This author used it at the recommendation of an ear specialist to ward off attacks of Minuere's syndrome. It did work for this purpose, yet it took a year or more for another specialist to find an acceptable substitute—and it is not as good. In the future, such edicts regarding products can be due to radiation, electromagnetic waves, defects in an airplane, and possibly cigarettes. However, in the case of cigarettes the product will still be available and sold in many foreign countries.

V.   PRICE/QUALITY RATIO

The price/quality ratio is an important *strategic* decision, as well as an operational decision. The reader should first review some of the things previously said regarding quality. Quality products do not cost more, if designed and manufactured correctly. In fact, as quality is improved the overall product cost is usually (for "commercial grade" of quality) reduced. This means that as quality is increased (by correct actions), the costs go down. However, if the quality improvement process is continued beyond commercial quality the cost does rise steeply. Beyond commercial quality, like for a space vehicle or for military equipment, the costs can become astronomical. The vast majority of U.S. firms operate in the region where increasing quality will decrease costs.

Based upon Strategic Planning Institute (SPI) research, high quality products can be sold at a somewhat higher price and the margins on such products are greater because of both a higher price and reduced product cost (due to higher quality). As quality is increased from a low level, corresponding increases in price may or may not be sustainable in market—it often depends upon what one's competitors are doing. While a particular price/quality ratio may bring on substantial problems, usually any one of a rather wide range of prices may be successful.

At one end of the spectrum customers are very price conscious, while at the other end they are very quality conscious *combined with* being price conscious. For industrial products, customers may be concerned with the best possible price/quality ratio for intermediate quality values—depending upon the buyers' perceptions of how much high versus intermediate quality products will benefit their firms. However, most firms are not sophisticated enough in quality management, and accounting to inform the purchasing agent or the buyer.

As to pricing high quality products, Mark Chussil and Sidney Schoffler

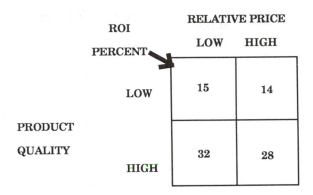

Figure 1   Adapted from PIMSLETTER on Business Strategy. Read text material
to understand what was eliminated from the original.[3]

of SPI have published useful research results, using the SPI data base. It
clearly shows that high product quality raises ROI regardless of whether
the firm uses a low or a high relative pricing strategy. Relative price is
low when a firm is selling its product at a lower price than competitors at
their product quality level. High relative price is the opposite.[3] Somewhat
similar and related information is in *The PIMS Principles.*[4]*

The general facts regarding the effect of relative price versus product
quality on ROI are shown in Figure 1. ROI is measured here prior to
income taxes and other financial charges. Note that the sectors for the
average spectrums are missing from Figures 1 and 2. The SPI research
also shows a similar effect of quality and relative price regarding market
share as shown in Figure 2.

If product quality is average or better and the firm sets a low relative
price, it seems that one can gain in both profitability (ROI) and market
share. However, if a firm gains significant market share, it will need to
spend more on producing the required output, maybe even on more plant
and equipment. The firm will then need a higher level of working capital,
which may require borrowing money (requires payment of interest).

Since very complex issues are being discussed here and nothing concerning these business factors is simple, one should always be careful before

---

*If the reader wants to use these data to ''fine tune'' quality vs price with respect to ROI
and market share they should use the additional information provided in both references!

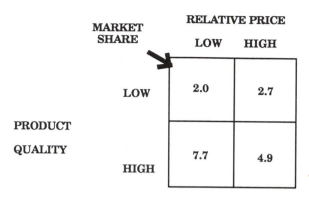

Figure 2   Adapted from PIMSLETTER on Business Strategy. Read text material
for more information.[3]

making a move. Value strategies vary in their effect with the kind of
business involved, how it is operated, and the kind of customers served.

VI.   PROCESSES

Manufacturing, paper processing, and personal services are different forms
of the basic process of adding value to fulfill customer needs. The system
characteristics of a TV manufacturer, an insurance company, or a motel
chain are alike—but the specific processes and equipment will differ.

In manufacturing a product, the production often requires certain kinds
of processing, and this will often determine the kind of equipment. However, in today's world there are often available very wide choices of usable
equipment. Moreover, the applicability of a given process has often to
be doubled or tripled in size. Flexibility and the economics of using the
equipment are of extreme importance—the example to think of here is
"flexible manufacturing" concepts (see Chapter 4).

Equipment is a capital investment and it is usually a long term consideration because of economic necessity and IRS rules—but the decision based
upon justification studies is often short term. An aside remark here
regarding the "pay-off" period is appropriate. Most American firms
expect new equipment to return their cost in 1, 2, or 3 years. If the
equipment is of the "flexible manufacturing" variety that can be pro-
grammed to shift from product to product with relative ease, the pay-off
or pay-out period can and should be much, much longer. This kind of
equipment (and many other pieces of new manufacturing equipment)
really represents a long term approach to competing, and the choice of
equipment is really a very important strategic decision.

VII.   USERS OF THE PRODUCT

The identification of present and potential users of a product is important to the specification of related strategies. Decisions about the expansion or contraction of markets can increase profitability. Contraction of geographical coverage, for example, may permit concentration on areas with more customers who may have more (or less) individual buying power — thus overall buying power will likely be "up."

A fresh and creative look at new potential applications for a product should also be a part of preparing strategies. For example, a corrugated cardboard manufacturing firm found that its sales had stabilized at a certain share of a highly competitive market, which was not growing. It could have fought harder for a small increase in this relatively fixed size market, but instead it sought new applications. It settled on the large market for packaging fowl. The company had to develop special foldout cartons with a coating that would resist ice and water. It then had to conduct a unique promotional venture to convince a major packer that the carton would work and was more economical than the wire reinforced wooden crates traditionally used.

VIII.   LOCATION OF PLANTS AND WAREHOUSES

Too often, companies fail to objectively evaluate present plants and locations. They know the costs of building new facilities, but usually they have no idea of the gains to be achieved through using these new facilities. This is an often forgotten area in planning.

Modernization or construction of new facilities may be suprisingly profitable because it can bring about or make possible increased efficiency within the company. Furthermore, a change of location may be beneficial if it puts the plants and warehouses nearer to suppliers and/or customers. This could be associated with the "just in time" supply technique. Differences in labor markets or costs of doing business in a particular state or area "tilt the scale" toward relocation.

IX.   INTEGRATION OF MARKET SHARE, INDUSTRY GROWTH, AND CASH FLOW FOR SETTING PRODUCT STRATEGY

For all but a few companies, there are more opportunities for the company to exploit than there is cash available for them. This is true if the firm keeps its eyes and options open to new ideas, concepts, products, and/or services. Therefore, companies should pinpoint the product strategies in terms of cash available, the present market share in the product or product

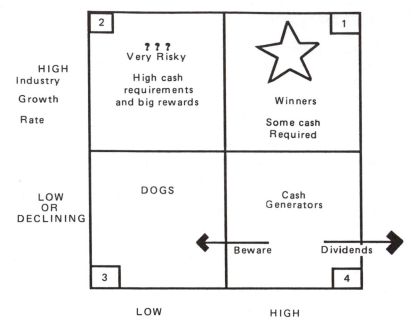

Figure 3   Industry/product line/product growth vs. market share matrix.[5]

line, and the potential and probabilities for growth or decline. Sam MacArthus, when C.E.O. of Federal-Mogul, suggested using the conceptual scheme shown in Figure 3 as a guide.[5]

Look first at quadrant 1 in the figure. If the firm has a high market share and is in a growth industry, it will have a tremendous edge over competitors because of the cumulative experience curve effect. Many text and reference books describe these experience curves and suggest ways of using them. This effect was discovered during World War I, so it is not exactly new information. The trouble is that most managers forget about its existence and importance.[1,6,7,8]*

Experience curves correctly predict that costs go down about 20–30 percent every time production experience doubles. Naturally, some organizations learn faster than others—meaning that the management of an organization can and often does affect the rate of learning. Some learn slower than the 20 percent rate, and some faster than the 30 percent rate. This phenomenon needs to be taken into account by all planning organizations—remember that the company can affect the learning rate.

*These are the most helpful references. Under references 6–8 is a short but helpful discussion of the thrust and orientation of each.

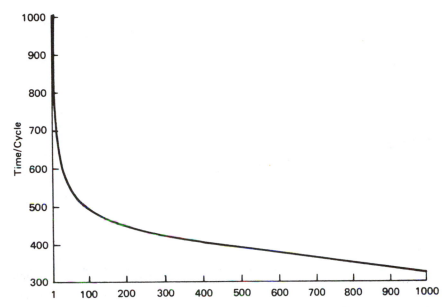

Figure 4   A 90 percent learning curve using linear coordinates.[7] Reproduced with the permission of the publisher of *Advanced Work Measurement*, copyright 1982 by Industrial Press, Inc.

The discussion will return to Figure 3, but a little more needs to be said about experience curves, a form of the "learning curve."

A.   Experience/Learning Curve Usage

The experience curve (or the production progress function) is essentially the same as the well-known learning curve which is usually expressed as the time required to perform a task. The ordinate is usually expressed in time per piece or labor hours per piece. The only real difference is that here we are discussing the "learning" of an organization and the ordinate is usually expressed in terms of cost or price per unit (of a product, but it could be a service).

Figure 4 presents a typical learning curve expressed in time per cycle which is taken from *Advanced Work Measurement*.[8] Figure 5 presents exactly the same data plotted on log log coordinates, which converts the difficult to handle curve to a straight line, and is also taken from *Advanced Work Measurement*.[7] The figures illustrate a 90 percent curve, and the costs (or time) go down 10 percent every time the production experience doubles. An 80 percent curve illustrates what happens when costs go down 20 percent every time production experience doubles. A 30 percent

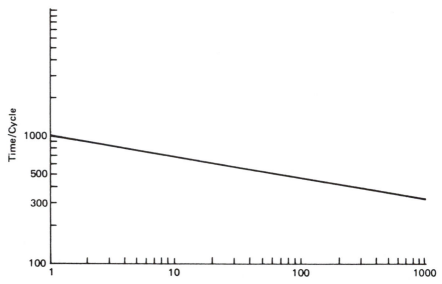

Figure 5   A 90 percent learning curve using log–log coordinates.[8] Reproduced with the permission of the publisher of *Advanced Work Measurement*, copyright 1982 by Industrial Press, Inc.

reduction results in a 70 percent curve. The greater the percent decrease, the greater (steeper) the slope.

Here is one more significant attribute of experience curves. Plot the price per piece, using log-log coordinates, against the same abscissa as the experience curves of the firm and the estimated curves of competitors. Then, when using a scale for the ordinate of the price curve that starts the price curve above the experience curves, it will be noticed that eventually the slope of the price curve will equal (for all practical purposes) the slope of the lowest cost producer.

This phenomenon makes possible some deductions of considerable practical value. First, however, it is also almost always true that when the price curve no longer changes slope periodically and remains steady, it is then very likely parallel to the experience curve of the lowest cost producer (they then have the same slope if plotted on log log coordinates). If the competitors in that product find this steady slope condition [there sometimes are slight variations over short ($\frac{1}{2}-1$ year periods] and their experience curve is of a shallower slope (not as steep), then they need to reassess what they will do about continuing to produce and sell that product. If the firm is a supplier of parts to the previously plotted situation, then it will have to consider the same set of facts. It should be understood by any firm in this position that it must decrease its costs at a rate faster than or at least equal to the slope of the price curve (this latter result will only maintain the the resultant profit margin), or it will be driven out of the market. This is just one illustration of how these curves can be used in a practical manner.

The use of the experience curve has value in a substantial number of areas. The following list identifies most of them:

1. Costs tend to be inversely proportional to market share. A high market share produces more production experience than that of competitors. Hence costs *should be* low relative to competitors.
2. The above condition (high market share) should make it clear that the greater the market share relative to competitor, the more the opportunity to acquire further share (by aggressive price action or by providing product enhancements—the last is the better way), since a profit margin greater than that of competitors likely exists.
3. Continuing with strategies for the high market share producer, the higher margin (over competitors) should make it possible to maintain a higher relative debt capacity, since earnings and cash flow will be relatively larger if the firm is properly managed. However, it should not be used unless there is a distinct and advantageous business use for the funds for improvements, acquisitions, or working capital.
4. If the above firm manufactures and sells other products and if some of the cost elements, especially parts or subsystems, can be shared, costs will go down faster for the above product *and* for the other products participating in the sharing.
5. To the extent that one wishes to measure whether the organization is improving or merely maintaining position, the slope of the experience curve can be used for cost control. Better yet, it can be used to force improvement by some form of incentive tied to such an improvement.
6. The above relations can even be used to affect product design, especially if the design team integration concepts identified in Chapters 3 and 4 are used. Knowing production rates, whether they can be maintained or possibly increased (or whether they are headed downward because some other competitor dominates the sale of the product) will help guide the selection between design element alternatives. It is then possible to really determine relative costs between the alternatives if one has the right design team composition, and if the firm has "backed the team" by providing proper software and a suitable data base. Merely lending or borrowing industrial engineers, marketing people, quality engineers, etc. will not work.

7. The above relationships can also have an effect upon actions concern-
    ing procurement negotiation and upon make-buy decisions—it is nor-
    mal to review make-buy decisions and procurement placements per-
    iodically in well run establishments. First, consider the "easy one,"
    procurement negotiation. The price of a purchased part should de-
    crease equal to your cost rate for the product being made and sold if
    the quanties produced by both firms are equal. If the supplier's part
    is used two or more times in each of the firm's product, then the cost
    of that purchased part should decrease faster than those of the firm
    using the product (or if only one is used per product, but the supplier
    is known to be selling the part to other manufacturers). Therefore
    the purchase part cost should decrease, in this latter instance, faster
    than the product cost.
        Now, consider the make-buy situation. Looking at the purchased
    cost, and knowing the production expectations, it might prove advis-
    able to reverse a buy decision to one of make—especially if two or
    more parts are used per product manufactured. Design engineering,
    manufacturing, and purchasing are all involved in developing the
    solution to this problem. This is still another reason why the design
    team composition needs revision in most plants.
8. The above relationships are complex, especially those involving com-
    bined product cost elements (points 4, 6, and 7 above). These in
    combination with the implications of experience curves can help evalu-
    ate the total economic effect of product line extensions.
9. Since the use of experience curves also requires examining the product
    price action, it is logical to compare market elasticity with the cost
    decline to help approximate market potential for the product (also
    take demographics into account).

   If more information is desired regarding experience or learning curves,
a start at such an objective is to read the references, especially those of
the Boston Consulting Group. Then, if more basic and somewhat more
scientific/engineering oriented information is wanted, one should read the
material in *Advanced Work Measurement*. Some of the early reference
material is listed in *Experience Curves as a Planning Tool* and at the end
of this chapter (9–16).
   Now it is time to return to the matrix displayed in Figure 3.

B. Market Share Matrix

The matrix displayed in Figure 3 is often pictured with the abscissa reversed as to "high" and "low," but in both cases the abscissa represents
market share. It too has "growth rate" on the ordinate, with the high

position at the top, just as in Figure 3. The ordinate in the figure developed and used by the Boston Consulting Group's matrix in *The Experience Curve Reviewed; IV*[7] *The Growth Share Matrix* has the abscissa reversed from that in Figure 3. However it also has the ordinate representing cash use. In the Figure 3 matrix it also *conceptualizes* the ordinate as representing cash. When the positions of the quadrants in each mentioned figure are represented by the ordinate and abscissa points, the "star" positions and their meanings are exactly the same. If growth rate is high and market share is high, the product or product line will require cash. However, such businesses generate much cash and eventually become "cash cows," because they then are in the low *growth*—high market share position.

What has been said above about becomming a "cash cow" is correct if the market cannot be expanded. However, if one does as McDonald's Corp. does, and begins the growth rate all over again in foreign countries, then one will have part of one's business in the high—high quadrant and part in the low growth (low cash use)—high market share quadrant (representing operations in the U.S. and Canada).

From this point on, only Figure 3 will be referenced since it identifies the same *conditions* in both representation schemes.

Next consider the "question marked" quadrant (number two). Here the company has a low market share in a high industry growth rate. This means meager profits since the market share is low (meaning low total sales volume) and the product or product line is continually requiring cash investment *just to maintain the low share of the market*. Unless the firm has some other advantages, like coming in late with a patent protected outstanding product, it will eat a lot of cash.

If money is available, if the product/product line is superior, if the marketing program is outstanding, and if engineering/manufacturing have managed to create a low manufacturing cost product, the firm probably should go forward with full speed. If it can capture a high market share, it will have a winner—in the "star" quadrant. If the firm only has one or two of the mentioned favorable attributes, it probably should not take the risk of trying to capture market share since the losses could be very large and it may never make a profit.

Products that are dogs almost always should be disposed of, one way or another. Generally they are money losers. Firms sometimes doctor the books to show a small profit or break even by hiding some of the costs in other related products. Usually such products have become someone's pet and the boss hates to admit a mistake. The best advice is to "bite the bullet" and write these products off and take whatever losses are necessary. They are real "cash traps."

Quadrant 4 in Figure 3 is labeled cash generators. The company likely got a product or product line into this quadrant because it had won a large market share and maintained this position. But, as often happens, the growth slowed (maybe because there were no more new customers to capture, like the McDonald's example for the U.S. and Canada). Since production capacity/sales outlets are all established, the cash need is low and profits are high. The fact that the firm is well established and way down on the learning curve means few will be foolish enough to try to break into the business area involved. If some of the excess cash is directed to dividends, this will keep shareholders happy and still make money raising relatively easy for some new promising enterprise. Oh yes, other uses for the excess money are to pay interest on debt and to help cover corporate overhead.

Obviously some clues have been given as what the planners ought to consider. Don't destroy the cash cows, get rid of the dogs, and keep most of the firm's activity in the "star" quadrant and the "cash generator" quadrant.

The reader may say, "what about quadrant 2, is not this a necessary starting place?" Not necessarily so. If the company is active in *creating new businesses with high potential* it will be far better off than trying to "slug it out" with a much larger opponent (the rival may already have a medium to large market share). If a firm starts in a new area at about the same time as others, it has a chance IF it has advantages like those mentioned earlier. One example would be the know-how required to learn quickly (meaning know how to design and produce at a low relative cost and how to further reduce costs after starting production), or having a good marketing department, and a first class engineering/manufacturing function. Cash also helps.

A good firm is one that maintains a superior growth rate in sales and earnings (especially the latter) and still keeps spawning successful new products and/or businesses. Earnings growth especially should be 15 percent or higher.

Another desirable attribute is a high return on equity or net worth, preferably above 15 percent. Pick almost any industry segment and examine this statistic (an easy place to look is Value Line since it presents 10 or more years of financial data on each firm followed). The reader will find that the leader almost always has the highest return on equity or net worth and that it is usually greater than 14%. However, some industries have characteristics which place the best ones below the suggested statistic.

Along the same line, a high net profit margin (NPM) is also the "mark" of a "winner." This author is an investor and uses multifactor models to analyze stock investment choices. Companies with an NPM of 4.8 or higher will usually have their stock rise faster than the average firm. However, this number has to vary with the industry, so look at the statistics in your industry. If you can't "see" a way to get close to the winners in NPM, beware.

Many people learned in the 1980s that high debt is unhealthy for a company. If long term debt/equity is greater than 52 percent, research of the Strategic Planning Institute shows it is detrimental to company performance in the market and as financial results. If it is below 33 percent, it generally will help financial results and stock market performance.

One more sort of general miscellaneous gauge to watch: Has the firm's financial head discussed the company's long term (both the five year and ten year) sales and earnings growth rates? In this investor's and management expert's opinion, the really good firms have rates (especially earnings) above 12%. Fourteen percent is better and twenty percent is the mark of a real high growth company. *Why* are the rates for your firm below these performance gauges? This is a valid question to consider in your planning.

High relative market share is always a big plus. Why does the firm not have a larger share of the market? All of the above and a significant number of others are in this author's investment analysis model. This is not likely to be believed, but it might get the attention of some of the readers. The above factors and other similar factors have yielded an aveage portfolio growth rate of 20 percent for almost two decades. Look at your company's performance very critically. Not every firm can be a high growth company, but it can at least try to be a medium growth firm.

X.   COMPETITIVE EDGE

If a firm has no identifiable factors comprising what it sees as a competitive edge for the firm, how can it have one for a product or product line? Many firms loose sight of this fact. There are carryovers from product line to product line, and if the firm is inconsistent, it will have a most difficult time establishing even a weak competitive edge. Sure, its edge will vary from product area to product area, but it must try for a consistent image.

Competitive edge is the sum of all factors which make the company different in some way from every other company, from the *customer's viewpoint*. This importance of competitive edge can not be over emphasized! A firm may have high morale, low production costs, well educated management, good sources of raw materials, or any number of *internal* operating advantages. If these are not translated into services and products with distinguishing features which are *recognized by the potential buyers*, they do not constitute a competitive edge.

The competitive edge may stem from operating advantages or other internal and external factors, but these eventually must be translated into identifiable items such as the following:

1. Unique and useful product features.
2. High product reliability.
3. Favorable price/quality ratio.
4. High integrity of the company.
5. Strong financial position.
6. Industry leader.
7. Modern plant and facilities.
8. Skillful marketing.
9. Excellent service provider.
10. Leader in technology, engineering, and design.

The competitive edge as viewed from the purchaser's side when comparing products involves:

1. Utility of the product function to the customer.
2. Price.
3. Quality of design, workmanship, and appearance.
4. Reliability of the product.
5. Life of the product.
6. Total life operating and maintenance costs.
7. Delivery lead time.
8. Status associated with product ownership.
9. Personal relationships with company and dealer or sales personnel.
10. Service on the product and company service to the customer.
11. Product warranty.

The definition of the competitive edge which the firm will try to create and maintain is vital to the survival of the firm in the marketplace. It must be recognized that merely thinking something is true will not make it true and discernable by anyone. Also, "talking it up" in the media will not work without having some real and tangible things to talk about.

As mentioned earlier, the mere projection of financial goals as the basis for strategic or proper long range plans ignores the reason for the firm's existence and healthy business "life." The focus must be on the *differentiation* of the company's products, services, and image from those of competitors. Success depends on having an edge over competition on a long range basis.

If no work has been done in developing such an image, one must start on the basis of what was learned in the environmental studies. If an image of sorts exists, it must be compared with what was discovered.

In the environmental analysis, a study of the industry and the strength of competitors will be developed. Gaps in product or service characteristics desired by market segments may be discovered. From the possible opportunities, the company's present positions, and desires from a business definition view, the company should try to find niches in the industry which it can fill. If it can and does fill such niches, this will be of considerable value in developing a statement of its desired competitive edge components. Moreover, any niches to be filled will represent a unique set of services and product strengths which the firm may be able to dominate. This will give the firm a limited monopoly, that is, an edge over the competitors beyond the other factors mentioned.

XI. Risk

Risk is a common companion in business. If there is an opportunity, there is a risk. Usually, the larger the opportunity, the larger the accompanying risk.

In its planning a firm should attempt to specify the risk and reward relationships that it considers reasonable or acceptable. This task probably can best be approached by expressing the meaning of risk in terms of company survival, rather than in terms of gains relative to losses. From this view, risk is a function of the probability of failure of a company venture and the ratio of potential loss of company equity.

For example, suppose General Electric were to consider the development of a new product line in which the possible loss of $40,000,000 could occur, probability of occurrence .40. GE's equity or net worth is over 23 billion dollars so that even though this would be a large loss, it would have little impact upon the survival of the company. It would not cause even a "flutter" in its financial strength rating.

Now consider EZ Co. with equity of $2,000,000. It develops a new product or engages in ventures where the potential loss is $1,000,000 per venture with a success probability of only .65. Just one loss of $1,000,000 would tend to cripple the company, two would certainly destroy it. If EZ Co decides to go ahead, it obviously has adopted a high risk strategy.

Many times, the above kinds of situations are the only ones examined with respect to risk. This is a BIG mistake since risk and the well being of the firm are associated with a very large number of both internal and external factors. These were somewhat discussed in Chapters 1–4. More such factors were mentioned in Chapters 6–9. However, only a few of the factors mentioned below were previously identified.

Many of the factors are "double edged," such as "synergism or lack of it." If there is synergism between existing products or with a proposed new product it reduces risk, whereas if there is no synergism in either of the mentioned cases it increases risk. It seems reasonable that the reader can make such connections regarding the identified factors. Ascertaining the degree of risk versus reward is not an easy task to accomplish. Give it a lot of thought in the firm's planning.

Internal	External
"Portfolio" of products	Rapid or unexpected change in
Synergism or lack of it	technology
Product innovation leadership	Change in consumer tastes, life
Level of commitment of resources	style, preferences
to fixed assets or programs	Change in customer needs or
affecting liquidity/illiquidity	or desires
Debt/equity ratio (<50% and <33%	Geographic shift of markets
is best)	
Information risk	Inflation or recession
Head-on competition vs. competitive	Diminishing natural resources
edge	Environmentalists' movements
Expediency management vs. strategic	New aggressive competitor
planning and management	Strong new management of an old
Operating on edge of legality,	competitor
social movement entanglements,	New or expected legal
etc. vs. "playing it safe"	restrictions
Investment in management	International events
Investment in communication and	Information ambiguities
computing systems	Net Profit Margin (>4.8% is desir-
Dividend/net earnings	able)
	Longterm growth in profits

XII. FACTORS TO UNDERSTAND AND KNOWLEDGE TO USE WHEN NEEDED

What follows will not be an all encompassing list, neither will the discussion present all available knowledge. However, it will provide some key information and concepts, and sources of more information will usually be provided.

A. Productivity

Increasing productivity is always better than stable or low productivity, right? No, this is not correct. There are practically always costs associated with an effort to increase productivity. Therefore, little study should be needed to arrive at a conclusion that says, productivity that costs more to achieve than the value of the benefits attained is not good productivity.

SPI produced PIMSLETTER Number 11 dealing with *Good Productivity vs. Bad Productivity*. It provides some excellent examples resulting from an analysis of ITS data base (members have access to all research results and to the computer data base).[17] However, each firm must perform its own cost benefit analysis, but some general guidelines can reduce the scope of the company analysis.

Actually, it was found that productivity improvement through actions requiring a large expenditure are generally bad—meaning that the benefit derived generally is less than the cost of the improvement. However, it also must be said that the original research was completed in 1978. Since then, with our international market, it probably is true that big money is required just to compete and stay alive when a competitor is from a less developed country (LDC) with low wage rates or when the competitor is a Japanese firm that has automated correctly. Nothing is simple in planning. Each situation must be carefully and separately examined.

One generalization that almost always holds true is that productivity improvement by low-investment means is usually good. Yet even here, if such an improvement merely reduces losses, it is NOT GOOD ENOUGH.

One other aspect of productivity, which emphasizes its importance, is that it increases the value added per employee. The more this is done, the larger the consequent profits that will be made—neglecting the capital or other cost of increasing productivity. The desirability of increasing value added per employee, among other such findings, is mentioned in *PIMSLETTER Number 1; Nine Basic Findings on Business Strategy.*[18]

B. Growth of Served Market

Growth in the market is generally favorable to dollar measures of profit, indifferent to percent measures of profit, and negative for all measures of net cash flow.[18] Intuitively, the ordinary person must conclude that market growth is good. But this also can have serious consequences for a small firm with low capitalization.

If the market grows and the firm tries to maintain its market share, it means it will have to spend big money (usually) in increasing production capacity and financing increased needs in distribution and marketing. Time needs to be devoted to studying this matter when a "smaller" firm is having the problem. Consider raising needed capital by either increasing debt and/or the sale of equity. If neither approach is viable, then maybe one needs to see if a niche can be found for the firm's product that allows the firm to stay both small and profitable. Merging with a larger firm must also be considered.

Raising money by selling stock (equity) was mentioned. Often a majority owner immediately resists such a move because it reduces the owner's ownership percentage. Such people need to consider that owning a smaller percentage of a company may easily mean owning more since net worth and/or equity will be increased. Moreover, the idea is to raise cash so the company can substantially grown. This is the usual result over a reasonable time period (2–5 years), and the real fact is that such people often then become *very* wealthy.

C.   Innovation (R & D),* Including Product Differentiation

R & D tends to be favorable if the firm has a strong market position (holds a larger share of the market); otherwise it generally has a negative effect. Nothing, not even R & D, is always good.[18,19,20,21] In fact, it is a very complex situation as illustrated by the SPI (described in Chapter 7) research upon which much of this discussion is based.

There are some generalized findings that should first be disclosed. First, the analysis of the SPI (PIMS) data base clearly shows that overspenders, greater than normal (where this the "spending" is indicated as a "percent of sales"), for the involved industry have a lowered ROI. It decreases from about 24 percent (for SPI database firms) to 18–19 percent. This is a large enough drop ($-25+$ percent) to give planners something serious to think about.

The above and all the additional findings are essentially disclosed in Figures 6, 7, and 8, which are presented by permission of the Strategic Planning Institute (see Chapter 7).

An examination of Figure 6 might lead the reader to the incorrect conclusion that increased spending over a small amount (about 1 percent of sales) will always lead to decreased ROI. This is not a correct conclusion.

A examination of Figure 7 shows that the winning procedure would be to not exceed normal spending. That is a correct conclusion (generally)

---

*R & D as used here includes all research, development, and engineering activities carried out by the technical function of a company (or in our case by an SBU). It includes product development and design and is the expenditure that manufacturing companies now must report in their 10K reports.

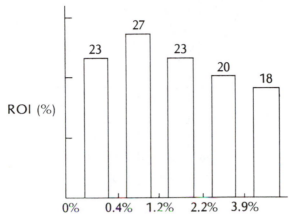

Figure 6   ROI vs. R & D/sales. By permission of the Strategic Planning Institute.

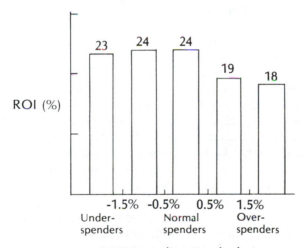

Figure 7   ROI vs. R & D spending. By permission of the Strategic Planning Institute.

if the firm does not have a major market share. If it does have a major market share, Figure 8 will disclose that overspenders (above normal) can succeed IF they have a high (above 28 percent) market share.

In view of the underspending advantage in its effect upon ROI, being a fast copier may not be a bad solution to new products if the leaders do

	Under-spenders	Normal spenders	Over-spenders
ROI (%)	-.75%		+.75%
Low	16	15	11
13%	22	25	18
28%	32	32	27
High			

Figure 8   ROI vs. market share and R & D spending. By permission of the Strategic Planning Institute.

not have a "mine field" of protective patents. Also, if the field is something like drugs or microchips, the firm that merely tries to copy is going to really have a hard time succeeding. Such firms have no choice but to innovate or become a "me too" supplier after patents expire.

However, as stated before, there is a big difference in the innovation efficiency of firms in a given field. The solution, is to learn how to be efficient in this area of activity. That is part of what the discussion in Part I regarding the design team composition was all about. High productivity in this area pays off, regardless of the business area involved.

Remember the Japanese consume about half the time required by U.S. firms between product conception and market introduction. Much of that advantage is generated by the design team composition. PIMSLETTER 29[20] speculated on the possibility of combining marketing and manufacturing into the product design time and the likely effect being a reduction in the lag between conception and market introduction. This speedup of the process would reduce the cost of R & D and reduce the lag in getting products to market, which also would help profitability.

The Japanese also have another advantage: they innovate as strongly in the process area as in pure product development, and this has a relatively quick payoff when compared to product innovation where the lag is about 4 years. Also the effect upon ROI per dollar spent is probably greater.

After all this, the reader may think that doing as little R & D as possible is being recommended; that would be incorrect. Remember that most companies and organizations start with a new product or service. Second, only continual innovation will keep most firms alive. As to the research results, remember the findings, but also remember the above statements and the basis for many of the comments.

There is considerable reason to suspect that the research, if (1) it was based upon firms using the proper design team integration, (2) it emphasized process research as well as product research, and (3) the firm used proper flexible and modular production and design techniques, would have produced considerably different results. For example U.S. R & D from product conception to introduction takes about 5 years, but the whole process can be accomplished in half the time (the Japanese have proven this fact). This would make our whole innovation process much more efficient, and this writer is certain that the if the SPI findings were based upon such results the findings would be significantly different. On the other hand, the findings would not eliminate most of the trends exhibited, only change their timing and impact.

D. Vertical Integration

Vertical integration usually pays off in mature and stable markets; otherwise it usually has a negative effect on corporate performance. The Japanese solve this problem with JIT inventory management. If one is in a high growth market, it is usually wise to delay integration attempts until the growth has receded and it begins to look like a mature market. Mature market does not mean it will evaporate, merely that it will not grow significantly—the product becomes "a cash cow." This is a fact well worth remembering.[18]

This does not negate nibbling at vertical integration by carefully examining the advisability of manufacturing certain parts currently being purchased when conducting "make-buy" studies.

E. Entry of New Competitors[22]

Business conditions identified in PIMSLETTER number 17[22] that were researched because they were believed to induce the entry of new competitors (a PIMS business was considered to have faced the entry of a significant new competitor if such a firm captured a 5 percent or larger share of the market) are as follows:

High industry growth rate tempts firms to "get in on a good thing." The probability of a new entry rises about 40 percent (from .23 to .33) if the growth rate is high (above 10 percent) rather than low. Actually, the researchers defined "probability of entry" as the *fraction of businesses* in the "data categories" which reported the entry of a major/significant competitor. When the growth rate is low (below 6 percent) about .25 of the firms experienced the entry of a major competitor regardless of profitability level. This rises to a high of .33 for high growth (10+ percent) and low profitability (below 10 percent ROI). Probibility is .38 for high

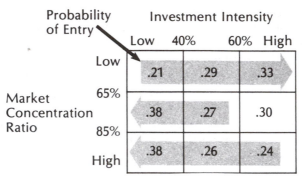

Figure 9   Probability of the entry of competitors based upon an analysis of investment intensity vs. market concentration ratio.

profitability (above 25%) and high growth. For profitability in the range
of 10–25 percent, there is very little *increase* in the probability of a major
new entrant when moving from low market growth to high market growth
(.26–.28).

High profitability of firms in a market obviously makes it tempting to
firms considering entry. They rationalize that they would be satisfied with
a little less profit, and so might capture a share of the market—ignoring
the fact that the other firm has the option to protect its position by
lowering price and decreasing its margin. SPI research indicates that the
probability does not go up significantly (only from .26 to .29 with firm
profitability above 10 percent) until the industry growth rate is about 10
percent or higher. Above 25 percent ROI and 10 percent industry growth,
the probability goes up to .38 (a rise of 46 percent from .26 to .38). The
same ranges of profitability and market growth apply to these data as to
that in the previous paragraph.

The next set of SPI research results to be examined involves "investment intensity" versus market concentration. "Investment intensity" is
defined as the percentage ratio of average book value investment to net
revenues. The "market concentration" ratio is defined as the combined
shares of the four largest sellers in the served market to the total market.
Probability of entry is defined as in the previous discussion of
PIMSLETTER number 17. What was examined here was the identification and evaluation of barriers to entry of new competition, and these
factors are what now will be discussed.

The Figure 9 matrix-type data display essentially reveals all of the
discovered facts. The PIMSLETTER contains four such displays and
three bar graphs, and is worth reading.

If you think that high investment levels will obviously discourage the entry of most competitors, you are partially correct. When the market concentration ratio is between 65 and 85 percent the probability of entry decreases from .38 to .30 as the investment intensity rises from below 40 percent to above 60 percent. Above a market concentration ratio of 85 percent, the probability of entry decreases from .38 to .24 for the same rise in investment intensity. For some reason it goes up with investment intensity if market concentration is below 65 percent, from 21 percent to 33 percent. SPI speculated that it could have been caused because the risks of entering investment intensive markets are reduced by lower levels of concentration. Also, an added advantage in this lower risk area might be the possibility of developing a quick competitive advantage via newer versions of plant and equipment. In any event, unless the new entrant can achieve a major advantage by virtue of its product design, efficient production, or an advantageous distribution system, the chances of failure or poor returns are very substantial.

The effect of advertising intensity (advertising and promotion as a percentage of revenues for the reporting business in each group statistic) versus the industry concentration ratio is the opposite of the statistics in Figure 9. Industry concentration, as defined by SPI, is the combined shares of the four largest sellers in the industry's Standard Industrial Classification group, at the four digit level. At a low industry concentration ratio, the probability of entry (regardless of advertising intensity) varies from .28 to .25. For an industry concentration greater than 70 percent, the probability of entry rises with advertising intensity—from .23 to .40.

Frankly, this author would summarize all the above into a simple statement that there is about a .23 to .38 chance of the entry of a significant competitor. But don't worry about it except to take the risk into account in your planning. The best way to combat any future entry is to act long before the event to drive down the planning firm's costs, further increase its market share, and develop an excellent reputation. Besides, that is what a firm should do in order to add market share and succeed in the business.

F.   Service Quality

Quality service does have an impact on corporate results. Service, however, can involve delivery, warranty, repair and maintenance, sales service, and other miscellaneous attributes such as advertising, promotion, financial condition, etc.

That having quality service is not a trivial attribute is indicated by a PIMSLETTER that says only 15 percent of the markets are service irrelevant in the customer perception of quality. Quality service can be a

powerful competitive weapon. PIMS found that the greater the importance of service, the higher the profitability of the businesses in it. It is
a way to counter foreign competition, and the inherent advantage is on
the side of U.S. firms who are home based in the U.S. The researchers
in this area are Philip Thompson, Glenn DeSouza, and Bradley T. Gale,
who completed their work in 1985.[23]

G.   Acquisition Factors and Variables

This topic was discussed in Chapter 3, mostly from the point of view of
how it appears to investors and the press. This discussion will look at the
process from a company perspective.

A company does not get very serious about acquisitions and divestitures
until it develops data on generally desirable criteria, such as blocking
factors, complementary businesses to acquire, and any other reasons for
engaging in such activities. These conditions should be discussed internally
and with the board of directors, who actually should participate in the
developing of specifications for the above matters.

Blocking factors are "go–no go" criteria that eliminate or very seriously
discourage considerations of candidates. These blocking factors (those
presented are representative of the planning firm's industry, market, technology, etc.) include items such as the following:

B1.   There is no "golden thread" of technical continuity.
B2.   The product(s) and/or marketing system does not match or comple-
      ment the company's products and/or markets.
B3.   The product may only be partially desirable since it does not support
      a finance division's customer lending operation since it is not a high
      ticket item that requires financing.
B4.   Sales potential must be over $25,000,000 annually for the acquisition
      to fit into the management scheme for the firm's other businesses.
B5.   The company does not exhibit the profitability and growth specified
      in acquisition criteria deemed desirable for an acquisition, and re-
      quires special study as to the reason for substandard performance
      and the possibility of improvement.
B6.   There is competition with major classes of current customers.
B7.   Labor history is terrible or very poor, such as many strikes or
      militant unionism.
B8.   Technology class and/or degree does not match "desired specifi-
      cations."
B9.   There is a strong probability of antitrust action.

It is also necessary to develop blocking factors if the firm is likely to be involved in divesting businesses or business lines. If such development is "left to the last minute," it is very likely that one or more important elements will be overlooked. The following are a few representative examples:

B1. High tangible and/or intangible assets that could be exploited even if the business is sold (in this case a "spin-off" might be worth considering).

B2. There is highly specialized equipment that discloses company trade secrets or know-how important to other company products.

B3. There will be a serious book value loss since the business involved is in trouble and the industry category is also at a low point.

B4. The plant involved is on strike.

B5. The product and/or business is involved in major government litigation.

Complementary attributes should be looked for in firms considered for acquisition. Some of these probably should be looked at from both views, those of the acquiring company and from the view of the acquired company—sometimes this sort of reverse look helps clarify the situation. Therefore, such attributes will merely be listed and it will be up to the acquiring firm to consider the mentioned "two way look."

C1. The acquisition will provide sales counter to the cyclical sales of the acquiring firm.

C2. Either firm could have a large cash position which would be advantageous.

C3. The potential acquisition provides help to the vertical integration of an important product of the acquiring firm.

C4. The firm to be acquired possesses needed technology (in this case the acquiring firm needs to be sure that the technology does not evaporate by having key technical people flee the firm).

Supplemental (somewhat indirect) factors could be exploited directly, or would reinforce or supplement existing factors or attributes of the acquiring company. Such synergism could result from factors such as the following:

S1. The firm being acquired will provide additional sales for subsidiaries or divisions since it uses acquiring firm's product(s) and/or will help produce sales of existing products because of its marketing strengths and/or customer categories.

S2. The manufacturing facilities can be adapted to produce needed parts or material for the acquiring firm, as well as continuing to produce for their existing customers.

S3.   The firm has a strong management team, some of which can be used in the acquiring firm.

S4.   Usable technological strength will be acquired.

It should be obvious that the lists were aimed toward product producing plants. Furthermore, all these lists can be expanded, especially by those who know the strengths, weaknesses, and other needs of the acquiring firm.

Also, it should be obvious that different, but similar, *kinds* of lists need to be prepared by firms such as those in "the service business" or merchandising. Moreover, it should be obvious that every acquiring firm needs to prepare a list of attributes that would be desirable in an acquired firm—a sort of wish list. Remember the story in Chapter 3 illustrating what happens when all of the above is not taken into account.

XIII.   PRODUCT PLANNING

New products and product planning are so important to the success and future well being of a company that this subject should be given considerable emphasis in strategic planning. If a product line is neglected or mismanaged, such as the U.S. automobile industries, the firm can become mired in BIG troubles. Our auto manufacturers neglected quality, advances in technology, and the desirable attributes of competing products, which caused them to lose 20–30 percent of the market. It might even get worse.[24]

Merely introducing new products is not a universal cure. There are some things that need to be taken into account, besides mere desire and the needs of the market. For example, research by Richard Morrison and Donald Tavel on the PIMS data base of SPI in PIMSLETTER number 28[25] rather clearly shows that while new product (NP) sales can improve market share, they at the same time depress ROI. The depressed ROI "negative" also relates to R & D effects on ROI which were discussed earlier. However, there are some things that can help negate the effect.

Since new products are to be discussed, it would be best to define how this term is being used. New products are *not* product line extensions or products with improved quality. They are such things as color TV when it first came on the market, or when a really new personal computer is introduced. They involve product development, product design, tooling a factory, starting production, establishing a distribution and marketing system, etc.

Furthermore, some definitions are required to understand the SPI research. The degree of new product sales versus existing (old) product sales is used here as a measure of new product (NP) sales. Relative market share (RMS) is defined as the planning firm's share of the market divided by the total shares accounted for by the top three competitors (note here that moving from an RMS of 40 to 44 represents a change of 10 percent).

ROI is always used by SPI as it exists before financial charges and taxes. It is obvious that NP sales improve market share. Below 20 percent new products versus existing products the effect on relative market share (RMS is defined as firm's share of market divided by the sum of the sales of the top three competitors) varies from 1.2 percent to 2.4 percent. Above 20 percent, the improvement is 5.6 percent.

New product sales do improve competitive position as measured by change in relative market share. On an annual basis, the effect of a change from 1 percent to about 10 percent of NP sales to total sales is about a 1.6 percent change in RMS. From 10 to 20 percent NP sales, the effect is a positive (+) change of 2.4 perecent in RMS. Above 20 percent NP sales the effect is +5.6 percent change in RMS.

Before deciding to act on the above statistics, you should consider that just 1 percent of NP sales equates to an ROI of 22 percent for the database being researched. Between 1 and 10 percent NP sales, ROI equates to about 25.5 percent. Between 10 and 20 percent ROI returns to 22 percent. Above 20 percent NP sales ROI is down to 18 percent. New product sales do depress profitability. Some firms can "live" with that statistic; others cannot do so because of other business attributes such as too much long term debt, inefficient processes, etc.

PIMSLETTER 15 presents the findings associated with the last three mentioned factors helping introduce NPs without incurring unmanageable handicaps. The findings are shown in Figures 10 and 11.

Note the robust change in RMS when the product line is narrow. Also note that ROI does not deteriorate greatly if the firm's product line is broad; in fact it *rises* substantially. These effects may be, so SPI researchers speculated, because such a firm would have marketing systems that could easily handle new products without incurring great additional marketing costs. Further, broad line firms tend to be known and respected in the trade and by customers.

SPI defines relative product quality (RPQ) as the percent of sales from high quality products minus the percent of sales from low quality products sold by the firm. Note that the effect on ROI is more positive for "high quality" (above 35 percent) than for a broader product line except that for NP sales above 8.2 percent (of total sales) the effect is about the same.

When Introducing a New Product,
a Broad Product Line Protects ROI

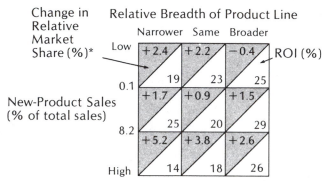

Figure 10   A broad product line protects ROI when introducing new products. The gain or loss in relative market share is shown in the shaded area, and the average ROI is shown in the clear area. By permission of the Strategic Planning Institute.

High Relative Product Quality
Reduces Cost of Gaining Share
Through New Products

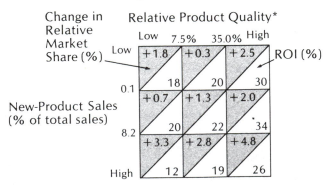

Figure 11   Effect of high relative quality on ROI and relative market share. Note that the figure illustrates the effect of initial/starting relative product quality (RPQ). See the text for a definition of this term. By permission of the Strategic Planning Institute.

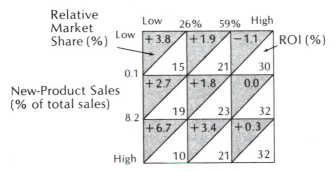

Figure 12   Results of having relatively low marketing expense/sales. This indicates that firms having a moderate level of marketing expense can attain an increase in market share and a stronger ROI than those who spend heavily on marketing. By permission of the Strategic Planning Institute.

However, the change in relative market share is substantially more positive in all of the specified measured ranges. Low quality is very expensive and this is clearly illustrated by the research results.

A strong relative market share does almost as well for protecting ROI as high quality, but it fails miserably in helping gain relative market share except when the relative market share is below 26 percent (the low measurement range). At the high end (59 percent and above), the three measurements for change in relative market share were (from top to bottom) −1.1, 0.0, and 0.3.

There is still one more research result that needs to be considered when developing strategy involving the introduction of new products. This is the effect of low marketing expense/sales, which is shown in Figure 12. The major characteristic of the results is that ROI is varies in a very small range over all categories of market expense/sales (the measures are "low–5%–10%–high"), from 21 percent to 26 percent.

Anyone involved in introducing new products should very carefully examine all the findings of SPI regarding new products! It should be obvious that the above findings taken from PIMSLETTER 28[25] clearly indicate what operational strategies should be pursued if it is at all possible or practical. If all are not possible, quality is probably the one most important factor. Also, if the planning firm can keep the marketing expense low (relative to the other "players"), it is well along the road to being in a position to benefit from new product development—assuming the design team and manufacturing recommendations were also accomplished.

There are some helpful suggestions about new products in *New Product*

Venture Management[1] and in the ASME paper,[21] but it would also be advisable to go to a major university library and call up "new product" books on their computerized library reference and catalog system. Then pull a representative sample of the books off the shelves and sit down and scan them. Many to most can be eliminated. Check out the others and copy the important parts for circulation among the concerned NP staff of the firm.

A.   The Product Life Cycle

Most products and many services experience a somewhat typical life cycle, although the length of the cycle varies greatly. Moreover, sales do not occur until considerable investment has been made. Initially sales rise very gradually.

As competitors enter the market, sales continue to increase, but at a slower rate. Once the market is essentially saturated, the sales begin to drop. Now the problem that results is that when production facilities are in full operation, each firm attempts economies, lowers prices, and tries to obtain a larger share of the declining market. This is when "competitive advantages" and other factors help. Prior to this problem's appearance, do build a reputation of selling a high quality product. Also, it would greatly help to be the dominent supplier.

Generally, at this stage it can be said that the product has started its demise. Yet up to here and beyond it *could be* a "cash cow" product. Obviously the product should be periodically examined for either revitalization through redesign or replacement based on new/improved technology, or considered for disposal. If it gets to the latter question, the firm needs to ask itself why it had not added related products and expanded the product line. Now is a poor time to attempt such an action.

As to the life cycle curve which typically shows sales versus time, profit margins tend to peak about half way up the curve and total annual profits tend to peak at the top of the life cycle curve. Since products do have a finite life cycle, the firm needs to keep introducing a stream of new and/or replacement products.

New product development and introduction is risky and this is why some companies tend to try to buy new product lines. This involves buying either part of a business line of a company or a total business purchase. Developing really new products requires a lot more than "throwing money at the problem" (never really works) or just asking "them" to create new products. How to do this is beyond the scope of this text.

XIV. CONCLUDING REMARKS

In case the reader is wondering when there will be a simple A,B,C procedure presented — there won't be. It is impossible to present a simple all inclusive procedure that everyone can use. What have been given are most of the obvious, and some not so obvious, factors that must be considered in planning. In addition the reader has been presented with guidelines and sometimes very specific advice and counsel as to what to do regarding a specific factor. Of course, there are many other possible factors than those mentioned. Only the most important could be covered in this writing.

Without knowing the industry, the company, the people, the competition, the customers, the distribution system, plant characteristics, etc., one cannot effectively plan. The external and internal environments must be researched, analyzed, and the planning data assembled, studied by all members of the team, and the team then assembled to plan the future of the firm.

From this point on the results depend upon how well the research is accomplished, how well it is analyzed, and how honest, perceptive, knowledgeable, and intelligent the planning team is in its actions. No one can do it for them. Others can merely assist and/or provide "expert" opinions and advice. Do seek expert advice if the "in house" team is deficient in some area of concern.

REFERENCES

1. D. W. Karger and Robert G. Murdick, *New Product Venture Management*, Gordon and Breach, Science Publishers, New York, 1972.
2. Delmar W. Karger, *The New Product*, Industrial Press, New York, 1960.
3. Mark Chussil and Sidney Schoeffler, *The PIMSLETTER Number 5; Pricing High Quality Goods*, The Strategic Planning Institute, Cambridge, MA, 1978.
4. Robert D. Buzzell and Bradley T. Gale, *The PIMS Principles*, The Free Press, New York, 1987.
5. D. W. Karger and R. G. Murdick, *Long Range Planning and Corporate Strategy*, Karger & Murdick, Troy, NY, 1977, 1978.
6. Patrick Conley, *Experience Curves as a Planning Tool*, The Boston Consulting Group, Boston, 1970. A good basic non-mathematical presentation.
7. Bruce D. Henderson, *The Experience Curve Reviewed* (Booklets I through V), The Boston Consulting Group, Boston, 1973, 1974, The series of five booklets is well worth obtaining, reading, and studying. Their goal is to aid planners in understanding and using the experience curve which represents the production progress function.
8. Delmar W. Karger & Walton M. Hancock, *Advanced Work Measurement*,

Industrial Press, New York, 1982. A technically and mathematically oriented presentation of learning curves (human learning and organizational learning), including the production progress function (the experience curves discussed in this strategic planning text represent the production progress function).

9.   Patric Conley, *Experience Curves as a Planning Tool*, The Boston Consulting Group, Inc., Boston, MA, 1970.

10. T. P. Wright, Factors affecting the cost of airplanes, *Journal of Aeronautical Science*, Feb., 1936.

11. S. A. Billion, *Industrial Time Reduction Curves as Tools for Forecasting*, University Microfilms, Ann Arbor, MI, 1960.

12. W. B. Hirschmann, Profit from the learning curve, *Harvard Business Review*, Jan.–Feb., 1964.

13. J. H. and Enuendy G. Perkins, Use of the learning curve to forecast trend of chemical prices, Am. Association of Cost Engineers, 10th Annual Meeting, Philadelphia, June 20–22, 1966.

14. R. R. Cole, Increasing utilization of the cost quantity relationship in manufacturing, *Journal of Industrial Engineering*, May–June, 1958.

15. F. J. Andress, The learning curve as a production tool, *Harvard Business Review*, Jan.–Feb., 1954.

16. J. E. Cohen, *Model of Simple Competition*, Harvard University Press, Cambridge, MA, 1966.

17. Sidney Schoeffler, *PIMSLETTER Number 11; Good Productivity vs. Bad Productivity*, Strategic Planning Institute, Cambridge, MA, 1978.

18. Sidney Schoffler, *PIMSLETTER Number 1; Nine Basic Findings of Business Strategy*, Strategic Planning Institute, Cambridge, MA, 1977, 1980, 1883, 1984.

19. Mark J. Chussel, *PIMSLETTER No. 13; How Much to Spend on R & D*, Strategic Planning Institute, Cambridge, MA, 1978.

20. David Ravenscraft and F. M. Scherer, *PIMSLETTER Number 29; Is R & D Profitable?*, Strategic Planning Institute, Cambridge, MA, 1982.

21. Delmar W. Karger, *Non Technical Considerations in Applied Research, Development, and Engineering Project Selection*, Published Speech given at A.S.M.E. Annual Winter Meeting, 1985, American Society of Mechanical Engineers, New York, Paper No. 85-WAMgt-1, 1985.

22. George Yip, *PIMSLETTER Number 17, Entry of New Competitors: How Safe is Your Industry?*, Strategic Planning Institute, Cambridge, MA, 1979, 1980.

23. Philip Thompson, Glen DeSouza, and Bradley T. Gale, *PIMSLETTER Number 33; Strategic Management of Service Quality*, The Strategic Planning Institute, Cambridge, MA, 1985.

24. Alex Taylor III, Why Toyota keeps getting better and better and better, *Fortune*, Nov. 19, 1990.

25. Richard Morrison and Donald Tavel, *PIMSLETTER Number 28, New Products and Market Position*, Strategic Planning Institute, Cambridge, MA, 1982.

III

MANAGING PER PLAN, MBO, AND PROFESSIONAL WORK STANDARDS

11

The Long Range and the Short Range Plans

Most of the important facts regarding strategic and operational planning have already been discussed. The remarks in this chapter will merely embellish what has been said, especially with regard to the actual planning sessions.

This chapter will be divided into two main parts. Part I will concern itself with long range planning and Part II will focus upon short range planning activities. Remember that the major benefits of planning are derived from the organization's agreement on the strategy and objectives of the firm. These must be reduced to written objectives and required actions, which will then serve as a guiding beacon for the firm. Finally, the firm must establish a system of guidance and control to assure achievement of plan objectives. Just having the plan achieves no tangible results in improving the performance of the firm.

I. MATTERS LARGELY PERTAINING TO THE LONG RANGE PLANS

The long range plans include both a strategic plan and a long range operational plan. The planning activities producing these plans will continue, as they are usually repeated every year. Over a 2 or 3 year time span these kinds of plans will change some of their objectives, occasionally eliminate one, and will add other objectives over the years—probably some entirely unrelated to prior plans. Naturally, the strategies in force will also be revised at times due to changing environments, and these, in turn, will require the establishment of new additional objectives. This is a normal occurrence and it in no way negates the value of the use of strategies, objectives, and major milestones to measure progress or the organization.

The financial plan largely represents the financial constraints of the system and is a measure and guide of the investment of the firm's financial resources.

The major strategies to be pursued should be stated at the front of the written planning document and should be coupled to the objectives required to implement the strategies. Each objective will require the establishment of milestones so progress can be measured, and corrective action taken if progress is inadequate.

Strategies essentially are based upon aspirations engineered down (by the planning process) to the realities of the external and internal environments—which naturally also include a consideration of the firm's resources.

The tactics required to achieve the milestones for each objective usually require the preparation of programs and tasks necessary to achieve the objectives and milestones. The programs need to be very specific for the first year in terms of tasks, subtasks, labor, materials, and returns. For the second year there is less detail and the items may be aggregated on a quarterly basis. For the third, fourth, and fifth years aggregations of labor, materials, expenses, and returns will likely be carried out only for milestones and for fiscal years. Naturally all of the second year material will be revised by the next planning cycle. If the strategies and tactics have not materially changed, the second year will be expanded as described for the first year and so on.

Work, performance, time, costs, and revenues are closely interrelated, and should somehow be illustrated so that these factors are understood by all planners. One method is to use a flow chart. With proper software, this could be accomplished on a computer in many cases. Often these relationships need to be developed over a 10 year period, especially if this is the time span of the long range plans.

The financial group should prepare separate detailed financial budgets, and pro forma P & Ls and balance sheet statements for the first 2 years. Beyond this point the material can be much less detailed. However, capital budgets and cash flow plans should be very carefully worked out and presented over the entire 5 year period.

Such a system of plans, that is, the interrelationships among an organization's plans, is shown in Figure 1. External development planning is

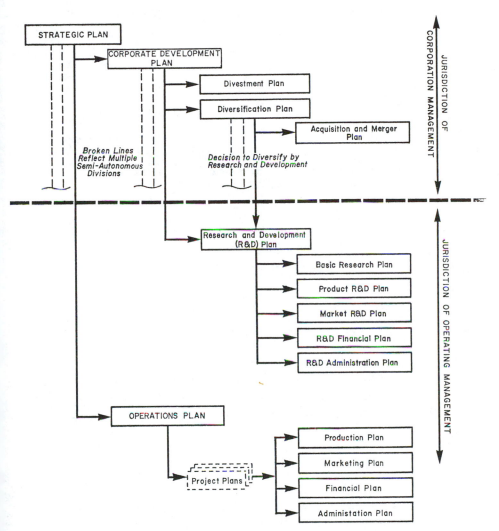

Figure 1   The system of plans. [1]*Long Range Planning and Corporate Strategy* by D. W. Karger and R. G. Murdick, published by Karger and Murdick, Troy, NY, 1977, 1978.

shown as the responsibility of top management. The development of internal growth and the operational plans are shown as the joint responsibility of top management and operating management. Naturally all such plans are subsidiary to the top level plans and should support and not hinder the achievement of overall strategies and objectives.

VOL. 1   Charter, basic mission of the company, values, statement
                by the President on LRP and responsibilities, organization
                for LRP, procedures, methods for measurement of performance.

VOL. 2   Environmental evaluation, potential opportunities,
                resources of the firm , profile of capabilities.

VOL. 3   Strategic objectives of the corporation as a whole,
                strategic objectives of divisions, subsidiaries, and
                functions.

VOL. 4   Long range plans: Corporate development plans and
                internal growth plans, organizational development plans,
                capital budgets, and cash flow plans.

VOL. 5   Divisional long-range plans, functional long-range plans.

Figure 2   Long range planning presentation.

The entire long range plan may be condensed into a single loose-leaf
notebook or distributed among several notebooks. The concept of multiple notebooks may facilitate keeping better control over the security of
the plans. This concept is shown in Figure 2.

A.   ESTABLISHING PROCEDURES, POLICIES, AND SCHEDULE

A procedure for the planning process should be established and dissemin-
ated. It should specify who does what and when to initiate, monitor, and
expedite the planning. The managers do the planning, but someone
also must establish each year's schedule and assist with the mechanics —
however, the planning director should also provide inputs to the planning
activity.

The creative part of long range planning is discovering "how" to achieve
the strategic objectives. Creative methods and means must be used for
analyzing the *strategic gap* and filling in the intermediate steps between
the present strategic posture and the new strategic objectives.

One of the largest parts of this procedure concerns the reporting techniques which permit easy visualization of the complexities of the final long range plan. Each company has to develop its own required unique procedures and report formats. No collection of these will fit all, or even most, organizations.

B.   Developing Milestones

Planners must start with the present strategic posture of the company in developing a set of strategic objectives. Naturally, this creates a gap, which must be bridged over time by establishing and achieving key intermediate goals and milestones. A milestone usually is a multifunctional goal. An example would be the functional combination required to create and launch a new product — engineering, manufacturing, marketing, finance/accounting, purchasing and legal activities. A market research project on a new product might also require such a combination.

Remember that product design teams must contain the integral members mentioned above, but the last three (finance/accounting, purchasing, and legal) often are parttime members. Engineering objects, even though the Japanese use it to reduce their time from product conception to the market to 50 percent below the usual U.S. time.

The construction of a new plant to expand production of a product could be classified as a milestone, even though it is primarily a goal of manufacturing, and secondarily of the financial organization.

Every time a major creation of new business/plant space or the rearrangement of the location of organizational units is involved, an attempt should be made to use this activity as an opportunity to relocate organizations and sub-unit organizations so that people who must frequently work and/or interact with each other are either intermixed or are located adjacent to each other. This nearness (close proximity) has a major beneficial effect upon performance that is dependent upon cooperation or where ideas and decisions must flow from one unit to another. It has been demonstrated that if individuals are to work together on projects or other organization endeavors, such activity is enhanced (made more effective and efficient) if they work in the same physical space — meaning that they can see and easily talk to each other. One management expert, Tom Peters, alludes to the above actions as "space management."

The relationship of milestones to strategic posture and strategic goals is illustrated by Figure 3, which admittedly is about a decade old as to specifics. However, it does illustrate the relationships.

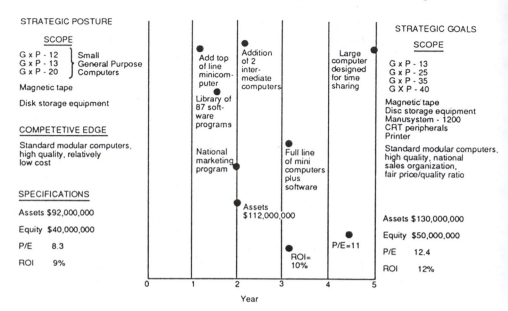

Figure 3   Milestones and their relationships with strategic posture and strategic goals. *Long Range Planning and Corporate Strategy* by D. W. Karger and R. G. Murdick, Karger and Murdick, Troy, NY, 1977, 1978.

C.   Developing Programs and Plan Resource Allocations to Achieve Milestones

The program required to achieve the overall company strategy starts with the identification of company strategies and then the objectives and milestones needed to be achieved in order to accomplish them. From there the program continues to the work and step breakdown illustrated below.

1. Establish milestones.
2. Establish basic division strategy.
3. Establish 5 year plans for the scope.
    a.   Product line definition.
    b.   Markets.
    c.   Price/quality product strategy.
    d.   Product line expansion, contraction, and innovation.
    e.   Milestones for the scope.
    f.   Financial plan for implementation of scope.
4. Program the development of competitive edge milestones for the 5 year plan.

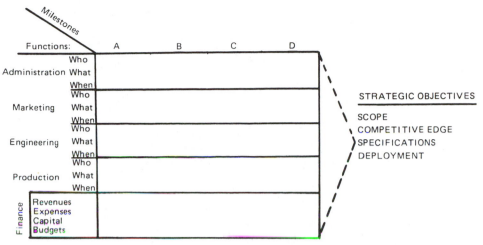

Summary Form for Implementation of Milestones

Figure 4   Relates the complex mix of milestones, objectives, responsibilities and work, with description of programs to achieve milestones. [1]*Long Range Planning and Corporate Strategy* by D. W. Karger and R. G. Murdick, Karger and Murdick, Troy, NY, 1977, 1978.

5.   Program for controlling risk.
6.   Program for achieving specifications milestones.
7.   Program for the deployment of resources to achieve scope, competitive edge, and specifications.
8.   Develop functional 5 year plans tied into the above programs.

Typical functional plans are those for:

1.   Administration.
2.   Marketing.
3.   Engineering and research.
4.   Manufacturing and production.
5.   Office systems.
6.   Development (natural resources, land development, financial package development, etc.) for various types of service industries.
7.   Facilities.
8.   Financial.
9.   Legal.

Each firm should develop standardized planning material, including forms and displays of information most suitable to its business and its

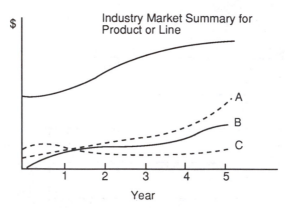

Figure 5   Product line summary chart, scope analysis. [1]*Long Range Planning and Corporate Strategy* by D. W. Karger and R. G. Murdick, Karger and Murdick, Troy, NY, 1977, 1978.

preferences. Figure 4 pulls together the complex mix of milestones, objectives, responsibility, and work. It will tend to expose gaps and overlaps. Figure 5 is a product line summary chart. Finally, a form for showing a summary of sales objectives by year is shown in Figure 6.

D.   Exploit the Future, Do Not Anchor to the Past

The proper approach to strategy development is to look at some point in the future and decide where one wants to be. Starting all the described tasks for developing strategies and long range plans from a past "base" or "the present" is a cruel trap since firms attempting this almost never arrive at the goals and objectives required for success. However, it is also true that *both* the "here" and the "future" must be considered in the firm's planning activity.

Just one more aspect of the last statement: This book was originally written as the two Germanys were preparing to unite. The event is now a fact and the U.S. now faces Germany as a potentially enormously strong competitor, as well as the EEC and Japan. East Germany had *very* low wages, but a well educated populace, and the combination may result in our strongest competitor nation.

II.   MATTERS LARGELY PERTAINING TO SHORT
       RANGE PLANNING

Short range planning is the detailing of the immediate-time portion (usually 1 year) of the long range plan. While short range plans may be

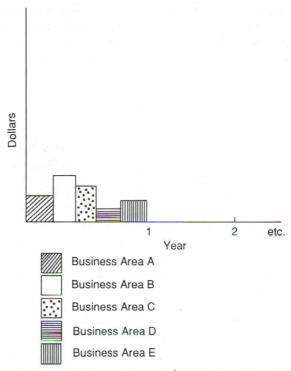

Figure 6   Summary of sales objectives by year. [1]*Long Range Planning and Corporate Strategy* by D. W. Karger and R. G. Murdick, Karger and Murdick, Troy, NY, 1977, 1978.

established for a firm's fiscal year if it varies from the calendar year, the plans really should be made to coincide with the calendar year since much valuable environmental planning data is presented on a calendar year basis. This includes economic and industry forecasts, which firms use in their planning. All of the related governmental material that is used in planning is on a calendar year basis. Moreover, tax considerations generally cause the fiscal year and the calendar year to coincide.

The short range plans provide the flexibility for a change in tactics within its broad strategic plan. They also tie together the various operational and functional activities into a unified system.

Subordinate to the functional plans are the departmental objectives and finally the objectives of the individuals in the various departments. Both professional and semi-professional employees may be guided and measured by the management by objectives (MBO) techniques, with or without an incentive program to reward excellent performance. However, since top managers claim they like incentives labeled as bonus payments, the same treatment can be used for all professional employees. It will boost performance as much as 20 + percent. MBO should really extend from the highest level of management to the individual professional at the operating level.

A.   Short Range Planning At The Corporate Level

Short range plans for the company must be established in consonance with the firm's overall plans for the organization. After these needs have been taken care of, then the other interests of subsidiaries, divisions, product lines, products, and sub-unit managers are considered. The short range plan consists of a system of activities which designate the specific objectives and responsibilities of each managed unit. The actual structure of this system of plans depends upon the organization of the company.

To help understand the above relationships, an example will be developed. Suppose that a firm is organized on a functional basis and that under scope, objectives, and strategy it plans to establish a new sales region in New York within 3 years. Also, current milestones have been established to (1) complete the design of new product NP15, (2) hire a sales manager, and (3) design and construct a 9500 square foot office building by the end of the current year. The functional departments obviously must perform many other regular tasks and continue normal operations.

The structure of a display of the mentioned milestones might be shown as in Table 1.

Each of the above objectives would be defined mutually by the appropriate functional manager and his superior. Each task would be one of several mutually established objectives for each manager under the MBO method — all as a part of the short range plan. Supporting descriptions of tasks, time schedules, and spread sheets for the various budget (month by month and for the year) would be prepared.

Again, the above is similar to many such cases. However, it is also likely that there will be variations in most firms.

Short range planning includes the development of methods of implementation of both top level strategies and the lower level strategies. Some typical subjects or areas that could involve the need for detailed short range plans are listed below. However, almost all of these items usually require board action before they can even be started. Therefore, it should be understood that the C.E.O. and his working top level team will usually gather data and make a presentation to the board for its

Table 1   Current Year Milestones Summarized

Function	Milestone 1	Milestone 2	Milestone 3	Functional costs
Engineering design	Design and engineering of NP15 ($82,500)	—		$82,500
Marketing		New sales manager, hire or promote, budget 1/2 year ($50,000)		$50,000
Manufacturing (industrial and plant engineering)	Equipment and tools, NP15 ($26,000)		Design and construct office building ($1,200,000)	$1,226,000
Accounting/ finance	Support and provide funds	Support and provide funds	Support and provide funds & equipment office building ($350,000)	$350,000
Purchasing	Support	Support	Support plus $\frac{1}{2}$ purchasing agreement ($13,000)	$13,000
Personnel	—	Support	Support	
Milestone costs	$108,500	$50,000	$1,563,000	$1,721,500

consideration. These are so important that they often are treated separately under strategic and operational long range planning.

Usually, such items are not voted upon during the presentation meeting, except for a somewhat routine item like authorization of a dividend payment. Furthermore, if the decision by the board is to go ahead, the items usually require extreme security measures. Such plans are therefore developed by a small but very competent team, often with the help of consultants. Such plans do not appear in the conventionally distributed planning books, except possibly as a generalized statement of intent to move in a particular direction.

This list of very significant and important items is now listed for the guidance of the planning director and top level planners:

1. Specific acquisitions and mergers.
2. Spin-offs and divestments.
3. Financial actions such as borrowing, increasing equity, purchase of

stock to reduce the number of outstanding shares, transferring of funds to or from subsidiaries, eliminating preferred shares, changing dividend policy, announcing a dividend, etc.

4. Establishment of a joint venture.
5. Creation of any subsidiary.
6. Major new product introduction, especially all those not closely related to existing product lines.
7. Reorganization of management structure.
8. Replacement or acquisition of major executives and important professionals.
9. Major decisions on, and implementation of, actions regarding company image, general corporate advertising, etc.
10. Restructuring the corporate board from a personnel or expertise view.
11. Design and implementation of a performance measurement and reward system tied to the planning process.
12. Implementation of a new (to the company) function such as a headquarters technical research and development laboratory, an overall new product management organization, etc.
13. Major decision making regarding the computer hardware and software.
14. Changes in the planning system, its major personnel, and its management.

The above is not an all inclusive list, but it could be helpful to beginning planners. There are many other similar items that could have been listed.

Item 11 indicates the creation of a reward system tied to plan achievement. This subject is covered in substantial detail in Part III of this book. However, it should be stated here that the establishment of a formal and specified *reward system* directly tied to plan achievement should be deferred until after (at least) the second year of long and short range planning.

There is nothing wrong with starting the MBO system (without a formal and specified reward) immediately after the *creation* of the company's first set of plans. Naturally, the possibility of increased salary for good performance is a part of a standard MBO system.

B.   Operational Short Range Planning

There are short range operational plans, just as there are long range operational plans. Both the short and long range plans are created or started by requesting each functional manager to work with his/her major staff and prepare a list of projects, including milestones, identification of major tasks, and specification of expected benefits.

The managers should be asked to concentrate on opportunities for improvement or the exploitation of opportunities. If any corporate strategies have already been identified that could affect any function, then functional managers should also include such items in their planning effort.

The correction of weaknesses must be included in the above list of projects. The same material as indicated in the above paragraph is needed. Of equal, and probably of greater, importance is the identification of projects related to the exploitation of strengths. The benefits can often offset costs associated with the correction of weaknesses.

Many of the short term actions identified by the function will likely be tactical in nature. For any important items, long or short term, managers should be asked to identify the significant milestones to be used for the measurement of progress toward the completion of the project.

The correction of weaknesses in each manager's organization was mentioned. It is necessary for the chief and a few top people to know the weaknesses, as well as the strengths, of each organizational element. However, in writing up and defining the purposes of the projects in long and short range plans that will be read by co-workers, projects and milestones should be defined in a way that does not disturb the firm's managers by exposing things *identified* as weaknesses.

Planning should not destroy the executive team; rather it should make it stronger. Elimination of weaknesses must be projected, but for the general inside corporate public such projects can be identified as building a stronger organization or as improving our ability to compete.

The execution of this phase of the planning cycle involves more than a list of projects, and all that will be said also applies to strategic and operational long range planning projects. Each project must be described (in writing) so that all the planners will be able to read the description and know what is to be acomplished. The time schedule must also be shown. It should define the "time frame" for all major events, milestones, and completion. Finally, some kind of cost-benefit analysis should be shown — it might even present some appropriate subjective data. Keep in mind that PERT techniques, Gantt charts, program manuals, and work breakdown material are all tools that can and should be used to organize and present the short and long range plans.

The Gantt chart format in combination with the use of logical identification symbols makes for relatively easy reporting of progress toward objectives and/or milestones — again this and the material below apply to both short and long range planning. If such reporting requirements are not established, the plans are essentially useless. By not requiring progress reports, management is signaling that it really does not care whether the plans are accomplished. If progress is not reviewed all the way "up the ladder" it too sends essentially the same message (we do not care too much). If reports and reviews are combined with pay for excellent performance toward plan/projects completion, then the IMPORTANCE message is greatly magnified.

Shortfall results should be discussed in detail with concerned individuals to ascertain why the plan was not achieved. In some cases it will not be caused by faulty execution, but by faults in the plan. In still others, unforseen events may have changed conditions, which require plan modification.

The frequency of checks on progress is at least partially organization dependent, hence there will be different schedules used by different organizations. However, the frequency must be often enough to assure continuing progress.

All planners in any type of planning session should be given the underlying material needed to do their job. In the case of short range plans, the applicable strategic and short-range planning materials should be distributed to all such operational planners well before a planning session. In some cases, it might be justifiable to withhold some ultrasensitive strategic material and present just that portion verbally at the planning session.

The planning director should see that the costs and benefits are summarized by the planning unit, both as to the totals involved *and* the cash flow. This analysis is also to be distributed to the planners before the formal short range planning session discusses this portion of such planning projects. Again, the same thing is needed for strategic and long range operational planning.

III.   AN OVERVIEW

While a big advantage appears to be gained by setting proper strategies and long term objectives in long term strategic and operational planning, actual results will be minor or insignificant if these are not implemented through the creation and use of proper tactics — which primarily relate to short range planning. It is the short term planning that determines what needs to be done during the year to achieve long term objectives as well as other short term required actions. Therefore, it can be said that both long and short term planning are of equal importance IF both kinds are accomplished. Only doing the short term planning or only the long term planning is no good.

Table 2   Steps in Long and Short Range Planning: Approximate Representation of the Iteration Experienced by Planners: Approximate Representation of the Iteration Experienced by Planners

	Initial goals	Analysis and prediction	Tentative goals	Feasible goals	Final goals
Objectives	1	2	3	22	29
Marketing	4	5	6	23	30
Finance	7	8	9	24	31
Engineering	10	11	12	25	32
Manufacturing	13	14	15	26	33
Facilities	16	17	18	27	34
Organization and staff	19	20	21	28	35

Often long range planning tends to be a bit exotic and intriguing to participants. Conversely, short range planning is hard work and requires great attention to detail. Many people do not like this aspect and will tend to be careless unless someone like the planning director carefully double checks items to make sure that all things have been properly considered, and reasoned decisions are made.

While it has been said before that short range plans are important since they help bring the long range into reality and also serve as the main standard for measuring performance against the plans, it seems that these facts often escape the understanding of many planners.

Both long and short range planning are iterative processes. If an overall goal or objective is conceived, the next step is to see what will be required by each of the firm's organizational elements. Moreover, strengths and weaknesses must be considered in relation to the tasks that each organizational element and/or individual must perform in order to attain the objectives. If this is properly executed it will be discovered that in many cases the original objectives must be modified because some organizational element or person can not meet the requirements.

Actually, the steps in the long and short range planning process almost always require several modifications of the first statement of goals or objectives. Planning is an iterative process that proceeds approximately as shown in Table 2. In some cases, what is discovered in the short range planning requires modification of one or more long range objectives. One final word of caution: just because of the previous statements, do not get the idea that it is only necessary to do short term planning. This is a sure way of reaping few to no benefits.

REFERENCE

1. D. W. Karger and R. G. Murdick, *Long Range Planning and Corporate Strategy*, Karger & Murdick, Troy, NY, 1977, 1978.

12

Achieving Plan Objectives and Attainment of Milestones (Specified Progress Points) through Performance Measurement Systems

I. INTRODUCTION[1,2]

Without performance measurement all planning activities are largely wasted effort. If there is no measurement of progress the plan will be "buried" in desk drawers and only dusted off when someone wants to know about it. In fact, if there is no formal feedback (measurement), how can one tell whether the firm is being managed in accordance with the plan? Moreover, there must be a resulting reward for good to excellent performance by the top executive group, especially by the C.E.O. Conversely there must be some sort of negative type response for unsuitable performance. If these aspects are missing it is a signal by management to the involved employees that plan objectives, milestones, and standards are nice — but not of much importance!

Aside from the importance to plan achievement, the proper establishment and application of job or performance standards for professional workers also produces as large (in many cases significantly larger) a positive economic impact on overall performance of the organization as does the establishment and application of standards for factory workers. This is in spite of the fact that the work standards cannot be nearly as precise or exact with respect to time or work content as the measurement of blue collar and clerical workers performing routine clerical tasks. Professional workers (engineers, scientists, managers, accountants, lawyers, etc.) tend to do more cerebral work and the main difference will likely be the degree and kind of education.

It must be recognized that for the kind of workers just described, performance against their work standards must be judged over a long term — 6 to 12 months. Measurements over a shorter term would not be meaningful in the vast majority of such cases. Only for a few less important standards can meaningful measurements occur over a shorter period, such as 3 months.

That the work of professionals needs to be measured and performance against such standards evaluated is attested to by the explosion in the number of such workers and the associated salary and support costs to almost all kinds of business firms, especially in manufacturing firms. Moreover, one of the functions of management and of managers is to control. No one can control anything or anyone unless there is a measurement (in our case, of the performance of knowledge/professional workers) that indicates what *kind* of control (and how much) is required. In addition, there is still one more important reason for measuring the performance of managerial and professional workers. These people have such a large effect on the performance of the organization that this really should be the overriding reason for measurement and control.

The above remarks emphasize the fact that performance standards in a typical factory or office (all kinds of offices) are established for only one reason — economic gain through increased and/or better worker performance. For example, earlier in this text we cited numerous reasons why business firms need to plan and run the business via the plan. In the case of top management (especially true in this area) they may not work harder, but if they make better use of their knowledge and skills to achieve plan objectives and milestones, the performance standards and possible associated financial incentives will have been worth all the trouble and expense involved. In the professional area, one is not so much interested in how hard one works, but in the quality of the needed output.

The approximate average performance of *direct labor employees* without good (engineered) standards is about 75 percent — meaning that the performance *before* standards were established is 75 percent of what the standards specify as 100 percent. When merely measured against standards, performance goes up to 86 percent (on the average). This represents a 14 percent gain in direct labor productivity for a very minor cost, the establishment and use of standards and making them known to the workers. In very well managed firms there are some that achieve 100 percent performance (or very close to it) without financial incentives — but this is *very* difficult to achieve since it requires shop foremen to continually being "on top" of the situation. With "one for one" direct labor incentives the performance rises to 120+ percent when the usual low task standards are used. The "one for one" incentive pay means that for each 1 percent above the performance standard the worker is paid 1 percent above his or her basic pay rate — some firms begin such payment at 95 to 97 percent of standard.

One other somewhat related thought: Ordinary office workers (typists, clerks, computer data entry operators, etc.), without proper standards (these can be ordinary engineered work standards), only perfrom at about 70 percent of standard, but with standards their performance matches that of direct labor.

While most readers understand the great benefits to the company by the above indicated performance improvement, some will wonder what *large* benefits go to the company since the *labor cost* per piece produced will be the same. Twenty-five percent greater production is possible in the same space, with the same people, with less equipment, and less money will be spent on employee benefit payments of all kinds since more new people will not be required. If the additional production cannot be utilized, then some workers can be eliminated until sales increase — also in this case it is possible that some equipment can be "idled." Then, in this latter case (where the excess 25 percent production is not needed) when sales increase no new equipment need be purchased, no factory additions are needed, and the employees like the chance to earn more money. If sales call for *greatly* increased production, the tangible benefits are even greater since one often does not need more building space and/or new machinery (and if so, 25 percent less than with a daywork payment scheme).

The vast majority of time and motion study standards are of the so-called low task standards, as are all the standards created by the use of the internationally used predetermined time system Methods-Time Measurement (this system only applies to manual work, for machine time the engineer must use a stopwatch or its modern computerized equivalent).[1,3] Actually the worker performance figure in these situations where a "one for one" (percent) incentive system is being used is 115–135 percent of "standard." Obviously the average incentive performance might reach 130 percent of standard in some cases. High task standards are based upon an *incentive performance pace* of about 120 percent when using a low task standard. This means that 100 percent performance of a worker approximately equals that of a worker performing at 120 percent of a low task standard.

Both of these standard concepts essentially exist because of *historical* developments (see *Advanced Work Measurement*[1] and *Industrial Engineering Terminology*[3]). With high task factory worker standards, the incentive system begins paying on a "one for one" (percent) basis at about 85–90 percent of standard so as to encourage the workers with earned incentive pay since workers cannot *greatly* exceed 100 percent performance against such standards (like 125–130+ percent with low task standards). The BIG thing to note is the great increase in performance over standard if excellent performance is significantly rewarded.

For a full discussion of low task and high task (high task is not applicable to professional work standards) see *Advanced Work Measurement*.[1] One other attribute of work standards is that they require maintenance (updating), since workers (without the help of management) will improve on the work place and work routine so that they average about 2–3 percent per year — think how far a job standard would be at the end of 10 years, about 25 percent too low for the job as it then exists. Many plants install such a system and then abandon it because they failed to maintain it properly, a not so smart action.

About 80 percent of this country's salespersons work under some form of incentive pay. Most C.E.O.s and senior officers of corporations receive some form of bonus — a payment that boards of directors allude to as incentive pay for good performance. In fact, many other high level managers receive bonuses for supposedly excellent performance. Even 30–40 percent of the USSR's managers have been receiving such incentive bonuses for good performance for several decades.

Most of the mentioned bonus payments, not sales incentives, are wasted because no *meaningful* (measurable) performance standards have been established. Corporate executives *should* work against meaningful objectives that will lead to future corporate success. These objectives can only be discovered and defined, especially for upper levels of management, through proper planning as defined in this text.

On a personal note, this author will say that when such standards are first developed and used for the C.E.O., the situation has a tendency to "scare the wits out of a person." The author knows because it happened to him. Yes, he did achieve the stated objectives.

II. PROFESSIONAL WORKER PERFORMANCE STANDARDS

Professional workers, individually and as a group, have a far greater effect upon the success of an organization than direct labor or other lower level employees. Therefore, it is also likely that an increase in their performance level will have a synergistic effect that compounds the benefits.

Of equal importance is the fact that if one does not have objective and measurable standards against which to judge performance, then this portion of the organization is sure to be out of control much of the time. Moreover, it often will be headed in wrong directions.

It has been mentioned that work performed by manual workers produces an immediate result that can be examined for volume produced and for defects caused by errors. The same holds true for *routine* office work. However, when measuring the work of professionals and many semi-professionals, the time span of the measurement must be lengthy since the effects of the actions of the workers often is 3 or many more months into the future. Sometimes, it is even years into the future. Moreover, the effect of day to day actions can be cumulative, and such actions could negate prior long term good actions — even though they produce short term profits.

This is why it is so important to identify good long term actions and why it requires the kind of planning previously described. Furthermore, this is why it is important to detect whether the firm is being run to attain the plan objectives or whether it is merely exploiting short term opportunities, which is what most U.S. companies do. Also, this is why the Japanese beat us.

As to performance standards, the long term actions obviously must be broken down to measurable steps (milestones) leading to the ultimate objective. Measuring output 2 or more years ahead is useless. This is why performance (progress) standards must be developed that permit measurement during the year ahead — preferably within 3 to 6 months. Such short term components (minor milestones) do exist, they just must be identified. Some milestones may require 9 to 12 months to detect progress. At all these intermediate measurement points the final result usually cannot be discerned. These facts complicate professional work standards, including those for individual performers such as engineers, scientists, technical salesmen, auditors, etc.

Many organizations that fail, do so because of poor professional worker performance — by their managers. However, other individual professionals have also caused the demise of an organization. The engineer that designs a deficient new product can produce the same bad result. Organizations should do everything possible to obtain top performance from all professional workers through proper planning, combined with the establishment and use of a proper and meaningful MBO program.

The last statement should make it clear that organizations should provide opportunities for further training and education — currently the half life of what professional knowledge has been learned is between 3 and 5 years, meaning that half will be worthless and/or forgotten in about 4 years (it used to be 5 years, but knowledge generation has been increasing at a faster rate).

The long range planning will not initially produce many measurable objectives or milestones. However, detailing the steps involved in a long term objective, if properly done, will produce an adequate number of measurable points. These then can be used to detect progress toward objectives — making performance measurement possible.

The top corporate long range plan will not produce many measurable objectives or milestones (measurement points) for anyone but for those in the top management group. However, the functional, divisional, subsidiary, and departmental *long range* goals and objectives, when detailed, will contain many measurable progress points (milestones) that will appear in the goal/objective statements for the year ahead for lower level managerial and some non-managerial professional workers.

The above means that the manager of other managers and/or individual professionals needs to check progress against objectives, goals, and/or milestones at least every 3 to 6 months, with a major review at the end of each year. Actually, the reviews can be accomplished on almost any schedule, but each year end performance review should happen at about the same time. Moreover, there should be a mid year review.

Other facets of professional work measurement must include a recognition of the fact that it deals with a very complex output, an output which has an important impact upon the organization. Therefore, one must also look beyond the obvious results, since factors such as the following affect the results achieved:

1. Complex mental processes.
2. Motivation.
3. Personalities, that of the performer and of those with whom he/she works.
4. Objectives, which must be very specific and measurable. They normally are not present unless an excellent MBO program accompanies the proper planning activity.
5. Knowledge, usually consists of many varieties and classifications. The quality of this attribute must be judged by educational records, professional achievements, speeches, articles, patents, etc.
6. Political aspects of the job, external and internal. External politics can change the business climate so that there must be significant adjustment of plans. Again, internal politics can adversely affect progress, just as proper use of internal politics can speed up progress.
7. Social impacts. Almost every day one hears or sees the effect of environmental factors that affect corporate performance. The same is true of any adverse or beneficial impacts that the firm has on any

element of our society. How the firm assists public education or some other similar public activity might be beneficial or detrimental to the firm.

8. Learning experience of the firm is beneficial. The more experience a firm has producing a product means costs *should* be significantly lower than those of less experienced competitors. The greater the job experience of the individual, the better should be his/her performance.

9. Government regulations, those of our government and those of governments in the international market with which the firm is involved, directly and indirectly.

10. Moral implications, internal to the firm or external to the firm.

11. Intelligence. One could argue that managers and other professionals should have the intelligence necessary to make rational decisions in most cases. Excellent managers produce decisions that are *consistently* good (based upon their effects).

12. Perceptions. Obviously these can cause effects, both beneficial and harmful.

13. Economic changes in the countries affecting the firm's results.

14. War, riots, mob actions, and many other such factors can cause changes in the performance of the firm and of the individuals.

These factors apply to the professional worker being measured and they also often apply to those affected by the actions of the measured worker. Considering all of the above, it should be obvious that any professional worker performance standards will be at least somewhat imprecise.

Based upon all the facts stated, the reader may decide that there is no way to win in view of all the variables. This would be an incorrect decision, since there are countless examples of superior performing professionals ranging from C.E.O. down to individual professionals. Just look at the records. Most readers know some such people who always perform at a superior level and some who are often failures or poor performers.

Many top C.E.O. types go from one company to another and always turn in a superior performance. It is somewhat like teachers in a school, college, or university. We all have experienced the superior teacher who always turns in a superior performance whereas others are always poor performers. In all kinds of organizations, the poor performers must be identified and encouraged to change their performance, and if they do not do so, the firm should try and eliminate them. Demoting them does not work satisfactorily. The good performers should be rewarded so they are happy and do not leave, and should be promoted when the opportunity arises. Without the help of good performance standards it is often impossible to identify the good from the average. The good performers can be identified through the use of good standards.

III.   MANAGEMENT BY OBJECTIVES (MBO)[1]

Before beginning this discussion, the author suggests to readers that they should read a short and excellent history of MBO, namely R. G. Greenwood's "Management by Objectives: As Developed by Peter Drucker, Assisted by Harold Smiddy," *The Academy of Management Review*, 1981.[4]

About the only useful measurement of progress involves the setting of meaningful and important objectives or goals (for professional work), which then must be expressed in measurable terms with regard to both the content of the goal and the time required to attain its completion. Such MBO goals must be identified and defined by the worker with his/her superior. These are then used to measure worker performance. Goals established by the supervisor and arbitrarily imposed upon the professional will NOT work.

Pragmatically, MBO goals must be established at three levels:

1.   The top executive level who are the prime movers causing the attainment of the corporate long and short range objectives.
2.   Functional, divisional, subsidiary, and departmental long and short range objectives. Here the prime movers usually are the upper level managers, but there are many milestones which apply to lower level managers and in the goals of individual professionals.
3.   Objectives and goals for each professional.

All lower level goals must be in consonance with and supportive of higher level goals. They also must not be in opposition to the welfare of the organization.

The overall organizational goals are primarily used to measure the performance of the C.E.O. and C.O.O.

The functional goals are primarily used to measure the performance of the functional managers.

The goals for divisions, subsidiaries, departments, and those of special programs are primarily used to measure the performance of the relevant managers.

Naturally, the goals for individual performers are used to measure their performance. Generally, the goals and milestones will consist of one or more of the individual goal segments illustrated in Figure 1.

Each manager should meet individually with each professional and

Goals related to organizational objectives	Goals related to functional, divisional, and/or subsidiary goals	Goals related to departmental goals	Goals only indirectly related to the welfare of the organization	Goals not related to the organization—private goals that often are not expressed before the individual performer's supervisor

Figure 1   Possible segments of an individual performer's goals. Taken by permission from D. W. Karger and W. M. Hancock, *Advanced Work Measurement*, Industrial Press, Inc., 1982.

semi-professional employee under his/her supervision and *help* them develop goals and milestones for the year ahead. The emphasis should be on *help*, since the manager should not set the goals and milestones for the employees. If it is perceived that a goal suggested by an employee is not suitable, then the reason for such unsuitablility must be explained in terms that the employee can understand and accept.

Goal negotiations and their establishment as goals are not between equals, a factor that can become a big handicap. One is the boss and the other is a subordinate. This is a *weakness* of MBO programs, and strong efforts must be made to neutralize the problem. Some managers and workers never seem to have problems, while the reverse is also true. The head of this program might want to call in an experienced expert to provide training assistance in an afternoon meeting.

Immediately after goal negotiations, one person should record "the understanding" in writing. It is suggested that the employee be asked to write up the goals and milestones upon the completion of their verbal development. These will tend to come back somewhat "fuzzy." However, a little further discussion and compromise by both parties should make it possible to finalize them to everyone's satisfaction.

There are a number of reasons why some employee suggested goals must be indicated as not being satisfactory. However it is necessary for the supervisor to discuss the matter and provide an acceptable explanation. The usual reasons are:

1. A goal that is either impossible to achieve or probably impossible to achieve within 1 year. Specified goals or milestones should be achievable with a reasonable expenditure of energy within 1 year — especially during the first year of a new MBO program. Here it is vital to the ultimate success of the plan that all goals or objectives be achievable without excessive effort, at least during the first year.
2. The goal is really not a goal because it is much to easy to achieve.
3. A proposed goal is in opposition, totally or partially, to one or more

of the company's overall corporate, functional, divisional, subsidiary, and/or departmental goals.

4. A goal is contrary to the best interests of the organization. Examples would be to get another job, or get a higher rated job in another company. This kind of goal is acceptable from a personal point of view, but it is not acceptable as an MBO goal.

It is important that the manager and the employee adequately cover the employee's work area responsibilities in setting goals.

That all goals should be stated in measurable terms cannot be overemphasized. A later subtitle of this chapter will discuss how this can be accomplished.

Secure agreement of all top executives as to a suitable starting date for measuring MBO achievement — all goal measurement should start at the same time. Almost always this should coincide with the starting date for the strategic and operational/tactical plans. Under no circumstance should there be a difference greater than 30 days.

It is usually found that functional, divisional, subsidiary, and departmental managers are essentially measured by short range goals (a number of these could be milestones in the long range plans) and only to a minor degree by top level overall long range goals. This is also true for C.E.O.s and other top officers. When such goals are "pure" short range goals, that is a wrong choice of goals, especially for the top level staff.

The short term emphasis in U.S. firms was extensively discussed in Part I of this text. This is why U.S. firms have generally failed to compete successfully with the long term oriented firms, such as the Japanese firms. The short term emphasis has been promoted by the bonus system for executives, which is not "tied" to long range plans. It has promoted job hopping, neglect of product development, as well as neglect of investment in manufacturing equipment, etc.

IV. STARTING THE MBO PROGRAM

MBO should be started after the first set of strategic and operational plans has been developed. During the process of educating the planners the concept of establishing standards for measurement will have been discussed. Also, it would be logical to have at least mentioned the MBO program and how it would tie into plan objectives and milestones. Furthermore, the reason for MBO's establishment and how it generally would work should have been explained to the main planning team and to all of the operational planners. This group should have also been told that MBO would not only help measure plan progress, but that it would help each professional gain a better understanding of what the company expects in the way of job performance.

With the above as the "background," the logical next action is to formally announce the start of MBO. An informative memo describing MBO's salient features should be distributed to all concerned personnel. In the case of this memo, while it should be personally addressed to the employee, it should be personally given to the employee by his/her supervisor, who *also* should indicate his/her availability to talk about the matter with the employee. It might even be worthwhile to hold a short meeting, make the announcement and statement, and then pass out the memos.

Concurrently with the preparation of the memo, all managers and supervisors who will be expected to negotiate MBO standards for the year ahead should be gathered into a meeting and receive a presentation of the MBO program that will be started. Otherwise they will not be able to answer questions from their employees.

This, in turn, brings forward another matter. The program to be started is NOT going to be a standard MBO program that centers attention on standards involving motivation, problem-solving, administrative-ongoing, and personal matters. It is why an MBO expert experienced in the original MBO format cannot be hired to make this presentation. However, practically all of the original MBO procedures can and should be used, except those concerning the kind of standards to be developed.

The standards for each employee will be personal to that employee and will concern no one else — except in the larger sense that plan objectives and milestone *may* be involved. As to classifying the objectives, almost any logical standard applying to the employee and the job is acceptable as long as the welfare of the firm will be enhanced by its attainment.

One could state that an employee's MBO standard could involve (1) plan objectives and milestones (all of these MUST be listed as an objective), (2) job improvement objectives (those that are doable and where progress can be measured), (3) objectives aimed at enhancing the knowledge and skills of the employee relative to his/her job or future job with the company (such as completion of educational courses, attendance at professional meetings, presentation of professional speeches, attendance at conferences and associated educational programs, etc.), and (4) more personal but still job related objectives such as developing a better "presence," becoming skilled as a public speaker in order to better serve the company in job situations or to represent the company better to the community, learning how to "make friends and influence people," etc.

Having accomplished the provision of training to all managers and supervisors who will be negotiating "standards" with employees, it is time for each supervisor and manager to call their *professional* employees into a small group meeting and provide them with the same information. At this point, this discussion is back to the second and third paragraphs of this sub-section of Chapter 12.

The establishment of such standards should not be overemphasized by rushing everyone through the process in a matter of few days. However, neither should the gradual attainment of having established an MBO standard for everyone involved be delayed for several weeks.

In each individual meeting the employee should be made to feel comfortable, he/she should be provided with writing materials if these were not brought to the meeting, and the employee should be encouraged to make a complete set of notes — telling the employee that he/she will be expected to draft the "standards" for the year ahead and beyond (some may extend to several years, like earning a graduate degree). If some aspect of the employee's performance has been outstanding, this surely should be mentioned early in the meeting. During the identification of "standards," the supervisor needs to also mention any aspect of the employee's performance that needs improvement and a "standard" involving it should be established.

The employee should be told to make sure the following suggestions are followed in his/her writing of the standards:

1. Start off with an action verb.
2. Identify a single key measurable result for each objective.
3. Give the exact date on which each objective is to be achieved.
4. Identify costs, time, materials, and any other important attributes.
5. List only objectives that can and are primarily controlled by the employee.

Before the employee returns to review his/her standards, be sure that copies have been typed and provided to the supervisor and the employee. A meeting between the employee and the supervisor should occur within a few days of the distribution of the copies. The personnel department may also want copies for each employee's official file.

Additional material on MBO can be obtained from G. Morrissey, *Management by Objectives*,[5] and J. B. Lasagna, "Make Your MBO Pragmatic," *Harvard Business Review*.[6] However, one should not fail to follow the precepts discussed in this chapter, and especially under this subtitle, if one wants to optimize one's chances for success.

V.   WRITING MEASURABLE OBJECTIVES

The material which follows is aimed at producing standards for managers and high level employees. However, the material will also help regarding the development of standards for ordinary employees.

It is difficult to phrase goals and objectives in measurable terms. However, it can be done if one gives the job enough thought and consideration.

First, it is suggested that the individual objectives, especially those for the non-managers, be written under categories such as:

1.   Related to the overall organization and organizational unit objectives.
2.   Related to specifically assigned responsibilities.
3.   Problem solving.
4.   Related to administrative and other ongoing matters.
5.   Motivation (as related to prior job performance).
6.   Professional development.
7.   Personal (but related to the job).

While the above suggestions are logical and should be followed, there is a task crucial to ultimate success that must precede the use of these categories. This is the identification of what the *real contribution* of the job is toward the success of the organization — what one really gets paid for doing. It must be done before trying to *establish* MBO objectives with the employee. Without this knowledge one not only cannot write meaningful measurable objectives, but the job incumbent, without this understanding, will not make a proper selection of goals. He/she will therefore fail to make a proper contribution to the organization's success, and will also fail to optimize career success.

Few people can give you a good answer if you ask them what they get paid for doing. The ordinary response is "I run a turret lathe" or "I manage the quality control function" or "I am the commercial loan officer of the City National Bank," etc. These are all functional statements of little real guidance to the man or woman trying to write significant measurable objectives.

In order to *begin* to discover the real contribution of a job one must ask a series of questions.

1.   Why do you get paid, and I do not want an answer like nursing, engineering, or accounting?
2.   Why should the organization really pay you?
3.   How can they afford to pay you? Why?
4.   How does the organization make money from what you do?

Recently this kind of thinking was applied by the author to the proper definition of a vice president and commercial loan (C.L.) manager of a substantial bank. First, he described his job as "making loans." Next as "making commercial loans." The next definition offered was "investing the bank's money." All of these were *functionally* oriented job descriptions. More questions brought forth the fact that about 65 percent of the bank's revenue came from the C. L. activity. That the C.L.M. and his staff adjusted loan interest rate to what he thought they could get and what rate would compensate the bank for the risk involved. This meant that the business(es) of the potential borrower had to be analyzed. The actions of competitive banks also had to be taken into consideration. Additionally, the C.L.M. and his staff had to go out and solicit business. Naturally, losses had to be kept to a minimum, and this sometimes required helping a borrower solve a serious business problem. Only now could one begin to formulate a valid definition of the C.L.M.'s job.

> "The Commercial Loan Manager is responsible for marketing the banks services, especially the Commercial Loan Services, so that the function brings in 65 percent (adjustable to each particular case) of the bank's revenue through investing the bank's funds in loans to professional people and commercial firms without incurring losses in excess of good acceptable practice (losses should not exceed X percent of loan revenue)."

Guidelines for the actual writing of measurable objectives are as follows:

1. Start with an action verb.
2. Identify the most logical measurable result for each objective — a result that gives a fair indication of the degree of attainment. Sometimes, two or more results must be used.
3. Identify the exact date each objective is to be achieved.
4. Costs, time, material, and manpower required for each objective are next identified.
5. Relate performance or improvements in terms of past history, company standards, and/or professional standards if at all practical.
6. Finally, only list objectives that are controllable by the individual.

A few examples may help the reader to more fully comprehend what is meant by the foregoing material. We will start with some middle-level managerial positions and end with an engineering worker level position. In each case measurability will be kept to the fore.

Our first example concerns the quality control manager. Logically he might be given as his objective "to achieve the number one quality reputation for our company within our industry." It sounds good, but how would one be able to measure such an objective? A rational and measurable substitute could be the following:

The desired quality reputation for our company will be achieved when the quality control function achieves the following:

1. Field service calls do not exceed X percent in 1 year and Y percent in 2 years.
2. Plant reject rate is reduced to no more than X percent in 1 year and Y percent in 2 years.
3. Warranty costs do not exceed X percent in 1 year and Y percent in 2 years.
4. Rework cost is less than X percent of manufacturing cost in 1 year.
5. The company's product is rated in the first position in *Consumer Reports* within 2 years and rated acceptable within 1 year. (Or, for an industrial product the statement might read "The company's product line has an operational experience or predictable life-reliability rating, or guarantee, at the end of the first year that is above the average for the industry and equal to or better than the best at the end of the second or third year.")

The first objective and also several of the others involve more than the quality control function. Product design by the engineering department is such a factor, since the design obviously will affect field service calls. However, a good quality control manager and quality control activity will identify design weaknesses, document the involved problems and their effects, and through "pressure" on engineering get the design deficiencies corrected. In addition, public distribution of these objectives by management will also serve notice to engineering and other functional managers that this is the official "word."

In like manner, poor manufacturing could be a major contributor to excess field service calls, even with a good inspection department operation. Again, deficiencies can be properly documented and "pressure" used to bring about corrective action.

Purchasing's selection of poor vendors again could be the cause of or a contributor to excess field service. Again corrective action can be initiated by quality control.

The objective is logical and rational if management "signals" by their actions and statements that they do want to achieve the desired objective. Naturally, the quality control manager will have to be knowledgeable, courteous but firm, objective and not subjective, cooperative and not obnoxious, etc. It *is*, properly, a measure of the quality control manager's performance if top management gives him or her reasonable support when he or she acts properly.

Objectives 2, 3, and 4 have similar complicated relationships involved, and indirectly so does the fifth objective.

There would logically be other objectives for the quality control manager. Some possible additional ones could be the following:

Obtain an assistant capable of "taking over" the quality control function by the end of the second year.

With the industrial engineering department develop sufficient engineering competence to "counterbalance" the egineering department.

Encourage learning and professionalism in quality control staff. This will be evidenced by X percent of the quality control staff being active ASQC members and Y percent having participated in quality control related to in-company training courses or in such an off-hours university course by the end of the year.

Complete personal work toward an MBA within the next two years, with emphasis on marketing and finance — as a preparatory step toward general management (incumbent already had an engineering bachelor's and a master's in applied mathematics).

One final example will be given for a project industrial engineer (PIE), but only with regard to the more generally recognized position attributes (as for the C.M. position).

The PIE's job is to provide all required IE services so that the manufacture of a new product proceeds on an optimal basis within the cost centers served by the PIE without delays, with costs that will not exceed the department's estimate by more than 6 percent, and with rework held to no more than 10 percent for the first 6 months of operation. This will deemed to be essentially accomplished satisfactorily during the year ahead when the project enters its manufacturing phase if the following are achieved:

1. Processes are written for each required operator position and "in place" before the operator begins the job.
2. Tooling, jigs, fixtures, etc., are all designed and in place before the work commences — and debugging is accomplished without incurring chargeable production loss in no more than 10 percent of the cases. Also such losses do not cause the production schedule to be missed or that the excess manhours involved do not exceed 500.
3. Engineered labor standards in accord with company policy are set via Company Standard Data and MTM before production starts, except where prior data do not permit determination of the process time.
4. Work is accomplished within ±10 percent of the tooling-equipment budget.

5. Labor manhours are within ±10 percent of the labor estimate.
6. All chargeable expenses to the estimated first lot production do not exceed 6 per cent of the total costs involved in the IE's pervue.
7. Cost reductions identified and approved prior to the end of the first year's production will amount to at least 15 percent of the manufacturing cost.

VI. INCENTIVE SYSTEMS FOR MANAGERS AND PROFESSIONALS

Frankly, there are few books or articles that deal in whole or in part with this subject, partly because managers and professionals are supposed to be motivated and always working at the limits of their capacity. This just is not correct: managers are human beings and act like human beings. Therefore an overview of the subject will be presented. The fact is that to some degree, each new and different incentive system for professionals will be "ploughing at least some new ground". At the same time it should be said that the examples provided are real and do exist, some in considerable number.

Boards of directors in a majority of the larger firms have a compensation committee that usually consists of the chairman (who usually is the C.E.O.) and about two "outside" directors who also are usually C.E.O.s (or have been C.E.O.s). Their first priority usually is to determine the bonus payment for the top *executives* (officers of the company). The typical three starting considerations are (1) this year's corporate financial performance, (2) the recommendations of the C.E.O., and (3) the previous year's bonus payment (possibly also to be considered is that year's corporate financial record).

There is a degree of rationality in the deliberations, but there also is a large measure of subjective thinking. The closest such groups get to looking at specifics is to review a few particular outstanding men/women who turned in unusually good performances (in the opinion of the C.E.O.).

This same group will also consider what should be paid as a bonus to any other managers eligible for such a reward. Such a group does not always exist in a firm. Again a recommendation is received from the C.E.O. and the same previously mentioned considerations for the top group are considered regarding this lower category of persons. The board's compensation committee does not alway review the details regarding this category of managers.

For both of the above groups there may exist some formal guides as to the percentage of gross or net profits that is to be paid as a bonus. Sometimes the last mentioned group is, in part, measured by performance against their activity's budget and if they "beat it" by a fixed percentage (can be two or more levels of measurement), their bonus is fixed as a percentage of the alloted (by the board) bonus pool.

If the reader has been thinking in terms of what has been said so far, he/she may well have thought that the goals, objectives, milestones, and other MBO objectives or goals could be used, at least in part, to determine the bonus received. This author agrees, but up to the present time he does not know of one specific case where this has been done. He hopes that some readers will respond and inform him where such procedures are utilized.

The problems in a given non-planning (per this text) firm are that the top management must first become convinced to start such planning, and then after a year or so, it needs to be persuaded by the board or through its own thought processes to utilize the plans and MBO objectives to install some form of incentive system for all the professional groups mentioned — top management, lower management, and individual professionals.

The same general approaches using the board's compensation committee can still be utilized, except that in this case the author recommends that the pools for each category of employees be decided by the board on the basis of a published guide or unpublished guide or a subjective determination. However, this last type of determination could get the board into deep trouble because it likely will be changed for various reasons. As to the top group, the performance of each individual based upon his/her plan objectives and milestones, plus any MBO goals, should be used as the final guide and determinant of amount. Ultimately, the committee will want to decide on some kind of formula so the decision process can be relatively simple and uniform.

Below this group, the committee will only need to determine the appropriate bonus pool. Company managers should then allocate it to individuals on the basis of their attainment of plan and MBO goals.

If this seems too complicated, get the help of a real compensation expert to assist in creating the system. However, do not stray far from the above general guidelines.

If the reader does get involved in the design of such an incentive system, it is recommended that the devised system be tested by pursuing various "paper strategies" to determine whether professionals (especially the managers) can evade the constraints and "milk the system" for rewards that are not properly due them. In other words, one should simulate the pursuit of various strategies to make sure that the system constraints upon a manager's performance will hold him/her in the desired direction and that excessive rewards cannot be obtained by other kinds of performance activities. Based on the author's experience, it is quite usual to discover weaknesses in the initially designed system.

It should be obvious that using compensation to motivate professionals is a complex matter. It can be used to increase performance on the job with respect to either current or long term objectives or for almost any mix of these. Compensation has traditionally been used to attract and hold people. Less popular is its use to move people out of the organization. It obviously is a management tool and should not be left to staff specialists without "heavy" oversight by management.

It was recommended that good performance should be rewarded. Typically, this is less than a 15 percent reward. If one gives 15 percent (often less) to the top performer and 5–10 percent to an average performer, the difference is rather meaningless at almost any level when one factors in a reasonable inflation rate. Another problem to be considered is that when an employee gets above the midpoint of his/her salary range, the raise increment to salary decreases. The inflation rate must also be considered.

Remember what the increase in good performance amounts to for a direct labor employee working under a "one for one" incentive system — 120–130 percent. This implies that the very top performers should be considered for at least a 20 percent incentive increment, especially if inflation is in the 7–10 percent range. Frankly, such a bonus should be earned by excellent performance, assuming that the performance *goals* were meaningful to the welfare of the organization.

The reader should now have enough information to begin the design of a professional employee incentive system.

VII.   CONCLUDING REMARK

If the reader has read all of the text, thought about it, and still is not sure about the need to properly plan and manage so as to achieve the plan, there is not much hope that one can succeed at the task of convincing him/her. However, he should do himself a favor and take a look at the world we live in by examining "Harper's Index"[1] and then try to write an essay as to why planning and managing by the plan are a waste of time. The reader will also find reference 7 to be of interest.

[1]A special note: "Harper's Index" is a registered trademark, and a copy of the index appears in each issue of *Harper's* magazine.

REFERENCES

1. Delmar W. Karger and Walton M. Hancock, *Advanced Work Measurement*, Industrial Press, New York, 1982.
2. D. W. Karger and R. G. Murdick, *Long Range Planning and Corporate Strategy*, Karger & Murdick, Troy, NY, 1977, 1978.
3. *Industrial Engineering Terminology*, American National Standard Z94.0 1982, Industrial Engineering and Management Press, Norcross, GA, 1983.
4. R. G. Greenwood, "Management by Objectives: As Developed by Peter Drucker, Assisted by Harold Smiddy," *The Academy of Management Review*, 1981.
5. G. Morrissey, *Management by Objectives*, Addison-Wesley, Reading, MA, 1970.
6. J. B. Lasagna, "Make Your MBO Pragmatic," *Harvard Business Review*, Cambridge, MA, Nov.–Dec., 1971
7. "Mexico: A New Economic Era," *Business Week*, Nov. 12, 1990.

APPENDIX

Planning Guidance for Sub-Unit Department or Division Planners in a Non-Long Term Planning Organization and Non-Business Type Organizational Planners

Long term planners located in a non-planning organization can develop a long term plan and can gain most of the benefits as far as their organizational unit is concerned. The actual amount of possible benefits achieved is dependent upon the kind of organization involved and the character of the top executives. These statements are based upon actual personal experience of the author as well as on discussions with others.

The instructions under each sub-title of this chapter will often refer to and make use of the material presented in the other chapters that can be applied in this type of situation. Often some change from the procedure originally described will be suggested.

Frankly, it will be impossible to identify and discuss all planning procedure possibilities because of the wide variety of organization types, purposes, characteristics of executives, degree of technology involved, markets, financial constraints, etc. If a little imagination is used, one will often be able to adapt the procedure specified for overall commercial organizational planning to any of the above special situations.

The examples and suggestions presented herein and what is presented in the chapters of this text should make it possible for any observant, imaginative, and thoughtful leader to select appropriate procedures and/or to devise appropriate procedures for most planning situations.

Overall organizational planning for a non-business organization should be easy to handle since there is a wealth of information in this text. Trying to plan for a sub-unit in an organization that does not plan (commercial or non-commercial) is a bit more difficult from a human relations viewpoint. However, it is possible to develop a valuable and usable plan that can accelerate progress and lead to eventual significant success.

Of course, the fact that the parent organization does not plan for the long term (L.T.) will place some handicaps upon the sub-unit organization's planning, aside from the human relations problems. However, in most cases these handicaps can be overcome. Further, implementing such an L.T. plan will not always be easy since there will be handicaps to overcome. It will be necessary to adapt and/or develop variations of the methods specified in this text—but the general format and thrust can be maintained.

Long term planning from a strategy viewpoint for a sub-unit organization of a governmental organization or of a non-profit organization will be significantly different from that of a sub-unit of a profit seeking organization. The same, not surprisingly, also holds true for overall planning in such an organization.

To supply a specific planning model for every possible variation is not a practical procedure, but such planners will be helped by the examples cited regarding this type of planning. These planners will find that the general planning steps and procedures for commercial organization planning are really not so difficult to adapt to sub-unit planning and to non-commercial total planning.

I. SUB-UNIT L.T. PLANNING WHEN PARENT DOES NOT PLAN FOR BOTH BUSINESS AND NON-BUSINESS ORGANIZATIONAL SUB-UNITS

The reasons for sub-unit L.T. planning are essentially the same as for total ogranization L.T. planning. It is possible by such action to make the sub-unit organization more effective and successful in achieving its organizational mission and objectives. The author has actually developed such plans in both types of organizations and realized outstanding accomplishment of mission and objectives in each. Moreover, similar planning by others and the attainment of objectives has been observed in a number of other cases.

Naturally, when the parent does not plan for the long term view, the sub-unit must be discreet in proceeding with such planning. This is not meant to imply or say that it should be done in secrecy—in fact the opposite is true.

The sub-unit head should prepare a somewhat formal statement of what it wants to do and what it hopes to achieve by such actions. He should take enough time to make sure that all positive and negative points are identified.

The lack of an existing overall planning effort is likely the result of the C.E.O. and/or the C.O.O. not wanting to engage in L.T. planning. Therefore, do NOT proceed to tell them that they ought to plan for the overall organization—at least not initially. They either subjectively or objectively do not want to plan because of one of more of the following negatives—that they either see (identify) or feel:

1. It would likely adversely affect yearly total remuneration.
2. The plan's L.T. objectives may be seen as constraining business decisions. (Be assured, plan objectives do not ever constrain *good* decision making! Hopefully, it *will* constrain bad decision making. When the reasons for modification are logical and valid, there is no impediment to modifying the plan.)
3. It is perceived that a plan's objectives would result in either unstated or stated performance standards. This will be instinctively perceived as being undesirable (for them) because of possible failure to achieve them. (This author had such thoughts the first time he led the creation of a plan for the organizational unit he headed—a university school of management.)
4. It could cause too much "light" to be shed on unfavorable past decisions and actions. This could be a possibility, but if the plan is designed to correct past errors it will do nothing but bring credit to all directly and indirectly involved executive(s).

Because of these and other such perceptions by the top executive(s), one must carefully present and bring to the fore one's desire and/or intent.

II.   HOW TO PROCEED

Generally the best procedure is to secure a personal appointment with the chief executive or other executive to whom the planning person reports by saying something like "I would like to see you to review and discuss some actions that I/we believe will make my function more effective and efficient." If it is a division making the request (in a profit seeking organization), add the words "more profitable" (but then this issue must be substantially addressed in the eventual plan). In other words, take the positive approach. Generally, it is best not to ask for *permission* to develop and use a L.T. plan. Merely tell what you expect to do and what you expect to achieve—and that you, of course, will bring it to him/her for review.

In the above paragraph, I/we was used in one sentence. If you have discussed this *very* informally with your staff, and they are in agreement, then use the word "we" in discussions with the superior manager.

When the above action is taken, be sure to know the facts extremely well. Present them orally and be prepared to discuss the various aspects in detail, but know the facts so well that you will not need a sheaf of reference papers. Unless it is requested or obviously desirable, do not leave a written request.

Do NOT ignore the matter of selling the employees on the concept of developing and using a plan—this applies to both sub-unit and overall organizational planning. Sometimes you will encounter an employee who objects to planning and he/she needs to either be converted, or neutralized by the vast majority in favor of planning. Usually, one of the strongest incentives for planning (both for the boss(es) and the workers) is that greater benefits will eventually flow to everybody involved. This last assertion is a fact, if the planning is properly accomplished and implemented.

The holding of planning sessions for sub-unit planning usually needs to be done in the office(s) involved. Otherwise too much attention will be called to the planning activity. The activity should not be hidden, yet it should not be done in a manner that will call significant attention to the activity.

National and worldwide economic and other considerations, for example, may not be of prime importance, or may even be of no importance, except for divisional and overall organization planning in business organizations. Possible likely exceptions are for planners at the departmental level who are located in marketing, manufacturing, engineering, or finance. However, even low level sub-units can not entirely ignore the effects of an economic boom or bust. Further, they are usually involved to a degree in non-profit institutions.

One area which will require heavy emphasis in sub-unit planning is the matter of strengths and weaknesses. In sub-unit planning these attributes may be more important and consume more time than almost any other factor. Moreover, the fact that the sub-unit will be examining itself will make the identification and the assessment of importance for each strength and weakness factor very difficult.

There is a further problem with strengths and weaknesses. Each sub-unit is often adversely affected by a weakness in another sub-unit because these sub-units must work together, in order to accomplish their respective tasks. If the reader looks at Chapter 9 to review the determination of internal strengths and weaknesses, he/she will find a statement that the weaknesses of a functional unit often are discovered through a disclosure from another organizational unit, which experienced difficulties in obtaining service because of a weakness in the servicing organizational unit.

There are two clues to problems in the above paragraph. First, finding your own weaknesses will require extreme candor on the part of all the planners. (Later will be discussed the second problem, a weakness in a servicing organization which causes problems to the planning organization.) A large department providing a necessary function for the firm usually is composed of sub-functions, and often each of these is headed by a supervisor.

The following are two varieties of sub-function examples in a relatively large firm:

Maintenance

1. Millwrights.
2. Machine repair department.
3. Welders.
4. Electrical construction.
5. Electrical repair.
6. Pipe fitters and plumbers.
7. Engineering support.

Plant and industrial engineering (combined)

1. Project/process industrial engineering for all but electrical engineering (E.E.) and electronic activities.
2. Project/process industrial engineering for E.E. and electronics activities.
3. Work standards engineering.
4. Tool and equipment engineering.
5. Cost estimating.
6. Plant engineering.
     Millwrights.
     Electricians.
     Carpenters.
     Welders.
     Construction.
     Plumbers and pipe fitters.

There always are some sub-functions in a functional organization, similar to those just illustrated, but often their number is less than those in the two examples. The sub-functions under the head of a functional department are treated in a manner similar to the functional departments in an overall organizational planning effort.

As to strengths and weaknesses, the sub-functions have them just as the overall function usually has them. Also, in a somewhat similar fashion, the sub-functional unit must also look for strengths and weaknesses that are (at least partially) outside of its area of responsibility.

Complicating the matter of identification of strengths and weaknesses is the fact that often a sub-function is headed by a supervisor/manager who has a limited breadth of experience and knowledge, and therefore cannot help a great deal in the identification of strengths and weaknesses. Because of the above complications, finding the strengths and weaknesses in the sub-units is just as "tricky" and difficult as it is finding them in overall functional units.

Furthermore, in a similar vein, it should be said that producing a good functional long range plan as a "stand alone" planner is not an easy task. It will probably be more challenging than producing a plan for a function when engaging in overall organizational planning.

The other problem is how to deal with a servicing organization (to the planning organization) that has a weakness which needs corrective action. In the overall planning effort, the other unit(s) are at times ignored until it becomes time to reconcile functional plans.

One should ask the head of the servicing unit to attend one of the planning sessions, the one where the problem will surface. Be very careful not to offend, merely let it become clear that a problem exists and that you are sure the head of the other organization will look into the matter and see what can be done to correct the apparent difficulty.

Once all the details have been settled in the planning sessions, the leader should draft the plan and a statement of its objectives. Make sure the other planners approve of the planning document. Also, from time to time, caution them to not discuss the planning activity or the plan's content with others. Do not bring up this subject in any conversation since it is difficult to predict how other subunits will react. At least keep absolutely quiet until it is decided how it is to be implemented, and preferably not until it has been approved. After that it is acceptable to talk about it IF it may have a useful effect; otherwise a discussion of its content with strangers should be avoided—it could have a significant negative effect.

The plan details should explain how the unit expects to achieve the objective, where required resources will originate, and when each objective will likely be achieved.

The required resources can be indicated as coming from the overall organization, but that means that the value of the benefits must be clearly stated and easily cover the costs in one or two years. The longer the time to recover costs, the more objections will be encountered. If the planning is in a non-profit overall organization, try to secure the resources from "benefactors" through some special action—such a move will be looked upon with favor by the head of the organization.

In the last cited example, it means that the head of the sub-unit must engage in fund raising, but such activity *must be* subject to the approval of the overall head of that activity. It can be done if the planning organization chief can get potential donors excited about what he/she is trying to accomplish.

Put the planning document in an attractive but subdued cover. Once you have reached this point, the leader should again approach "the boss" to make a presentation. Usually this is best accomplished in a low key private meeting. Do not get into boring details unless it is requested. Take a very positive stance. Present the plans as if you are fully expecting to implement them. Do not ask for approval to proceed.

If the boss agrees and says he approves without your asking for approval, you obviously have won. If he wants to generally expose the plan in a "staff meeting," agree—but "don't hold your breath until this happens." However, it is a distinct possibility. If you get the opportunity, do not try to start talking about the good things that would happen if overall organizational planning were to commence. Getting the whole organization to actually plan is usually very difficult, and how to do it should first be cleared with the reader's boss if the reader is in a sub-unit or heads a sub-unit.

Such plans usually do not garner many objections simply because the plan objectives tend to serve the welfare of the parent organization in a significant manner. If some of the actions are going to require money, the plan should indicate when it will be needed and exactly how the money will be used. Also, be sure to clearly state the returns to be expected by the parent organization. If certain reservations are raised by the chief they need to be discussed and rationalized so that his apprehensions are eliminated.

It sometimes occurs that when plans are presented and a copy is left (always leave a copy with the boss after presenting the highlights), they will be received, thought about, but then no response will be received from the boss. This author has had that happen. In a non-profit organization he was even asked to present the plans to the board of trustees, and still no response was received. Yet he and "his group" proceeded to implement the plans, secured needed funds from outside sources (not secretly, and with the approval of the fund seeking department head), and by good management secured 90 percent of the predicted benefits. All this is why it is a good idea to present such plans as if the developer plans to proceed exactly in accordance with them. Incidently, the president of the organization and the academic vice president never once directly alluded to the completion of the plans. Yet from their actions they obviously were very pleased with the result.

The plans can usually (this author's guess is that "usually" equates to about 85–90 percent of the time) be implemented with relative safety, even if no formal approval is received, *providing no significant money or other tangible assets are required from the parent organization.* However, be sure to say at some time that seems appropriate that you are proceeding and have started the implementation of the plan. This author has had three or four such personal experiences.

If you really need organization money when located in a commercial firm, try to so formulate your plan that the needed funds are associated with one or two objectives that have overwhelming advantages to the organization. Hopefully the remainder of the plan can be accomplished, more or less, within budget. If you can't get money for the one or two projects needing extra funding, then implement the remainder of the plan—that which can be accomplished within the budget. Then, the improved results from your function may "open the door" to the needed funding for the remainder of the plan.

One other possibility: If your plan is producing significant benefits, do not be too afraid to exceed budget expenditure limits. Often nothing at all will be said, but expect to be "called" on such an action. This author has also used this "ploy" to acquire needed resources. Some overspending will likely be tolerated if other than budgeted money is producing significant achievements for the overall organization.

Another possible ploy would be to submit one of the projects requiring funds as a "special" work or project request—justify the request by savings and/or increased profits or revenue. Again this author has succeeded with this approach.

Such plans usually do not garner many objections, simply because the plan objectives tend to serve the welfare of the parent organization in a significant manner. If some of the actions are going to require money, the plan should indicate when it will be needed, how and where you expect to secure it, and why it likely will be available.

Naturally, if certain objectives are questioned by the chief, such objectives need to be discussed and rationalized so that his apprehensions are eliminated.

One final comment: Do not feel discouraged by "no response" from the boss. Go ahead and implement the parts of the plan for which you have the funds required. Do NOT HIDE the action, neither should you flaunt the act. Is there danger? Some, but in most cases not too much. This danger is balanced by an opportunity to become an above average performer—an accomplishment of obvious value.

As to the danger in a non-profit organization where outside funds were secured from impressed donors, they will be the planner's shield if trouble develops from "above."

The following will be a repeat of a former remark: Do not take any tangible steps to hide the existence of the planning activity. Rather, treat it as a normal and natural one. Also, do not emphasize it or call attention to it—you will do this if you try to hide the activity.

Make the goals and objectives real and important milestones. Then expand the near term portions (for the next year) of the actions required to achieve the goals and objectives—just as in overall organizational planning. Also try to establish "benchmarks" for the next year of the progress toward achieving the established objectives. These should be used to measure progress and should be reflected in MBO statements. Furthermore, they should be specifically mentioned with respect to their achievement in discussions with the boss.

Finally, revise the L.T. plans each year. Just because it is an L.T. plan does not mean it will not require change as new knowledge is acquired.

III. HOW TO ADJUST OVERALL COMMERCIAL PLANNING PROCEDURES FOR NON-PROFIT OR GOVERNMENTAL ORGANIZATIONS

The adjustments that are required are logical and of a practical nature, all of which makes the adaptation relatively easy. Moreover, the factors affecting overall plans tend to be politically and/or socially oriented. This reduces the exterior environmental factors affecting overall planning.

The fact that government plans often involve "heavy" political considerations may increase the complexities of the plan and the planning activity. People who work in elective offices and those who work for elected officials can not ignore political considerations. However, if a particular function of government involves "processing" of either paperwork and/or benefits, generally the more efficiently the process is executed the more the function will "serve the people," and the more the head will be "liked." Therefore, planning how to make the process more efficient and effective should not encounter impediments from the political connection.

Planning in a college or university, or even in the lower grades of primary and secondary education, poses no real problems or handicaps to the planning process. Consider all the problems, handicaps, and opportunities, and proceed to create a plan with objectives. The only word of caution here is to let each academic department create its own plan, subject to the limitations established by the head of the school.

In a college or university the chief academic officer (the provost and/or academic vice president) should sit in on the the final planning session of an academic unit if he expresses this desire or exhibits enthusiasm for the planning activity. The author knows of no primary or secondary school producing such a plan, but he suspects it would work as previously described. School superintendents, in his experience, are almost deathly afraid of real overall planning.

If the planning is to be accomplished by a sub-unit in a university/college which is not a planning organization, then the provost should not be invited to sit in on the planning sessions. He merely must be told about the activity and later presented with the plans as discussed under the other subtitle. Also note that an academic department in this situation likely can raise enough money to implement the plans from wealthy alumni if it is an old enough school and if the academic department properly clears its actions with "the money raising department."

Planning in a church organization can be a "can of worms"—excuse the metaphor. This author once helped do some planning for a diocese of a church. He was then a member of a church in the diocese, but was on the committee because of his expertise. When the plan was finished and was to be presented at the yearly diocesan meeting, his church would not send him as a delegate, which would have given him an official "voice" in the proceedings.

He was only allowed to present the plan as a special dispensation to the planning committee, but he was not allowed to answer any questions. The priests immediately instituted their right to call for a vote by "orders"—meaning approval of the motion required getting a majority of the priests to agree and a majority of the lay delegates to agree. The planning committee/commission won, but only by one or two votes from the priests. The vote was overwhelming by the lay delegates.

The situation was not caused by a matter of religion, but a matter of how the bishop should organize the diocese. As it turned out, he was afraid to implement the plan since too many priests felt they would experience more pressure "to perform." A canon of the church had headed the committee at the request of the bishop, and he invited the author to join the group and provide outside expertise. The author's priest said to him, "Del, how could you do it?" The author thought (and still does) that he was helping the church.

The above tale merely illustrates some of the peculiarities encountered in planning. While the plan did not get completely implemented, the bishop used part of the plan.

If you wondered why the bishop did not participate in the planning directly, it was because of "political" considerations—he was acting exactly as secular politicians act. They always try to escape being blamed for something that others might not like.

IV. CONCLUDING REMARKS

It really is not too difficult to generate useful and significant plans in the organizational units discussed. In most cases they can be implemented and they will produce significant improvements in the operation(s) of the organization or organizational sub-unit.

Index

Acquisitions & Mergers, 214–216

Benchmark Spying, 151, 152
Board of Directors, 165–168, 181, 182

C.E.O. Role In Planning, 116, 121
Competition, 5–28
  in 21st century, 10, 11
  beating competitors, 5–28
  gathering intelligence, 21–23
  global, 6–14
  Japanese, 13, 14, 17–19, 25, 26
Competitive Edge, 203–205
Competitive Research, 22, 23
Computer Integrated
    Management, 65–79

Corporate Culture, 129, 130
Corporate Image, 129, 130, 138–140
Corporations, 9, 12–18
  downsizing, 9
  governance, 9
  future, 9
  unbundling, 9

Environmental Analysis, 145–160
  benchmark spying, 151, 152
  data sources, 154–157
  forces in environment, 149–155
  general description, 145–149
  industry study, 157–160
  need for, 145–160
Environments, 1–3, 10–14

corporate, 1–3
Europe, 10–14
external, 2
internal, 2
Experience/Learning Curves, 197–
  200
External Environmental Analysis,
  145–160
  benchmark spying, 151, 152
  data sources, 154–157
  forces in environment, 149–155
  general description, 145–149
  industrial spying, 151, 152
  industry study, 157–160
  need for, 145–160
External Factors, 49–59
  acquisitions, 56, 57
  mergers, 49–56
  selling businesses and/or SBUs,
    58, 59
  spin-offs, 57, 58

Fears Of Executives, 115, 116,
  119–121
Flexible Manufacturing System
  (FMS), 72, 73

Halal Research, 88–93

IDEF$_0$ (Planning tool), 79–83
Incentive Systems For Managers
  and Professionals, 241–244,
  257–259
Industrial Spying, 151, 152
  benchmark spying, 151, 152
Integrated Management/
  Enterprise (CIM), 67–79
  computer integrated
    management/enterprise

(CIM), 67–79
flexible manufacturing system
  (FMS), 72, 73
just-in-time (JIT) inventory, 71,
  72
planning for, 73–79
Intelligence Gathering, 21–23
  benchmark spying, 22, 23
  competitive research, 22, 23
  spying 21–23
Internal Environmental Analysis,
  161–183
  board of directors, 165–168,
    181, 182
  C.E.O. role, 161–163
  engineering and research, 176–
    179
  financial evaluations, 172–175
  managers, professionals and
    craftspeople, 168, 169
  manufacturing, 179, 180
  marketing evaluations, 175, 176
  organization dynamics, 181
  personnel policies, 170, 171
  strength and weakness
    determination, 163–183
  vendor relations, 180, 181
International Trade, 8–15
  alliances, 9
  future factors, 8–15
  reciprocity, 8, 9
Inventory, 71, 72

Just-In-Time (JIT) Inventory, 71,
  72

Long Range Plans, 225–232
  milestone development, 229, 230
  policies, 228, 229
  procedures, 228, 229
  schedules, 228, 229

Malik Research, 94–98
Management By Objectives
        (MBO), 225–271
    starting the program, 250–252
    writing objectives, 253–257
Management Per Plan, 223–259
Manufacturing, 65–79
    background, 65–67
    increasingly integrated, 67–73
    increasingly integrated
        enterprise, 67–79
Market Growth Effects, 207, 208
Markets, 6–12
    international/global, 6–12
    populace characteristics, 7, 8
    redesigned products, need for,
        7, 8
Market Share vs Growth, 200–203
Milestones, 229–259
    assuring achievement, 241–259
    development of, 229–230
    resource allocations, 230–232

New Competitors, 211–213

Organization Image, 138–140

Performance Standards, 244–248
Planning, 1–30, 41–46, 49–59, 85,
        161–183, 197–203, 208–211,
        216–220, 236–238
    internal, 161–183
        board of directors, 165–168,
            181, 182
        C.E.O. role, 161–163
        engineering and research,
            176–179
        financial evaluations, 172–175
        managers, professionals and

    craftspeople, 168, 169
    manufacturing, 179, 180
    marketing evaluations, 175,
        176
    organization dynamics, 181
    personnel policies, 170, 171
    strength and weakness
        determination, 163–183,
        237
    vendor relations, 180, 181
operational/functional, 2–5, 25–
        30, 41–46, 85, 236–238
    process of, 5, 30, 85, 236–238
    social factors, 41–46
strategic, 1–28, 41–46, 49–59,
        185–222
    acquisitions and mergers,
        214–216
    competitive edge, 203–205
    educational factors, 41–46
    environmental, 5–28, 49–62
    market share vs growth, 200–
        203
    product life cycle, 220
    product planning, 216–220
    research and development,
        208–211
    social factors, 41–46
Planning Director, 99, 100
    characteristics, 99
    qualifications, 99
    representative tasks, 99, 100
    sources, 99
Planning In General, 5, 14–16,
        23–25, 29–36, 85–111, 116–
        128, 134, 238, 239, 241–259
    benefits, 5, 85–98
        Halal research, 88–93
        long range, 14–16, 23–25, 29,
            94–99
        Malik research, 94–98
    C.E.O. role, 116, 121–125

defining future horizons, 104, 105

definition of the business, 134

director, 99, 100

essential elements, 95, 96, 101–104

factors, a discussion of, 116–119

fears of executives/managers, 115, 116, 119–121

governmental factors, 31–36
    Japanese, 31–35
    political actions, 31–35
    U.S., 30–36

manual, planning, 100, 101,

materials needed, 127, 128

measuring
    progress/achievement, 109, 110
    assuring achievement, 109–111, 241–259

in non-planning organizations, 113
    sub-unit planning, 113

organizing the process, 122–125

process illustrated, 238, 239

site of planning, 105

standard view creation, 126, 127

steps in process, 96, 98

strategic components, 105–108

Planning In Non-Planning Organizations, 261–271

how to proceed, 263–269
    in non-profit organizations, 261–271

Planning Manual, 100, 101

Planning Process, 238–239

Planning Tool (IDEF), 79–83

Political Actions, 31–35
    Japanese, 31–35
    U.S., 30–36

Political Weapons, 33–35
    import rules, 34, 35
    money, 33–35

Product Design Engineering, 59–62

design team composition and organization, 60–62, 69–71

Product Life Cycle, 220

Product Planning, 216–220

Product Redesign Requirement, 5, 6

Professional Worker Performance Standards, 244–248

Quality, 8–20
    importance of, 18–20

Research & Development, 17, 25, 26, 208–211
    funding by government vs industry, 17, 25, 26

Risk, 205, 206

Service Quality, 213, 214

Short Range Plans, 232–238
    operational plans, 236–238
    planning at corporate level, 234–236

Social Factors, 41–61

Spying, 21–23
    benchmark, 22, 23
    competitive research, 22, 23
    corporate, 21–23

Standard View of Organization, 101–104
    areas needing coverage, 103, 104
    facilities, 103, 104
    manpower evaluation and determination, 102–104
    marketing evaluation and determination, 103, 104

Strategic Management Defined, 2
Strategic Planning Institute (SPI),
    140–142
Strategy Development, 185–222
  acquisitions and mergers, 214–
    216
  competitive edge, 203–205
  components of strategy, 188, 189
  experience learning curve, 197–
    200
  market share, industry growth,
    and market share research
    results, 200–203
  market share vs growth, 200–
    203
  price quality ratio, 192–194
  product life cycle, 220

product portfolio, 190–192
research and development
    (R&D), 208–211
risk, 205, 206
service quality, 213, 214
scope of business, 189, 190
vertical integration, 211
Sub-Unit Planning in Non-
    Planning Organization, 113
Successful Small Corporations, 9

Value Set Development, 133, 134
Value System of Individuals, 130,
    131
Value System of Organizations,
    131, 132
Vertical Integration, 211